Publishers:
Plan-A-Home,
Glencrow, Moville, Co. Donegal.
Tel: 077 - 82258
(Int. Code 01035377)
Fax: 077 - 82341
(Int. Code 01035377)

Book origin/make-up:
DBA Publications Ltd.,
56 Carysfort Ave., Blackrock,
Co. Dublin.

Colour separations:
Litho Studios, Kylemore Road,
Ballyfermot, Dublin 10.

Printed by:
Task Printers, Limerick Road,
Naas, Co. Kildare.

ACKNOWLEDGMENTS

Designs & layouts:
Harold McGuinness

Typeset & plan drawings:
Michael Hannigan
George McGuinness
Rosaleen McDaid
Junior staff:
Cathy Doherty
Brendan Porter

Construction costings:
Harold McGuinness
Liam Cotter

Artists illustrations:
Paul Gallagher
Assisted by:
Mark Collins

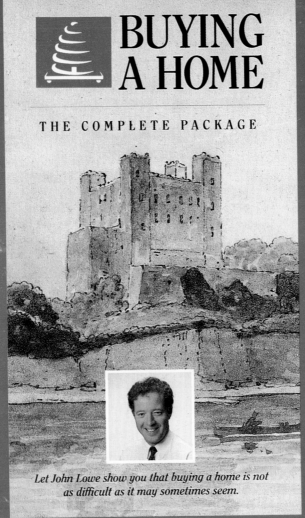

Architects & Surveyors
Glencrow, Moville, Co. Donegal
Republic of Ireland.

Dear Customer,

If this is your first introduction to Plan-A-Home we welcome you on board, and hope that you find the content of this, our first full coloured, 4th edition book of home plans, both informative and helpful.

To avoid any confusion, our front covers differ for Ireland and the U.K., as one of our counterparts in the U.K. trade under a similar name, therefore the "Design-A-Home" cover was decided upon after coming to an amicable agreement.

We, at Plan-A-Home, have been keeping a very close eye on the natural progression towards custom designed homes and felt that the time had come to produce a book of this quality, as choosing to have your home built on your own plot, means that there will be much more careful planning required throughout the entire operation, therefore, we have endeavoured to give you as much clarity of information as we can, in both plan layouts and illustrations, in order to help you make the correct choices.

As with our previous editions, we ask that you use this book as a guideline in choosing what aspects of layout and design best suit your requirements, site, etc. Our speciality at Plan-A-Home, is preparing "one-off" designs and working drawings for individual clients, so therefore, we ask you to avail of the opportunity to change any of our enclosed designs, and on ordering, to complete your own individual choice of specification at the rear of the Order Form.

We would ask that you obtain professional, or well informed advice, on your choice of design or alterations to same, before ordering, to ensure that it blends harmoniously into it's site setting, and surrounding environment.

Please bear in mind that your new home will probably be your most important and expensive undertaking in your lifetime, so time and care should be taken in choosing your preferred design. We would hope to be able to assist you in any queries or problems that you might encounter while making the all important decisions, and hopefully, use of our Pre-Order Enquiry form may assist you in these matters.

I take this opportunity in wishing you well in the future and every happiness in your new home.

Harold Mc Guinness

Yours sincerely,
Harold McGuinness.

£3,000 NEW HOUSE GRANT

A grant of £3,000 is available for building or purchasing a new house/flat, provided house is constructed by a registered contractor and the floor area does not exceed 1,346 sq.ft. (125 sq.m.). The following conditions also apply:-

a) You our your spouse, either individually or jointly, must never have previously purchased or built for your own occupation another dwelling in Ireland or abroad.
b) You must occupy the dwelling on completion as your normal place of residence.
c) Your application must be received in the Department within a year of occupying the house.
d) The dwelling is new.
e) The dwelling must be built in accordance with good building practice and with the Building Regulations 1991.
f) The dwelling is built by a contractor registered for VAT who holds a current Form C2 or tax clearance certificate. In the case of a house built on an applicant's own site VAT registered work of not less than £15,000 must be undertaken under contract by the registered contractor(s).
g) In the case of house located in the Dublin City or County (including the Borough of Dun Laoghaire, but excluding certain largely rural ares of Co. Dublin) it will be necessary that the dwelling has a principal means of space and water heating which uses electricity, gas, oil or a solid fuel burning appliance which will satisfactorily limit smoke emissions. In addition, an ordinary fireplace which is not the source of water heating for the house and is used solely to heat the room in which it is located, is permitted.

In your own interest, you are advised to make application before work on the house has commenced, or at the time of payment of a deposit, so that a decision on eligibility can be given in good time and a provisional approval issued.

The following documents must accompany the completed application form in any case where the applicant is building (and not pruchasing) the house on his own site:-

(i) Site location map
(ii) House plan, elevation and section (slace 1:50)
(iii) Specification
(iv) Planning permission

In all cases, Form NH2B - certificate from Inspector of Taxes-must be submitted with your application.

Applicants may also be required to produce any other documents (e.g. Contract of Sale, evidence of title, etc.) deemed necessary.

In any case where title to the new dwelling is being taken out in the names of two or more persons, details of title including the names of other parties, should be given.

If you are deemed to be eligible for a grant, and the plans and other documents submitted comply with requirements, provisional certificates of approval will be issued to you.

No changes should be made to the approved plans without the prior approval of the Department.

PAYMENT OF GRANT

When the house is finished and occupied, you can claim payment, provided:-

1. All work has been completed in accordance with the approved plans to the Department of the Environment's outline specification
2. You are in occupation of the house as your normal place of residence on a year round basis.

Claim for payment is followed by a final inspection and then payment. This can easily take up to six months.

Application for grant must be made on appropriate form, accompanied by house plans, site location and layout maps, and planning permission, and forwarded to Dept. of Environment in your area.
Head Office, O'Connell Bridge House, Dublin 1.
Telephone (01) 6793377

FLOOR AREA FOR GRANT PURPOSES

The total floor area of a house for grant purposes must be at least 35 sq.ft. and not more than 125 sq.m. (1,346 sq.ft.). In the case of flats, the maximum is the same (125 sq.m.) with minimum floor area at least 30 sq.m. These limits are designed to allow the construction of reasonably sized houses and are strictly enforced.

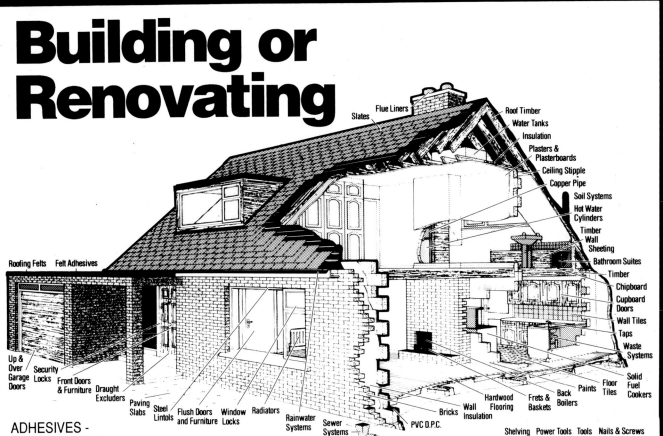

BRADSTONE

Bradstone captures the eye and the imagination.

Build in harmony with the landscape. For the time honoured tradition of stone, Bradstone is the natural choice.

Information on the walling and complimentary Quoins, Cills and Lintels available in Ireland can be obtained from our free Bradstone Homebuilders Information Pack.

Your new home checklist.....

Energy-efficient design	☐	☐	**Gold Shield Specifications**
Low Running Costs	☐	☐	**Gold Shield Specifications**
Clean and Smoke-free	☐	☐	**Gold Shield Specifications**
Best use of Nightsaver electricity	☐	☐	**Gold Shield Specifications**
Kind to the Environment	☐	☐	**Gold Shield Specifications**
Comfortable and Convenient	☐	☐	**Gold Shield Specifications**

When you select your new house design why not incorporate in it the heating specifications which will make it a Gold Shield Home.

A Gold Shield Home is a modern, energy-efficient, all-electric home designed to make the best use of less-than-half-price Nightsaver electricity.

Gold Shield Home owners get as much as 80% of all the electricity they use at less-than-half the standard price.

ESB's Gold Shield Homes design services will prepare a detailed specification - free of charge - for your selected house design.

Simply phone your ESB Regional Office.

GOLD SHIELD AWARD
NEW 2000 STANDARD

ELECTRIC
ENERGY EFFICIENT HOMES

ESB

EXCLUDED AREAS:

Fully detached garages, carports and out-offices.

A garage (or carport) attached to, or forming part of a house which complies with the conditions for garages or a single storey, undeveloped garage, which is attached to, or forms part of a house, and complies with Dept. regulations. It must also comply with the fire requirements, have provision for not more than two windows, and the entrance must normally be from the front of the house, but consideration will be given in cases where this is not possible due to the restriction of the site. It should not have a fireplace opening or be capable of having a fireplace.

Undeveloped attics which may be floored for storage purposes: One window in each of two gable ends, or one dormer window or rooflight not exceeding 2.8 sq.m. (30 sq.ft.) to provide light and ventilation, is also permitted.

Undeveloped basements: Walls must be unplastered internally, and only works necessary to secure the structural stability of the house may be carried out. Separate rooms with external access from the house, may not be provided.

A boiler house/fuel store with external access only, and a floor area of not more than 4 sq.m. (43 sq.ft.).

Small open front porches.

INCLUDED AREAS

As a general rule you may take it that areas which are capable of being converted into habitable or useful floor space, even if there is not direct access to the rest of the building, and irrespective of the state of finish, will be regarded as part of the floor area.

You are advised to have your plans approved by the Department before you start work, and to check that the dimensions of the house being constructed, are in accordance with approved plans, particularly where the floor area is near the maximum limits.

PLANNING PERMISSION (REP. OF IRELAND ONLY)

After choosing your site, and having given some thought as to the nature of the development, the first stage is to apply for planning permission to the Planning Authority in your county, or to the Urban District Council, or in the case of cities, to the City Borough Corporation.

There are three types of planning applications which can be made, i.e. outline, approval, and full permission, and these are outlined below.

OUTLINE PERMISSION

In some cases, persons may wish to ascertain whether or not planning permission would be granted for a particular development/site, and on the advice of your architect/engineer, it may be advisable to apply for outline permission to determine whether or not, your development would be permitted. Outline permission allows you to make an application without having gone to the expense of preparing working drawings, detailed specification, etc.

An outline permission must by accompanied by:-
a) **Completed application form**
b) **Planning fee of £24 per house**
c) **Proposed site layout and location maps, showing location of proposed development on site, and giving brief description of same.**
d) **Copy of notice of application to Planning Authority inserted in local newspaper, or alternatively, copy of notice on site.**

Note: grant of outline permission does not permit carrying out of any works.

APPROVAL

Approval can only be sought where outline permission as described above, has already been granted, and must be accompanied by complete working drawings and specification, together with all documents as listed for outline. Planning fee per house - £16.

FULL PERMISSION

Full permission is a combination of outline and approval as previously described, and is a more direct and speedier method for sites where it is considered that planning permission should be relatively easy to obtain.

GENERAL PROCEDURE

In all above cases, when an application is made, the Planning Authority have two months in which to notify the applicant of their decision, and a further month in which to grant the permission.

Should the Planning Authority decide that insufficient information has been supplied, they are entitled to request further information, whereby, the three months processing period commences only after they have received a full replay to the further information requested. Therefore, in some case, incomplete or awkward applications, can take longer. So, as you may have deducted from the foregoing information, application for outline permission, followed by approval, takes twice as long as an initial application for full permission.

In all cases, when a decision is made, the applicant is notified within two months, of the decision to grant, or refuse, the permission applied for, and provided there is no objection to same, the planning approval is issued one month later.

PUBLIC NOTICE

This may be done by means of a newspaper notice in a locally distributed newspaper, or alternatively, by a notice on site, provided it is placed in a convenient position so as to be legible from main thoroughfare, and must remain in place for the duration of the application.

SITE LAYOUT MAPS

4 no. layout maps, showing clearly boundaries of the site, site entrance, storm and foul drainage details, water supply, etc.

Letter of consent from any group schemes or landowners to right-of-ways, etc., to accompany application.

SITE LOCATION MAPS

4 no. site location maps, being extracts from Ordnance Survey sheets, and showing clearly the location of site and adjoining developments in relation to any churches, crossroads, towns, etc., or any other distinct landmark in the area.

HOUSE PLANS

4 no. copies of detailed plans and specifications, clearly illustrating layout, elevations, sections, details of finishes, and all materials, etc., to be used in the construction.
Note: These need not accompany outline application.

OBJECTION

Objections can be made in writing as follows:-

a) **By the applicant to the Planning Authority in relation to it's decision to refuse, or to object to some of the conditions relevant to the Grant of Permission. The applicant has one month from the date of receipt of a decision, within which to object.**
b) **Objections can be lodged by a third party against a planning application, and if an objection is made, the objector is notified of the Council's decision, at which stage he has a further 21 days to appeal the Council's decision. In all cases, the objections must be forwarded in writing, with the reasons for the objection, fee, etc., to An Bord Pleanala, Block V1 & V11, Irish Life Centre, Lower Abbey Street, Dublin 1. Details of fees will be outlined on the Planning Authority's "Decision to Grant Permission" form.**

Details of complete documents required for planning applications, as follows:-
a) **Application form, completed accurately, stating all details as requested.**
b) **Completed Addendum - Application Fee form, with remittance of planning fee, as follows:-**
Full permission - £32
Outline permission - £24
Approval - £16

The previous information is a simple guide, which is basically sufficient for the majority of applications for single house developments, as it would only complicate matters to include all the different variables. It is advised, if you are in doubt as to any detail, that you contact your local Planning Office who will be glad to assist you with any other relevant information concerning your site and application.

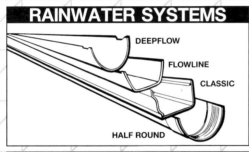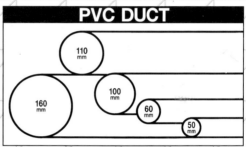

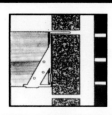

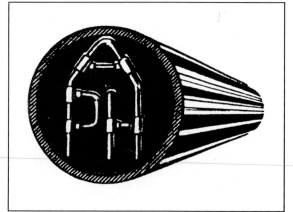

PLANNING APPLICATIONS (U.K)

Application forms are obtainable from your Divisional Planning Office or Local Authority Office. Complete these accurately and submit with your planning application including plans, maps, etc. Ensure the correct fees accompany your application. Advertisements if required, are placed in local papers inviting anyone interested to inspect your application, and they will have a limited period in which to object. Your local planning office will advise you on these matters specific to your area.

Your application is required to be dealt with within eight weeks unless the applicant agrees to a longer period. Carrying out the necessary consultations takes several weeks and requests to you for further information, or the timing of planning committees, could delay the process beyond the eight weeks period. If a decision is not given within eight weeks you may lodge an appeal with the Planning Appeals Commission as if the application had been refused. Again your planning office will advise you further.

PLANNING APPEALS

If permission is refused, the decision notice will list the reasons. You have the right to appeal to the Planning Appeals Commission against a refusal, or the conditions of an approval, but you must appeal within six months of the decision.

There are two principal kinds of appeal - Public Hearing or Written Representations.

PUBLIC HEARING

You are entitled to have a public hearing and as this can be a costly method, professional planning advice should be sought.

WRITTEN REPRESENTATIONS

The majority of domestic appeals are processed by this method. You will have to send a full statement, in writing, of your case and comments to the relevant authority.

As a rough guideline, the average length of time to process an appeal from the time the the the relevant authoirty receives all the relevant information is approximately four to six months. You will be required to furnish a written statement and any supporting information which you feel would help your case. Your local planning office will furnish a similar report stating their case for refusal. You will usually have an opportunity to comment on this. However, lengthy correspondence tends to delay the process.

You can only challenge the decision on a point of law, or if you feel the requirements of planning legislation have not been carried out. The challenge must be made through the Court system, and you will need legal advice.

It is important to make sure your information is up-to-date, on planning policies and any other information to help in your appeal.

NEIGHBOUR NOTIFICATION

When the relevant authority receives an application for planning permission, it will notify certain occupiers of buildings on land adjoining the application site.
"Neighbouring land" means (i) land which adjoins the boundary of the application site, (ii) land which would adjoin the boundary but for an entry of a road less than 20 metres wide.

Only occupiers of buildings on neighbouring land, which are within 90 metres of the boundary of the application site, will be notified. Neighbour

notification forms are obtainable from your Divisional Planning Office, and these should be completed and submitted along with your application.

The procedures of some borough councils, etc., may vary but again they will advise you on this.

YOUR PLANNING APPLICATION

The following documents should accompany your full planning application for a new house on your site:-

House Plans - full detailed plans and specifications, clearly illustrating layout, elevations, sections and all materials and finishes intended in use.

Site layout and location maps - these must show clearly boundaries of site, site entrance details, storm and foul drainage details, water supply, all if any necessary right-of-ways, consent from any group schemes or any landowners granting right of ways, location of site, etc.

Planning forms - these include forms such as permission to develop lands, planning fees, neighbours' notification, permission to develop in agricultural green belt areas.

Planning fee - appropriate fees are required for outline permission, reserved matters or full permission.

All previous information on planning is a simple outline which basically is sufficient for the large majority of applications for single house developments, as it would only complicate matters to include all the different variables. It is advised if you are in any doubt as to any detail, that you contact your Local Planning Office, and they will be very glad to inform you of any other relevant information concerning your site and application.

BUILDING CONTROL

Your plans must also be submitted to Building Control for inspection to ensure that all materials and proposed use, comply with all building regulations. This may be done, either concurrently with planning application, or after grant of permission. The decision is yours, depending on your time limits. If you wish to expedite matters, concurrently would be best, although you risk the waste of building control fee in the event that planning has been modified or refused.

The following is a list of important issues which you should ensure are in place before commencing construction on your new home:-

1. Conveyancing:

Ensure that the legal conveyancing of your site has been completed thoroughly in regard to site boundaries, easements for access or services, and any liability towards common accesses, or services clearly defined and highlighted. Have your site boundaries checked independently to ensure that they comply with your transfer documents.

2. Mortgaging:

If you are arranging a mortgage this should be done before or in tandem getting your house designs and permission, so as to:-

i) to ensure that you can obtain sufficient funds to complete your home

ii) to ensure that you comply with the many conditions laid down by your mortgage company in relation to structural checks, supervision, etc.

3. Planning Permission:

Full planning permission must be received before any work can commence. Ensure also that any statutory objection periods which may exist, have elapsed, and any conditions as outlined on your planning permission, are complied with during construction

4. Building Regulations:

All plans and specifications should be to Building Regulations standards, and passed by the relevant authorities if applicable in your area. Likewise, you should ensure that contractor is fully conversant with the current Building Regulations, and fully intends to construct dwelling in compliance with same.

5. Commencement Notice:

If building in the Republic of Ireland you are currently obliged to submit a "Commencement Notice" stating your intention to commence work within fourteen days. These forms can be obtained from your local authority.

6. Insurance:

Insurance cover is vital during course of construction to protect your investment. If under contract, then ensure that your builder has a policy to cover this, but if your building by the self-build method then insurance cover can be easily obtained through any broker.

7. Structural inspections:

a) **National house building guarantee scheme/registered builders**
Builders registered under this scheme can offer you the additional security of a six year structural guarantee, against any major defects which may occur. Opting for a builder registered in this scheme, can often help to simplify mortgage applications, as it is a desired requirement with a lot of loaning agencies. The scheme is administered by the National House Building Guarantee Company, and inspections are carried out at three different stages during the course of construction, i.e. foundation trenches, roof and completion.

b) **Supervision by architect/engineer:**
This is an alternative option if your builder is not registered in the above scheme or if you are going the self-build route, you should ensure that the persons employed to carry out the inspections are covered by professional indemnity insurance, although this may be a standard requirement of your mortgage.

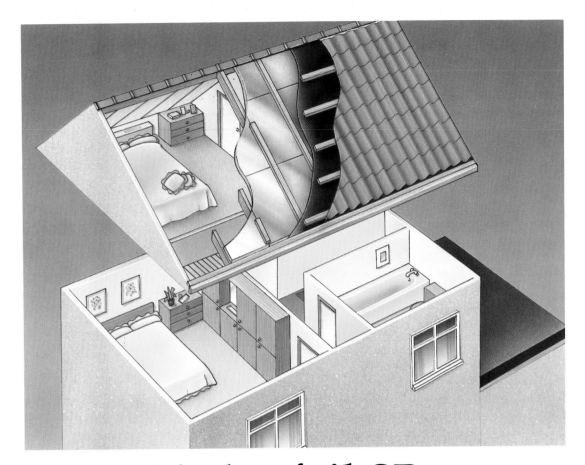

Getting The Most From Your Insulation
by Frank Fitzmaurice, Marketing Director
Kingspan Insulation Limited

Taking a closer look at the differences between various insulation materials can enable building designers to make informed choices about which product to use. In many instances, surprising benefits over and above the provision of thermal insulation to meet Building Regulations can be obtained.

This is well illustrated by the product range made by Kingspan Insulation - Rigid Urethane (Polyurethane) Foam Insulation boards. Combining the high thermal efficiency of the urethane foam core with a variety of purpose-designed facings, this product offers considerable benefits over and above ordinary fibrous or polystyrene insulation. Consider the following applications.

PITCHED AND DORMER ROOFS

Tradtionally, mineral fibre insulation has been used, either rolled out between the joists in the attic floor, or pinned up between the rafters in polythene. There are several drawbacks to this method.

• **Bulky Thickness:** due to mineral fibre's relatively poor thermal efficiency, as much as 150mm (6 inches) of this material is now needed to meet the Building Regulations for roof insulation. This thickness is greater than the depth of joist or rafter normally found in housing (100mm/4 inches).

• **Insulation Sag:** mineral fibre depends on retaining trapped air between the fibres for its thermal efficiency. Excessive packing during installation will seriously impair its insulation performance. Over time, the trapped air tends to escape as the weight of the fibres causes the material to settle down, again accompanied by a loss of thermal efficiency. In dormer roofs, the weight of the fibrous insulation could cause it to slip gradually down towards the bottom of the roof. Insulation sag (visible in many attics after a period of time) means that mineral fibre insulation can save less heat as time goes by.

• **Condensation:** because of mineral fibre's loose and open structure, it is advisable that a vapour barrier is placed between the insulation and the ceiling, that all possible points of vapour escape up into the attic are sealed and that there is adequate ventilation in the attic to dry out any condensation that may occur. Should condensation occur in a poorly ventilated attic, it will tend to saturate the water-absorbing mineral fibre insulation from the top down, diminishing its insulating values as the saturation increases. Ironically, the risk of heat loss due to saturated mineral fibre can be greatest during winter, the time when we most want our insulation to work!

• **Chill Factor:** an adequately ventilated attic will experience atmospheric temperatures, underlining the need for insulation of tanks and pipes. Cold air circulating through the top 25% of the mineral fibre can greatly reduce its effective thickness.

• **Thermal Looping:** it is essential that insulation be fitted down tight between the joists, flat on the top of the ceiling boards, to prevent air movement occurring between the top of the ceiling and the bottom of the insulation. Any such air movement will mean that warm air from below may become cooled before it comes into contact with the insulation. Ironically, while the temptation might be to pack the insulation tightly down between the joists, doing so with mineral fibre (as we have seen) could impair the thermal efficiency of this material.

One answer to these problems would be to use a rigid, higher performance insulation material, ideally fitting it between the rafters in the roof rather than the attic floor. This technique, called sarking insulation, creates a warm roof space instead of a cold attic, with obvious benefits in terms of eliminating both the need for attic ventilation and the need for insulation of tanks and pipes. A warm attic, which can represent 15% of the total building space, could be designed for use as storage space or extra living accommodation.

Kingspan Insulation's product for this application is Shelterfoil S.B. (see our advertisement). It is a foil-faced board which meets the Building Regulations with just 75mm thickness.

HOLLOW BLOCK WALLS

The traditional method of insulating hollow block walls has been to use timber battens, with mineral fibre packed in behind a vapour barrier, followed by the plasterboard.

Apart from the inherent drawbacks with mineral fibre due to insulation sag or collapse described above, this is a time-consuming and costly tradition. The alternative is to use insulated plasterboard, a composite panel combining thin rigid urethane insulation and gypsum plasterboard. Kinspan Insulation's board, called Shelter Plasterboard Laminate (Shelter PBL), offers the following advantages:

* One fix operation: the board can be fixed directly to the wall in a variety of methods.

* Eliminates condensation: the urethane foam insulation core has a high resistance to vapour transmission which prevents warm air coming into contact with the cold block wall.

Saves on thickness: because it has a superior thermal efficiency, 38mm of urethane insulation is equivalent to 64mm of Glass Fibre quilt (source: NHBGS Housing Insulation Guide) to meet the Building Regulations. This space saving feature can be very significant. Shelter PBL is ideal for existing uninsulated buildings where the same benefit of quick response heating without much loss of space can be achieved.

CAVITY WALLS

In a two leaf cavity wall construction, most designers favour partial fill insulation to avoid the risk of moisture penetration or the ingress of driven rain. Normally, this means that after insulation is applied, a 50mm clear cavity remains. However, ordinary insulation materials now need to be so thick (Mineral Fibre 65mm, Expanded Polystyrene 56mm) to meet the Building Regulations that either the traditional cavity width needs to be increased to exceed 100mm or the concept of a partial fill must be compromised.

An alternative is again provided by considering the higher performance rigid urethane insulation option. For cavity walls, Shelterwall is a foil-faced rigid board from Kingspan Insulation which meets the Building Regulations with a thickness of just 35mm. This thickness leaves a clear cavity of 65mm, providing a true "partial fill" solution for this problem. The foil facing increases the resistance to the passage of water vapour as well as almost doubling the thermal resistance of the cavity.

Apart from the retention of a clear cavity, Shelterwall doesn't break easily during handling and installation. Any breakage or excessive puncturing of brittle cavity insulation could create a gap in the insulation coverage of the wall leading to a potential cold bridge. This problem cannot be easily remedied once the wall is built so the robustness of Shelterwall compared with expanded polystyrene is an added benefit. Other advantages include compatibility with PVC wiring, piping and damp-proof courses.

FLOORS

The proper insulation of floors has been receiving increased attention in recent years. Traditionally, perimeter or edge insulation has been favoured, and for certain floor sizes this will still meet the Building Regulations.

Kingspan Insulation recommend full floor insulation for two simple reasons.

Firstly, using the earth as a heat store doesn't make good sense from an energy conservation perspective, particularly if local water table levels are high. Secondly, full floor insulation will considerably enhance user/occupier comfort. Creating a warm floor by placing insulation beneath the screed means that the screed offers a useful thermal mass, providing a quick response heating benefit back into the room.

Shelterfloor is a rigid urethane foam insulation board from Kingspan Insulation for use on solid or suspended floors. Thanks to urethane's superb insulating efficiency, a thickness of 25-30mm is usually adequate to meet the Building Regulations. Compared with 55mm of expanded polystyrene, Shelterfloor's thinness reduces the amount of soil excavation and removal, yet provides even greater compressive strength so important for this application. The full size boards won't easily blow off-site during high winds and will be much more resiliant than expanded polystyrene to the rigours of foot/wheelbarrow traffic, or to the pouring of a floor screed.

The extra benefits obtained by using the higher performance urethane insulation boards mean that their Value for Money can be properly established. Above all else, the advantages of space saving and long term insulation values make rigid urethane foam the growing choice for people who take the trouble to look into the difference between insulation materials.

Kingspan Insulation, who have accumulated over 70 years experience in rigid urethane foam insulation, manufacture a full range of insulation boards in Castleblayney, Co. Monaghan. Marketed under the Shelterboard brand name, the products are available from stockists nationwide.

Full product details, stockists locations and technical advice on insulation problems are available by calling us on (042) 40631.

Kingspan Insulation

GARAGE NO. 1

PROPOSED SIZE	Metric	Imperial
Floor area	54 sq.m	.581 sq.ft.
Double garage	5850 x 6000	19'2" x 19'8"
Store	3000 x 6000	9'10 x 19'8"
Compound	2750 x 2900	9'0" x 9'6"

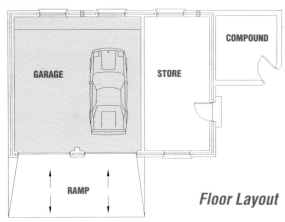

Floor Layout

GARAGE NO. 2

PROPOSED SIZE	Metric	Imperial
Floor area	42 sq.m.	452 sq.ft.
Garage	6000 x 7000	19'8" x 23'0"

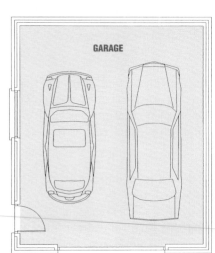

Floor Layout

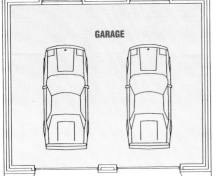

Floor Layout

GARAGE NO.3

PROPOSED SIZE	Metric	Imperial
Floor area	44 sq.m.	472 sq.ft.
Garage	7300 x 6000	24'0" x 19'8"

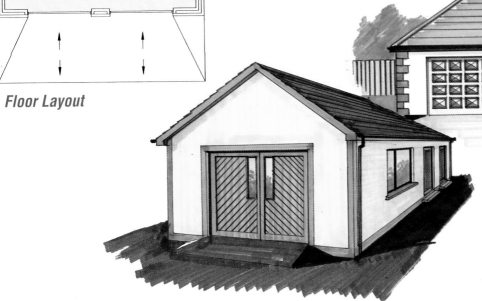

Floor Layout

GARAGE NO.4

PROPOSED SIZE	Metric	Imperial
Floor area	27 sq.m.	291 sq.ft.
Garage	4100 x 5000	13'6" x 16'5"
Store	2500 x 1500	8'3" x 4'11"
W.C.	1500 x 1500	4'11" x 4'11"

GARAGE NO.5

PROPOSED SIZE	Metric	Imperial
Floor area	20 sq.m.	219 sq.ft.
Garage	3700 x 5500	12'2" x 18'0"

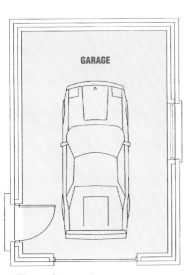

Floor Layout

DESIGN
1001

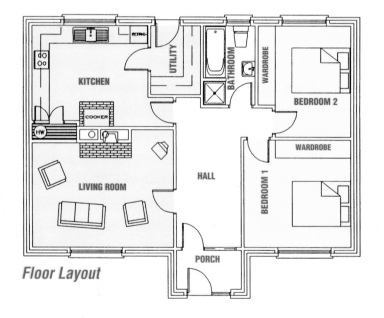

Floor Layout

A basic design with economical use of space while incorporating interesting porch feature. Roof can be raised and allowance made for initial or future attic conversion.

Construction Cost
See page 57

DETAILS	Metric	Imperial
Overall length	11.700 m.	38'5"
Overall width	9.450 m.	31'0"
Floor area	86 sq.m.	924 sq.ft.
Kitchen	4050 x 3200	13'4" x 10'6"
Utility	1750 x 2300	5'9" x 7'6"
Living room	4950 x 3500	16'3" x 11'6"
Bathroom	1800 x 2650	5'11" x 8'8"
Bedroom 1	3200 x 3750	10'6" x 12'4"
Bedroom 2	3700 x 3600	12'2 x 11'10"
Porch	2250 x 1300	7'4" x 4'3"
Main hall width	2250	7'4"

DESIGN
1002

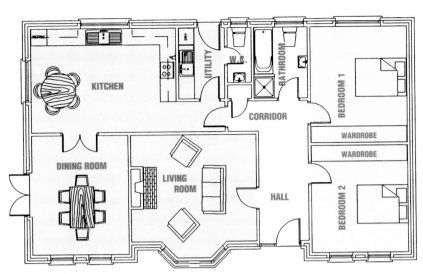

Floor Layout

DETAILS	Metric	Imperial
Overall length	14.700 m.	48'3"
Overall width	8.900 m.	29'0"
Floor area	115 sq.m.	1238 sq.ft.
Kitchen	5450 x 3800	17'10" x 12'6"
Utility	1750 x 2600	5'9" x 8'7"
W.c.	900 x 2000	3'0" x 6'7"
Bathroom	2000 x 2600	6'7" x 8'7"
Bedroom 1	3600 x 4250	11'10" x 13'11"
Bedroom 2	3600 x 3950	11'10" x 13'0"
Living room	4750 x 3950	15'7" x 13'0"
Dining room	3600 x 4400	11'10" x 14'5"
Main hall width	1850	6'1"

Luxurious 2-bedroom home with enhanced entrance. Also having large living quarters to facilitate future extension. Ideal for first home or retirement bungalow.

Construction Cost
See page 57

DESIGN
1003

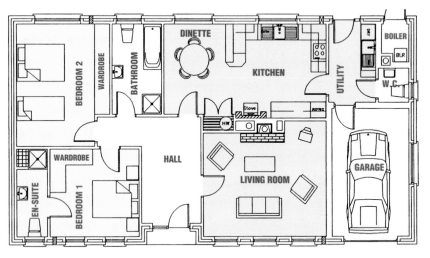

Floor Layout

A spacious 2-bedroom with traditional styling incorporating garage to one end.

Construction Cost
See page 57

DETAILS	Metric	Imperial
Overall length	16.350 m.	53'08"
Overall width	8.600 m.	28'2"
Floor area	105.5 sq.m	1137 sq.ft.
Boiler	26.5 sq.m	177 sq.ft.
Kitchen/Dinette	6500 x 3400	21'4" x 11'2"
Living room	4900 x 3900	16'1" x 12'10"
Utility	1875 x 2925	6'2" x 9'7"
W.C.	1225 x 1300	4'0" x 4'4"
Bathroom	2000 x 3400	6'7" x 11'2"
Bedroom 1	3600 x 3300	11'10" x 10'10"
Bedroom 2	3750 x 4600	12'4" x 15'1"
En-suite	1250 x 3300	4'2" x 10'10"
Main hall width	2400	7'11"

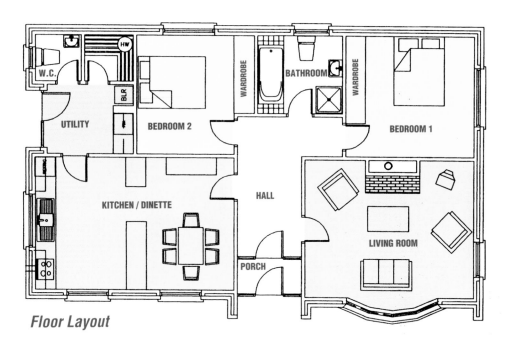

Floor Layout

DETAILS	Metric	Imperial
Overall length	13.560 m.	44'6"
Overall width	8.310 m.	27'3"
Floor area	96.5 sq.m.	1039 sq.ft.
Kitchen/Dinette	5900 x 3850	19'4" x 12'8"
Living room	5000 x 3800	16'5" x 12'6"
Utility	2050 x 2600	6'9" x 8'6"
W.C.	1350 x 1300	4'6" x 4'3"
Bathroom	2500 x 2250	8'2" x 7'4"
Bedroom 1	3600 x 3500	11'10" x 11'6"
Bedroom 2	2900 x 3450	9'6" x 11'4"
Main hall width	1900	6'3"

A traditional home incorporating many modern features. Kitchen/dinette is located to front of house making this design ideal for smaller sites with views and aspects to South.

Construction Cost
See page 57

DESIGN
1005

DETAILS	Metric	Imperial	DETAILS	Metric	Imperial
Overall length	12.32 m.	40.5"	Living room	4500 x 4200	14'9" x 13'9
Overall width	8.400 m.	27'6"	Bathroom	2600 x 1500	8'6" x 5'0"
Main body width	6.420 m.	21'1"	Bedroom 1	3500 x 4200	11'6" x 13'9"
Floor area	73.5 sq.m.	790.5 sq.ft.	Bedroom 2	3500 x 3000	11'6" x 9'10"
Store	2.80 sq.m.	30.5 sq.ft.	Hall width	1100	3'7"
Kitchen/dinette	5300 x 1900	17'4" x 6'3"	Porch	1800 x 1100	6'0" x 3'7"

An economical but interesting 2-bedroom house. Ideally suited for use as a holiday home.

Construction Cost
See page 57

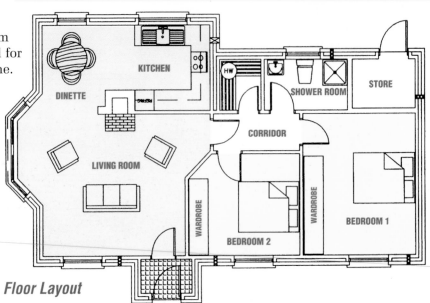

Floor Layout

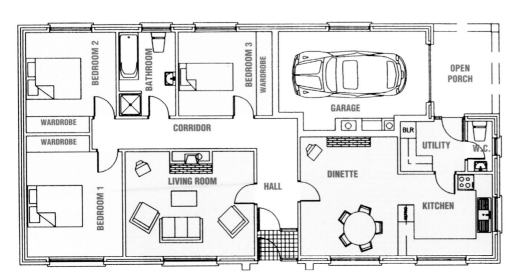

DESIGN
1006

Floor Layout

DETAILS	Metric	Imperial
Overall length	17.750 m.	58'5"
Overall width	8.700 m.	28'6"
Floor area	111 sq.m.	1199 sq.ft.
Garage	18 sq.m.	191 sq.ft.
Kitchen	3500 x 2950	11'6" x 9'8"
Dinette	3600 x 3800	11'10 x 12'6"
Living room	4800 x 3800	15'9" x 12'6"
Bathroom	2100 x 3050	6'11 x 10'0"
Utility	2400 x 1800	7'11 x 5'11"
W.c.	900 x 1800	3'0" x 5'11"
Bedroom 1	3500 x 3800	11'6" x 12'6"
Bedroom 2	3300 x 3050	10'10 x 10'0"
Bedrood 3	3500 x 3050	11'6" x 10'0"
Hall width	150	5'0"
Garage	5445 x 3050	17'10 x 10'0"

This compact 3-bedroom bungalow, has some excellent features in that the entire living quarters and main bedroom extend to the front of the dwelling. A standard size garage, incorporated access through covered open porch. Economical design-considering all the features.

Construction Cost
See page 57

DESIGN 1007

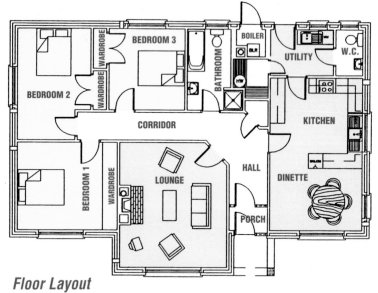

Floor Layout

Traditional 3-bedroomed home, with large kitchen/dinette and lounge to front. Suiting site with views and aspect to South and East.

Construction Cost *See page 57*

DETAILS	METRIC	IMPERIAL
Overall length	14.800 m.	48'9"
Overall width	10.150 m.	33'4"
Main body width	8.650 m.	28'5"
Floor area	119 sq.m.	1280 sq.ft.
Kitchen/Din.	3800 x 6050	12'6" x 19'10"
Lounge	4400 x 5000	14'5" x 16'8"
Bathroom	1800 x 3250	5'11" x 10'8"
Utility	2600 x 1850	8'7" x 6'1"
W.c.	1100 x 1850	3'8" x 6'1"
Bedroom 1	4100 x 3500	13'6" x 11'6"
Bedroom 2	3000 x 3350	8'10" x 11'0"
Bedroom 3	3100 x 3250	10'2" x 10'8"
Hall width	1600	5'3"

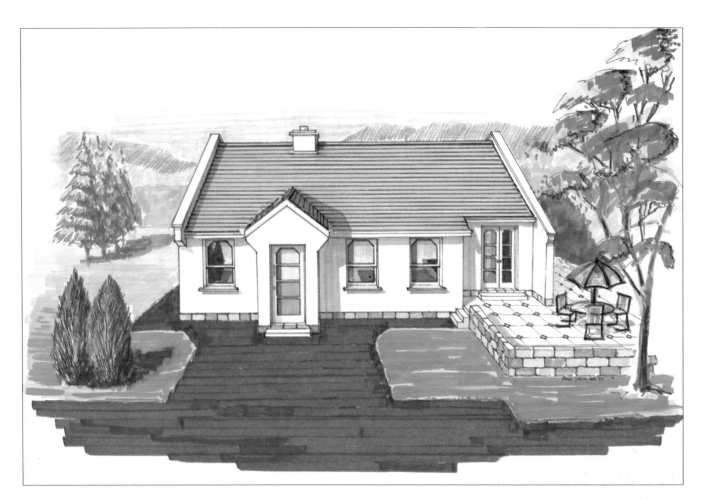

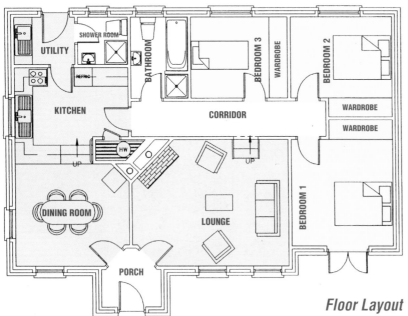

Floor Layout

DESIGN
1008

A compact split level cottage with traditional styling incorporating raised barges and entrance porch. The elimination of unnecessary hallways helps maximise internal room sizes.

Construction Cost
See page 57

DETAILS	METRIC	IMPERIAL
Overall length	13.145 m.	43'2"
Overall width	9.950 m.	32'8"
Main body width	8.650 m.	28'4"
Floor area	103 sq.m.	1108 sq.ft.
Kitchen	6400 x 3775	21'0" x 12'4"
Lounge	5220 x 4085	17'2" x 13'5"
Bathroom	1920 x 2600	6'3" x 8'6"
Utility	2000 x 1500	6'7" x 5'0"
Shower room	1675 x 1500	5'6" x 5'0"
Bedroom 1	3350 x 4085	11'0" x 13'5"
Bedroom 2	3350 x 2600	11'0" x 8'6"
Bedroom 3	3200 x 2600	10'6" x 8'6"
Hall width	1100	73'8"

DESIGN
1009

Compact 3-bedroom dwelling with garage and store incorporated, with a rather pleasing and attractive facade.

Construction Cost
See page 57

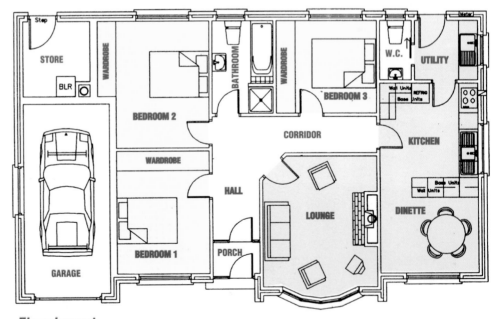

Floor Layout

DETAILS	Metric	Imperial
Overall length	14.950 m.	49'1"
Overall width	8.860 m.	29'0"
Floor area	91 sq.m.	983 sq.ft.
Gar/store	20 sq.m.	215 sq.ft.
Kitchen/Din.	3100 x 5800	10'2" x 19'0"
Living room	3600 x 4000	11'10 x 13'2"
Bathroom	1950 x 2750	6'5" x 9'0"
Utility	2000 x 1800	6'7" x 5'11"

DETAILS	Metric	Imperial
W.c.	1000 x 1800	3'4" x 5'11"
Bedroom 1	2950 x 3750	9'8" x 12'4"
Bedroom 2	2950 x 3850	9'8" x 12'8"
Bedroom 3	3150 x 2750	10'4" x 9'0"
Hall width	1500	4'11
Store	2100 x 2275	6'11x 7'6"
Garage	2700 x 5800	8'11 x 19'0"

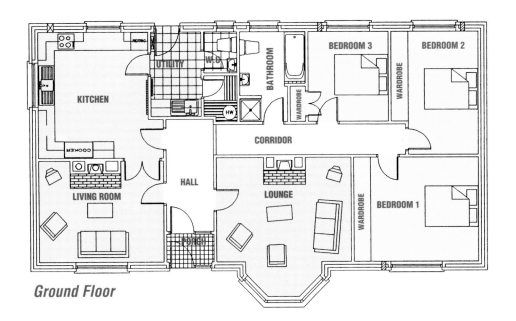

Ground Floor

DESIGN
1010

DETAILS	METRIC	IMPERIAL
Overall length	9.810 m.	32'2"
Overall width	8.570 m.	28'2"
Floor area	125 sq.m.	1345 sq.ft.
Kitchen	3925 x 4250	12'10" x 14'3"
Living room	4450 x 3500	14'7" x 11'6"
Lounge	4850 x 3610	15'11" x 11'10"
Bathroom	2375 x 3080	7'9" x 10'1"

DETAILS	METRIC	IMPERIA
Utility	1800 x 3080	5'11" x 10'1"
W.C.	1200 x 1400	3'11" x 4'7"
Bedroom 1	4450 x 3610	14'7" x 11'10"
Bedrood 2	3100 x 4240	10'2" x 13'11"
Bedroom 3	2850 x 3080	9'4" x 10'1"
Hall width	1700	5'7"

A very comfortable 3-bedroom home, with an attractive bay window to front. Bay window design can be altered to suit alternative preferences.

Construction Cost
See page 57

DESIGN
1011

Traditional, cottage-style home which has proven to be one of our best sellers in this price range, in that it offers everything you would require in a home of this calibre.

Construction Cost
See page 57

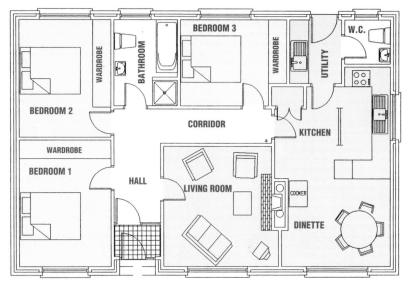

Floor Layout

DETAIL	METRIC	IMPERIAL		DETAIL	METRIC	IMPERIAL
Overall length	12.630 m.	41'5"		Utility	1700 x 2040	5'7" x 6'8"
Overall width	8.335 m.	27'4"		W.C.	1500 x 1420	4'11 x 4'8"
Floor area	97.5 sq.m.	1050 sq.ft.		Bedroom 1	3050 x 4060	10'0" x 13'4"
Kitchen/Din.	3350 x 5790	11'0" x 19'0"		Bedroom 2	3050 x 3765	10'0" x 12'4"
Living room	3600 x 3860	11'10 x 12'8"		Bedroom 3	2950 x 2750	9'8" x 9'0"
Bathroom	2100 x 2750	7'0" x 9'0"		Hall width	155	5'1"

DESIGN
1012

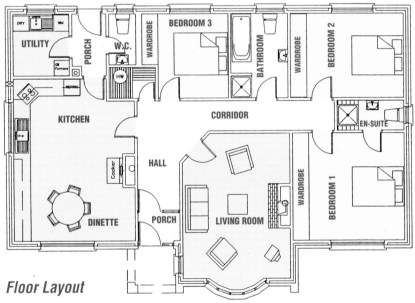

Floor Layout

DETAIL	Metric	Imperial
Overall length	14.960 m.	49'1"
Overall width	10.235 m.	33'7"
Floor area	122.5 sq.m.	1320 sq.ft.
Kitchen	4500 x 5800	14'9" x 19'0"
Living room	4000 x 5150	13'1" x 16'11"
Bathroom	2100 x 3000	6'10" x 9'10"
Utility	2050 x 2200	6'8" x 7'3"

DETAIL	Metric	Imperial
W.c.	910 x 1800	3'0" x 6'0"
En-suite	2450 x 1100	8'1" x 3'7"
Bedroom 1	4100 x 3800	13'5" x 12'5"
Bedroom 2	4150 x 3000	13'7" x 9'10"
Bedroom 3	2625 x 3000	8'8" x 9'10"
Hall width	1500	5'0"

An elegant 3-bedroom home incorporating large kitchen/dinette area and en-suite to main bedroom.

Construction Cost
See page 57

DESIGN
1013

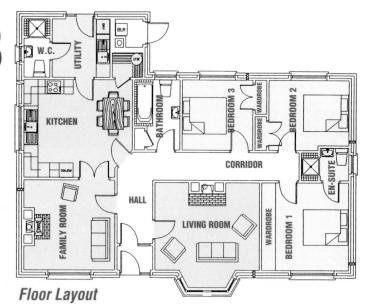

Floor Layout

This home comprises a compact yet spacious layout with the added feature of bay window to living room and all modern utility facilities. This design incorporates attractive bonnet hips which can be replaced with traditional gables or hips if desired.

Construction Cost
See page 57

DETAILS	METRIC	IMPERIAL	DETAILS	METRIC	IMPERIAL
Overall length	14.570 m.	47'10"	Bathroom	1950 x 2900	6'4" x 9'6"
Overall width	11.020 m.	36'2"	Utility	2475 x 2400	8'2" x 7'10"
Main body width	8.520 m.	28'0"	Shower room	1100 x 2400	3'7" x 7'10"
Floor area	122 sq.m.	1313 sq.ft.	En-suite	2000 x 1350	6'7" x 4'6"
Boiler	1.5 sq.m.	15.5 sq.ft.	Bedroom 1	3700 x 3650	12'2" x 11'11"
Kitchen	3650 x 4050	12'0" x 13'3"	Bedroom 2	3400 x 2700	11'2" x 8'10"
Family room	3900 x 3750	12'9" x 12'4"	Bedroom 3	3050 x 2900	10'0" x 9'6"
Living room	4500 x 3650	14'9" x 11'11"			

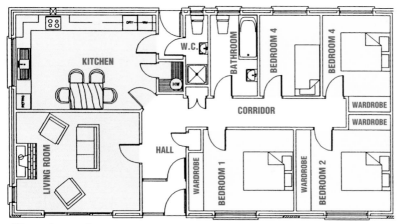

Floor Layout

DESIGN
1014

An economical 4-bedroom home with generously sized kitchen and living rooms. Brick quoins and roof over entrance, add extra character to overall appearance.

Construction Cost
See page 57

DETAILS	METRIC	IMPERIAL
Overall length	15.650 m.	51'4"
Overall width	8.160 m.	26'9"
Floor area	115 sq.m.	1235 sq.ft.
Kitchen/Din	5600 x 3700	18'4" x 12'2"
Living room	4900 x 3800	16'1" x 12'5"
Bathroom	1900 x 3150	6'2" x 10'4"

DETAILS	METRIC	IMPERIAL
Rear porch	1000 x 1700	1'3" x 5'7"
W.C.	900 x 2700	3'0" x 8'10"
Bedroom 1	3650 x 3150	11'11 x 10'4"
Bedroom 2	3850 x 3150	12'7" x 10'4"
Bedroom 3	2750 x 3150	9'10 x 10'4"
Hall width	1800	5'9"

DESIGN
1015

DETAILS	METRIC	IMPERIAL		DETAILS	METRIC	IMPERIAL
Overall length	15.010 m.	49'3"		Utility	2900 x 1200	9'6" x 4'0"
Overalla width	12.850 m.	42'2"		W.C.	1360 x 1650	4'6" x 5'5"
Main body width	8.300 m.	27'3"		Bedroom 1	3660 x 3200	12'0" x 10'6"
Floor area	125 sq.m.	1345 sq.ft.		Bedroom 2	3200 x 3200	10'6" x 10'6"
Kitchen/Din	5030 x 4420	16'6" x 14'6"		Bedroom 3	3400 x 3200	11'2" x 10'6"
Living room	5030 x 4270	16'6" x 14'0"		Bedroom 4	3095 x 3200	10'2" x 10'6"
Bathroom	1980 x 3200	6'6" x 10'6"		Hall width	1625	5'4"

Compact 4-bedroom with utility and second w.c. located in rear projection. Bay to living room, stone to quoins and under bay, make very attractive features.

Construction Cost
See page 57

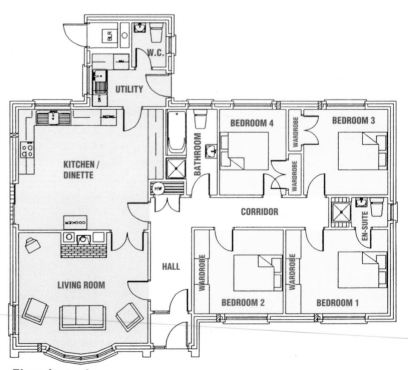

Floor Layout

DESIGN
1016

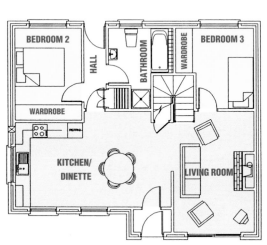

Ground Floor Layout

First Floor Layout

DETAILS	Metric	Imperial
Overall length	10.160 m.	33'4"
Overall width	8.560 m.	28'1"
Main body width	7.600 m.	25'0"
Floor area	102 sq.m.	1094 sq.ft.
Ground floor	72 sq.m.	771 sq.ft.
First floor	30 sq.m.	323 sq.ft.
Kitchen/din.	6400 x 3300	21'0" x 10'10"
Living room	3200 x 4750	10'6" x 15'7"
Bathroom	2600 x 2250	8'6" x 7'4"
En-suite	2060 x 2040	6'9" x 6'8"
Bedroom 1	3340 x 4888	10'11 x 16'0"
Bedroom 2	2700 x 3600	8'10 x 11'10"
Bedroom 3	2300 x 3150	7'6" x 10'4"

A traditionally styled holiday home, making use of roof space to accommodate master bedroom and en-suite, while incorporating a spacious open plan layout with full height sloping ceiling, and first floor balcony over living room.

Construction Cost See page 57

DESIGN
1017

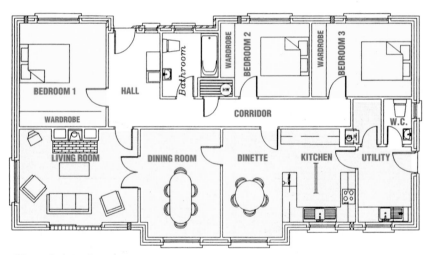

Floor Layout

DETAILS	Metric	Imperial
Overall length	16.650 m.	55'6"
Overall width	9.100 m.	29'10"
Main body width	8.500 m.	27'11"
Floor area	125 sq.m.	1345 sq.ft.
Kitchen	3000 x 3700	9'10" x 12'2"
Dinette	2500 x 4300	8'3" x 14'1"
Dining room	3300 x 4300	10'10 x 14'1"
Living room	4800 x 3700	15'9" x 12'2"
Bathroom	2300 x 1750	7'7" x 5'9"
Utility	2150 x 3000	7'1" x 9'10"
W.C.	1125 x 1800	3'8" x 5'11"
Bedroom 1	3500 x 4100	11'6" x 13'6"
Bedroom 2	4050 x 2900	13'4" x 9'6"
Bedroom 3	3100 x 2900	10'2" x 9'6"
Hall width	2100	6'11"

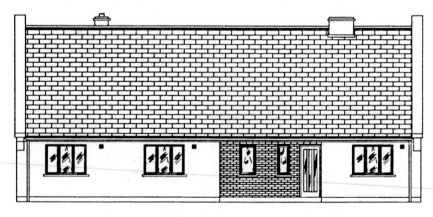

Rear Elevation

Designed along traditional lines, this home features raised barges and recessed stone/brick porch to rear, but has the benefit of modern internal layout, incorporating utility room and generous living accommodation.

Construction Cost
See page 57

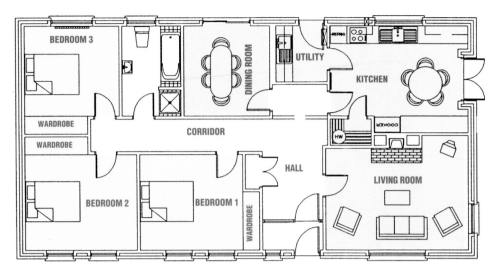

Floor Layout

DESIGN
1018

DETAILS	Metric	Imperial
Overall length	16.350 m.	53'8"
Overall width	8.400 m.	27'7"
Floor area	122.5 sq.m.	1316 sq.ft.
Kitchen/din.	4900 x 3135	16'1" x 10'4"
Dining	3050 x 3135	10'0" x 10'4"
Living room	5075 x 3550	16'8" x 11'8"
Bathroom	2100 x 3135	7'0" x 10'4"
Utility	1825 x 1935	6'0" x 6'4"
Bedroom 1	3965 x 3350	13'0" x 11'0"
Bedroom 2	4260 x 3350	14'0" x 11'0"
Bedroom 3	3350 x 3135	11'0" x 10'4"
Hall width	2150	7'1"

This 3-bedroom home
has been designed along
traditional lines and is
particularly suited to the
West of Ireland.

Construction Cost
See page 57

DETAILS	Metric	Imperial
Overall length	14.560 m.	47'9"
Overall width	8.710 m.	28'7"
Floor area	113.5 sq.m.	1221.5 sq.ft.
Kitchen/Din.	6600 x 3300	21'8" x 10'10"
Living room	4700 x 3950	15'5" x 12'11"
Bathroom	2000 x 3350	6'7" x 11'0"
Utility	1700 x 2050	5'7" x 6'9"
Bedroom 1	3600 x 3500	11'10 x 11'6"
Bedroom 2	3600 x 3500	11'10 x 11'6"
Bedroom 3	3400 x 3350	11'2" x 11'0"
Hall width	1800	5'9"

Elegant, traditionally-styled home with large kitchen/dinette and sizable living room. This design is available with modifications, i.e. straight roof with gable ends, single windows etc.

Construction Cost *See page 57*

Floor Layout

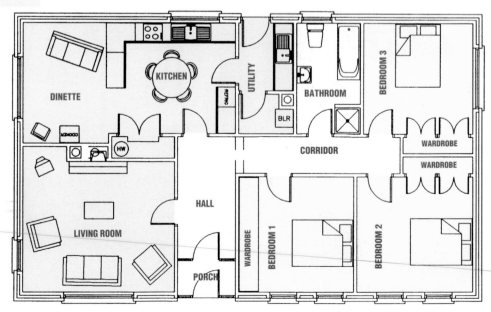

DESIGN
1019

Floor Layout

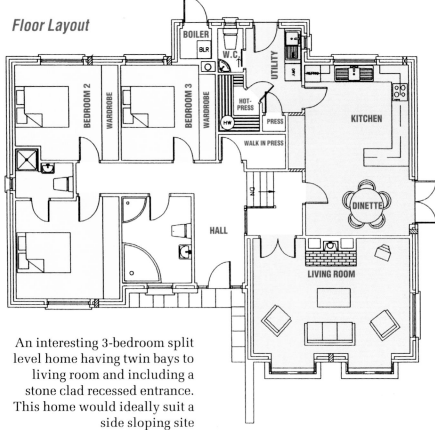

DETAILS	Metric	Imperial
Overall length	14.700 m.	48'3"
Overall width	11.850 m.	38'10"
Main body width	8.700 m.	28'6"
Floor area	125 sq.m.	1345 sq.ft.
Kitchen/Din.	3700 x 5900	12'2" x 19'4"
Living room	5600 x 3650	18'4" x 12'0"
Bathroom	2500 x 3000	8'2" x 9'10"
Utility	2000 x 2900	6'7" x 9'6"
W.C.	900 x 1500	2'11" x 4'11"
En-suite	2050 x 1200	6'9" x 4'0"
Bedroom 1	3700 x 3400	12'2" x 11'2"
Bedroom 2	3700 x 2800	12'2" x 9'2"
Bedroom 3	3400 x 3300	11'2" x 10'10"
Hall width	1800	5'11"

An interesting 3-bedroom split level home having twin bays to living room and including a stone clad recessed entrance. This home would ideally suit a side sloping site

Construction Cost *See page 57*

DESIGN
1020

DESIGN
1021

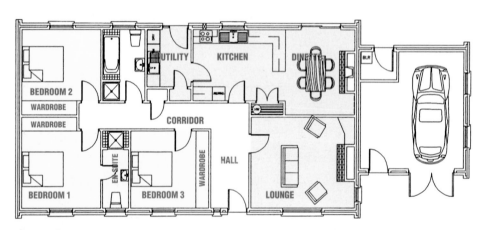

Floor Layout

A good sized 3-bedroomed home, with spacious kitchen, dinette and large main bedroom, with adjoining en-suite. Raised barges and projecting gables give a more traditional look to this design. Garage is optional according to your needs.

DETAILS	Metric	Imperial	DETAILS	Metric	Imperial
Overall length	21.140 m.	69'4"	Bathroom	1950 x 3050	6'4" x 10'0"
Overall width	8.560 m.	28'1"	Utility	2050 x 2450	6'9" x 8'0"
Floor area	119 sq.m.	1284 sq.ft.	En-suite	1200 x 3350	3'11 x 11'0"
Gar/boiler	24 sq.m.	258 sq.ft.	Bedroom 1	3650 x 3350	12'0" x 11'0"
Kitchen	4350 x 3050	14'3" x 10'0"	Bedroom 2	3650 x 3050	12'0" x 10'0"
Dinette	2750 x 5650	9'0" x 12'0"	Bedroom 3	3650 x 3350	12'0" x 12'0"
Lounge	4800 x 3950	15'9" x 13'0"	Hall width	1800	5'11

Construction Cost
See page 57

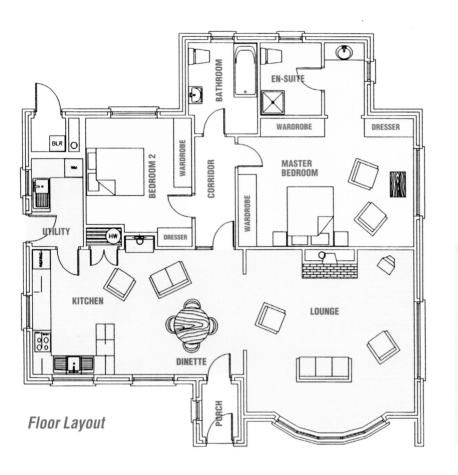

Floor Layout

DESIGN
1022

A 2-bedroom home with corridor space all but eliminated, allowing for larger rooms and service areas.

Construction Cost *See page 57*

DETAILS	Metric	Imperial
Overall length	13.200 m.	43'4"
Overall width	13.200 m.	43'4"
Main body width	10.800 m.	35'5"
Floor area	125 sq.m.	1345 sq.ft.
Kitchen/din.	7000 x 4000	23'0" x 13'2"
Lounge	5500 x 5800	18'0" x 19'0"
Bathroom	2300 x 2900	7'7" x 9'6"
Utility	1700 x 2800	5'7" x 9'2"
En-suite	2000 x 2300	6'7" x 7'7"
Master bedroom	5750 x 4100	18'11 x 13'6"
Bedroom 2	3500 x 3400	11'6" x 11'2"

DESIGN
1023

An economical 3-bedroom home with the added feature of brick lintels, quoins and plinth if desired.

Construction Cost
See page 57

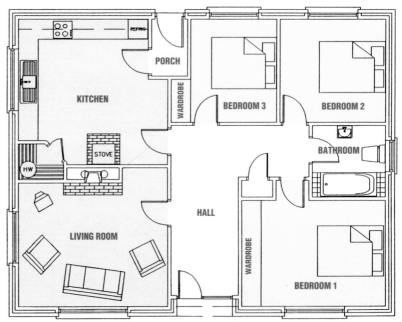

Floor Layout

DETAILS	Metric	Imperial
Overall length	11.800 m.	38'9"
Overall width	9.050 m.	29'8"
Floor area	95 sq.m.	1024 sq.ft.
Kitchen	4000 x 4250	13'2" x 14'0"
Living room	4550 x 3650	15'0" x 12'0"
Bathroom	2200 x 2100	7'3" x 6'11"
Bedroom 1	4350 x 3150	14'3" x 10'4"
Bedroom 2	3200 x 3050	10'6" x 10'1"
Bedroom 3	2650 x 3050	8'8" x 10'1"
Hall width	2100	6'11"

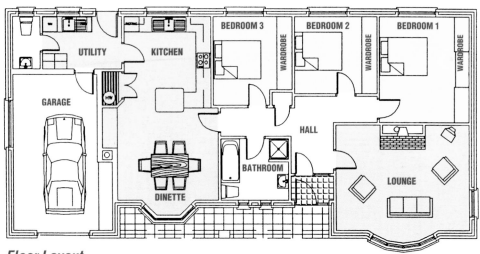

Floor Layout

DESIGN
1024

DETAILS	Metric	Imperial
Overall length	19.000 m.	62'4"
Overall width	8.950 m.	29'4"
Floor area	120 sq.m.	1293 sq.ft.
Garage	22 sq.m.	240 sq.ft.
Kitchen/Din.	3500 x 7150	11'6" x 23'5"
Lounge	5350 x 4150	17'6" x 13'7"
Bathroom	2750 x 2400	9'0" x 7'10"
Utility	3200 x 2050	10'6" x 6'9"
W.C.	1100 x 2050	3'8" x 6'9"
Bedroom 1	3600 x 4100	11'10 x 13'6"
Bedroom 2	3300 x 3000	10'10 x 9'10"
Bedroom 3	3200 x 3450	10'6" x 11'4"
Hall width	1700	5'7"
Garage	3400 x 6085	11'2" x 19'11"

A modern design featuring attractive recessed entrance and bay to lounge and incorporating generous garage/workshop.

Construction Cost
See page 57

DESIGN 1025

This pleasant 3-bedroom house has the advantage of a spacious kitchen/dinette suitable for every day living (leaving the lounge available for those special occasions).

Construction Cost
See page 57

DETAILS	Metric	Imperial
Overall length	16.760 m.	55'0"
Overall width	8.810 m	28'11"
Floor area	125 sq.m.	1345 sq.ft.
Kitchen/Din.	3350 x 7400	11'0" x 24'3"
Living room	5250 x 3750	17'3" x 12'4"
Bathroom	2200 x 2835	7'3" x 9'4"
Utility	1900 x 2335	6'3" x 7'8"
W.C.	1300 x 1400	4'3" x 4'7"
Bedroom 1	3750 x 4100	12'4" x 13'6"
Bedroom 2	2750 x 4050	9'0" x 13'4"
Bedroom 3	3000 x 2835	9'10" x 9'4"
Hall width	1800	6'0"

Ground Floor

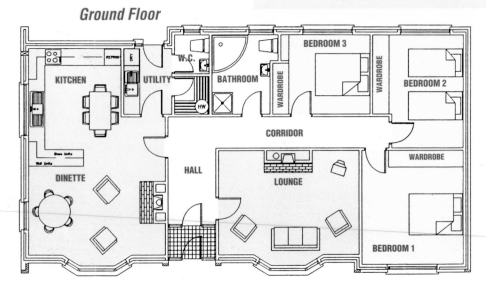

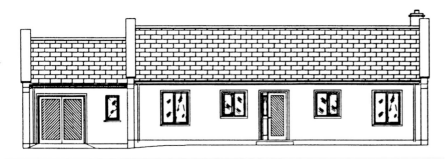

DESIGN
1026

DETAILS	Metric	Imperial
Overall length	18.400 m.	60'4"
Overall width	9.000 m.	29'6"
Main body width	7.900 m.	25'11"
Floor area	92 sq.m.	991 sq.ft.
Gar/boiler	24 sq.m.	258 sq.ft.
Kitchen/Din.	5600 x 2500	18'4" x 8'3"
Lounge	4375 x 5400	14'4" x 17'9"

DETAILS	Metric	Imperial
Bathroom	1950 x 2500	6'5" x 8'3"
En-suite	1700 x 2300	5'7" x 7'6"
Bedroom 1	3175 x 2850	10'5" x 9'4"
Bedroom 2	3350 x 2850	11'0" x 9'4"
Bedroom 3	3150 x 3050	10'4" x 10'0"
Hall width	1500	4'11

Compact 3-bedroom, with en-suite adjoining main bedroom and including gabled projection of large open plan kitchen /lounge area.

Construction Cost See page 57

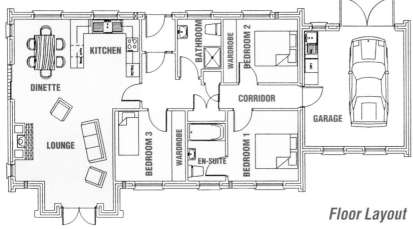

Floor Layout

DESIGN
1027

Ideally approached from the rear, this home includes large lounge and 3 spacious bedrooms, 1 with en-suite. Location of living room and lounge make it best suited to a site with views to front.

Construction Cost
See page 57

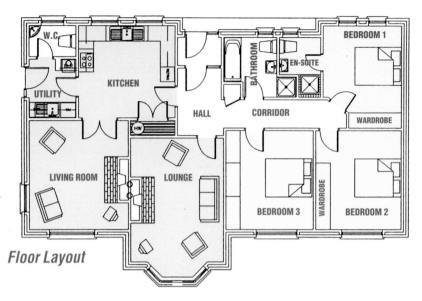

Floor Layout

DETAILS	Metric	Imperial		DETAILS	Metric	Imperial
Overall length	15.800 m	51'10"		*Utility*	1900 x 2300	6'3" x 7'7"
Overall width	9.900 m	32'6"		*W.C.*	1900 x 1200	6'3" x 3'11"
Main body width	8.600 m	28'3"		*En-suite*	1700 x 1450	5'7" x 4'9"
Floor area	124 sq.m	1332 sq.ft.		*Bedroom 1*	3200 x 3600	10'6" x 11'10"
Kitchen	3900 x 3600	12'10" x 11'10"		*Bedroom 2*	3500 x 3900	11'6" x 12'10"
Living room	4000 x 4300	13'2" x 14'1"		*Bedroom 3*	3600 x 3900	11'10" x 12'10"
Lounge	3800 x 4900	12'6" x 16'1"		*Hall width*	1900	6'3"
Bathroom	2100 x 2350	6'11" x 7'9"				

DETAILS	Metric	Imperial	DETAILS	Metric	Imperial
Overall length	18.425 m.	60'5"	Utility	2500 x 1900	8'3" x 6'3"
Overall width	9.700 m.	31'10"	W.C.	1500 x 1200	4'11 x 4'0"
Main body width	8.300 m.	27'3"	En-suite	1900 x 1975	6'3" x 6'5"
Floor area	123 sq.m.	1326 sq.ft.	Bedroom 1	4000 x 3700	13'2" x 10'10"
Gar/boiler	23 sq.m.	248 sq.ft.	Bedroom 2	3600 x 3050	11'10 x 10'0"
Kitchen/Din.	4100 x 5400	13'5" x 17'9"	Bedroom 3	3500 x 3200	11'6" x 10'6"
Living room	4300 x 4500	14'2" x 14'9"	Hall width	2000	6'7"
Bathroom	2400 x 3200	7'10 x 10'6"	Garage	3300 x 5500	10'10 x 18'1"

DESIGN
1028

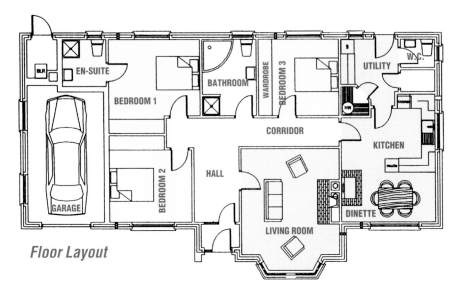

Floor Layout

Brick quoins, plinth and entrance add particular interest to this 3-bedroom home, also included are dormers to roof, which serve as lighting for storage space or future conversion.

Construction Cost *See page 57*

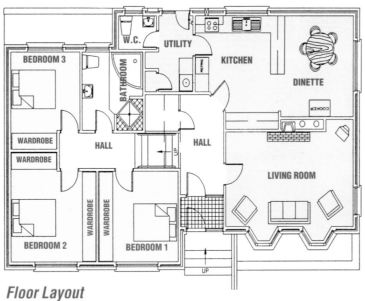

Floor Layout

An exceptionally attractive split level home ideally suited for a side sloping site, incorporating 3-bedrooms with spacious living quarters and dual level bathroom internally, while having a raised recessed entrance along with projecting bays in feature random stone externally. The provision of dormers at roof level allow for future conversion of attic with stair located in hall cupboard area.

Construction Cost *See page 57*

DESIGN
1029

DETAILS	Metric	Imperial
Overall length	15.460 m.	50'9"
Overall width	9.595 m.	31'5"
Main body width	8.260 m.	27'1"
Floor area	119 sq.m.	1277 sq.ft.
Kitchen	6850 x 3700	22'5" x 12'5"
Living room	5500 x 3500	18'0" x 11'6"
Bathroom	2650 x 2850	8'8" x 9'4"

DETAILS	Metric	Imperial
Utility	1500 x 2790	5'0" x 9'2"
W.C.	1650 x 1235	5'6" x 4'0"
Bedroom 1	3500 x 3350	11'6" x 11'0"
Bedroom 2	3700 x 3350	12'2" x 11'0"
Bedroom 3	3000 x 2850	9'10" x 9'4"
Hall width	1900	6'3"

DESIGN
1030

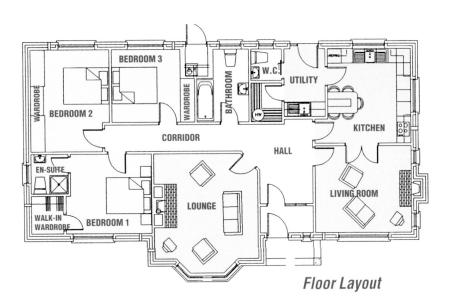

Floor Layout

DETAILS	Metric	Imperial	DETAILS	Metric	Imperial
Overall length	16.720 m.	54'10"	Utility	1750 x 2800	5'9" x 9'2"
Overall width	9.270 m.	30'5"	W.C.	1300 x 1300	4'3" x 4'3"
Main body width	8.220 m.	26'11"	En-suite	1350 x 1650	4'6" x 5'5"
Floor area	125 sq.m.	1345 sq.ft.	Bedroom 1	3600 x 3300	11'10 x 10'10"
Kitchen	3550 x 3900	11'8" x 12'9"	Bedroom 2	3300 x 4200	10'10 x 13'9"
Living room	4100 x 3600	13'5" x 11'10"	Bedroom 3	2900 x 3000	9'6" x 9'10"
Lounge	4400 x 4350	14'5" x 14'2"	Hall width	2250	7'5"
Bathroom	1500 x 3000	5'0" x 9'10"			

A spacious 3-bedroom bungalow with projecting lounge and bay, also, incorporating en-suite and walk-in to main bedroom.

Construction Cost
See page 57

DESIGN
1031

A dormer residence comprising
3 spacious bedrooms and
exceptionally large living/kitchen
area, for a home which still comes
within grant size.

Construction Cost *See page 57*

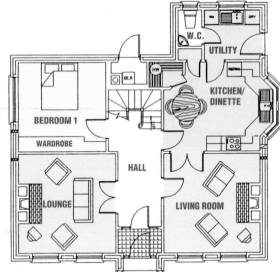

Ground Floor Layout

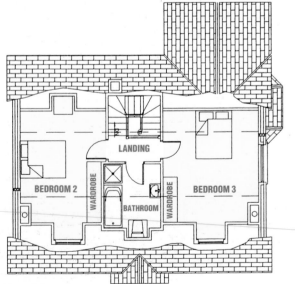

First Floor Layout

DETAILS	Metric	Imperial
Overall length	10.620 m.	34'10"
Overall width	10.820 m.	36'6"
Main body width	8.320 m.	27'3"
Floor area	125 sq.m.	1345 sq ft.
Ground floor	81.5 sq.m.	877 sq.ft.
First floor	43.5 sq.m.	468 sq.ft.
Kitchen	4000 x 3600	13'1" x 11'10"
Living room	4000 x 4000	13'1" x 13'1"
Lounge	4000 x 4000	13'1" x 13'1"
Bathroom	2400 x 2565	7'10 x 8'5"
Utility	2300 x 2000	7'6" x 6'7"
W.c.	1000 x 1450	3'3" x 4'9"
Bedroom 1	3600 x 3600	11'10 x 11'10"
Bedroom 2	3600 x 4450	11'10 x 14'7"
Bedroom 3	4000 x 4450	13'1" x 14'7"
Hall width	1800	5'11"

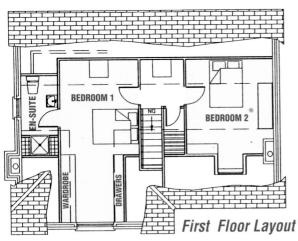

First Floor Layout

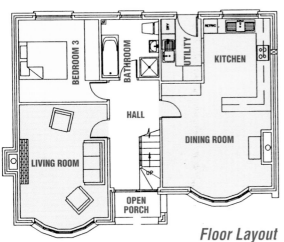

Floor Layout

A grant size "L" shaped home, which incorporates luxurious master bedroom with adjoining dressing area and en-suite. Bay windows and open porch combine with dormer to give this dwelling a somewhat charming appearance.

DESIGN
1032

Construction Cost *See page 57*

DETAILS	Metric	Imperial
Overall length	11.160 m.	36'7"
Overall width	8.610 m.	28'3"
Main body width	7.590 m.	24'11"
Floor area	125 sq.m.	1345 sq.ft.
Kitchen	2850 x 3800	9'4" x 12'5"
Dining room	4650 x 3050	15'3 x 10'0"
Living room	3650 x 4600	12'0 x 15'1"
Utility	1700 x 2500	5'7"x 8'3"
En-suite	1525 x 3200	5'0"x 10'6"
Bedroom 1	3265 x 3815	10'9" x 12'6"
Bedroom 2	3700 x 3815	12'2" x 12'6"
Bedroom 3	3350 x 3350	11'0" x 11'0"
Hall width	2100	6'10"

DESIGN
1033

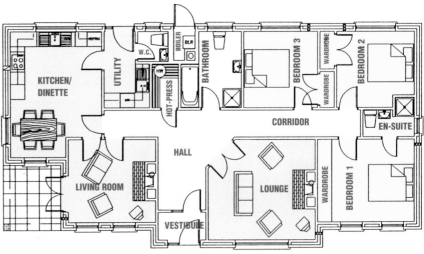

Floor Layout

Here we have a spacious 3-bedroom bungalow, with traditional lines while incorporating very generous living areas with patio off living room and en-suite to main bedroom.

Construction Cost
See page 57

DETAILS	Metric	Imperial
Overall length	17.750 m.	58'3"
Overall width	9.020 m.	29'7"
Main body width	8.320 m.	27'3"
Floor area	125 sq.m.	1345 sq.ft.
Kitchen/din.	3800 x 4250	1'5" x 13'11"
Living room	3650 x 3350	12'0" x 11'0"
Lounge	4450 x 4050	14'6" x 13'3"
Bathroom	1800 x 3050	5'9" x 10'0"

DETAILS	Metric	Imperial
Utility	1300 x 3050	4'3" x 10'0"
W.c.	1275 x 1200	4'2" x 3'11"
En-suite	1100 x 2150	3'7" x 7'1"
Bedroom 1	4050 x 3350	13'3" x 11'0"
Bedroom 2	3250 x 2550	10'8" x 8'4"
Bedroom 3	3150 x 3050	10'4" x 10'0"
Hall width	2000	6'7"

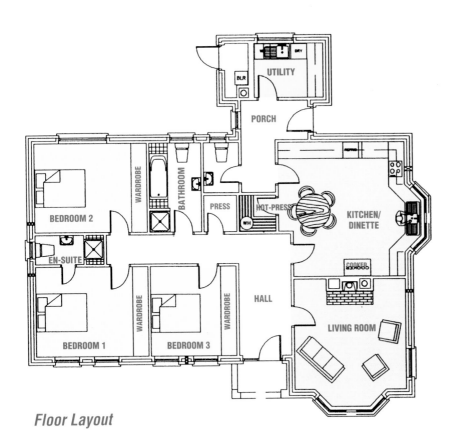

Floor Layout

DETAILS	Metric	Imperial
Overall length	14.770 m.	48'5"
Overall width	13.500 m.	44'3"
Floor area	125 sq.m.	1345 sq.ft.
Boiler	1.8 sq.m.	19.5 sq.ft.
Kitchen/din.	4950 x 5000	16'3" x 16'5"
Living room	4250 x 4100	14'0" x 13'5"
Bathroom	2000 x 3300	6'7" x 10'10"
Utility	2625 x 2000	8'8" x 6'7"
W.C.	1300 x 1840	4'3" x 6'1"
En-suite	1100 x 2600	3'7" x 8'6"
Bedroom 1	4300 x 3300	14'2" x 10'10"
Bedroom 2	4300 x 3300	14'2" x 10'10"
Bedroom 3	3300 x 3300	10'10" x 10'10"
Hall width	2000	6'6"

This 3-bedroom home maximises available space while remaining within grant size. It includes a rear annex incorporating utility room, and features a brick open entrance porch and half hip roof.

Construction Cost *See page 57*

DESIGN
1034

DESIGN 1035

A very pleasant 4-bedroomed home, having 2 large double bedrooms (one with en-suite) and 2 medium sized double bedrooms, also incorporating generous kitchen/dinette and living rooms.

Construction Cost *See page 57*

DETAILS	Metric	Imperial
Overall length	17.820 m.	58'6"
Overall width	8.070 m.	26'6"
Floor area	125 sq.m.	1345 sq.ft.
Kitchen	6900 x 3200	22'8" x 10'6"
Living room	4700 x 4150	15'5" x 13'8"
Bathroom	2225 x 3050	7'3" x 10'0"
Utility	2050 x 3050	6'9" x 10'0"
W.C.	1500 x 1310	4'11" x 4'3"
En-suite	2200 x 1100	7'3" x 3'8"
Bedroom 1	3850 x 3100	12'8" x 10'2"
Bedroom 2	4000 x 3050	13'2" x 10'0"
Bedroom 3	3500 x 2920	11'6" x 9'7"
Bedroom 4	3250 x 2920	10'8" x 9'7"
Hall width	1500	4'11"

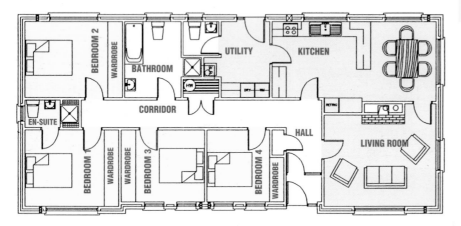

Floor Layout

DETAILS	Metric	Imperial
Overall length	15.120 m.	50'4"
Overall width	11.020 m.	36'2"
Main body width	8.320 m.	27'4"
Floor area	98 sq.m.	1048 sq.ft.
Kitchen.Din	5000 x 4000	16'5" x 13'2"
Lounge	5400 x 4200	17'8" x 13'9"

DETAILS	Metric	Imperial
Bathroom	2110 x 2400	6'9" x 7'9"
Bedroom 1	3600 x 3500	11'10 x 11'6"
Bedroom 2	3300 x 3500	10'10 x 11'6"
Bedroom 3	3400 x 3000	11'2" x 9'10"
Hall width	1500	4'9"

DESIGN
1036

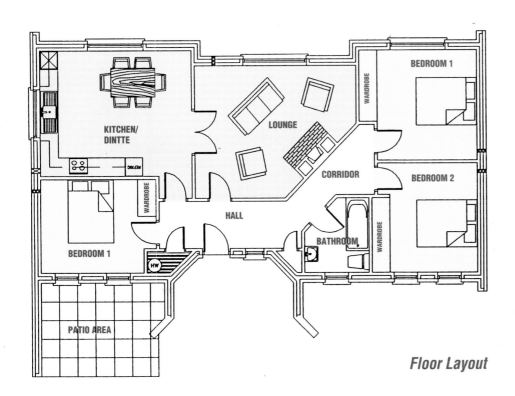

Floor Layout

A 3-bedroomed holiday home, with large living accommodation and featuring interesting curved entrance porch.

Construction Cost
See page 57

DESIGN
1037

DETAILS	Metric	Imperial
Overall length	12.050 m.	39'8"
Overall width	9.050 m.	29'8"
Main body width	6.900 m.	22'10"
Floor area	127 sq.m.	1344 sq.ft.
Ground floor	80 sq.m.	846 sq.ft.
First floor	47 sq.m.	498 sq.ft.
Kitchen	2700 x 5050	8'10" x 16'7"
Dinette	2350 x 3450	7'9" x 11'4"
Living room	4300 x 4500	14'2" x 14'10"

DETAILS	Metric	Imperial
Bathroom	2415 x 2125	7'11" x 7'0"
Utility	1900 x 1850	6'3" x 6'1"
W.C.	1550 x 1150	5'1" x 3'10"
Bedroom 1	3375 x 3900	11'1" x 12'10"
Bedroom 2	3375 x 4400	11'1" x 14'6"
Bedroom 3	3650 x 3800	12'0" x 12'6"
Shower room	1400 x 2150	4'7" x 7'1"
Hall width	1900	6'3"

An attractive and economical styled dormer, with the use of Velux windows to minimise cost. Kitchen/dinette designed large enough to be utilised for family living area, also.

Construction Cost *See page 57*

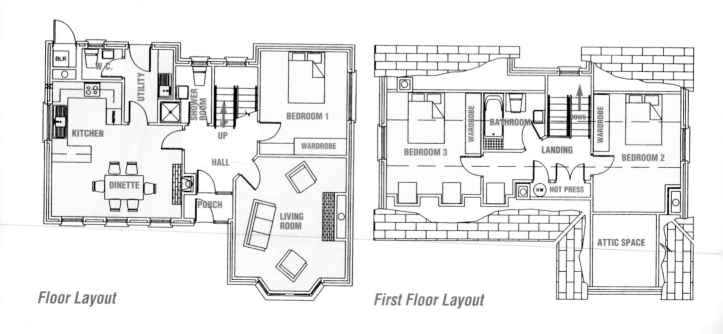

Floor Layout   *First Floor Layout*

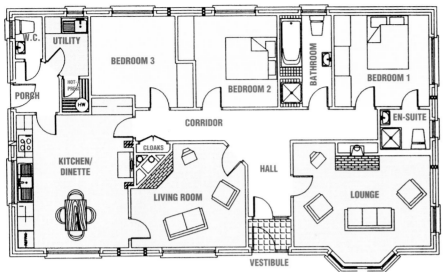

Floor Layout

DESIGN
1038

A practical 3-bedroom bungalow, best suited to a southerly facing site with view. Emphasis here given to large kitchen and lounge, with three adequate bedrooms, en-suite, and family room. Side door eliminates the necessity to drive around the rear of house.

DETAILS	Metric	Imperial
Overall length	15.850 m.	52'0"
Overall width	8.850 m.	29'0"
Main body width	8.850 m.	29'0"
Floor area	125 sq.m.	1346 sq.ft.
Kit/din.	4100 x 4750	13'6" x 15'7"
Living room	4250 x 3650	13'11"x 12'0"
Lounge	5000 x 3250	16'5" x 10'8"
Bathroom	1900 x 3250	6'3" x 10'8"

DETAILS	Metric	Imperial
Utility	1600 x 2100	5'3" x 6'11"
W.C.	1000 x 1500	3'4" x 4'11"
En-suite	1800 x 1435	5'11" x 4'8"
Bed. 1	3450 x 3250	11'4" x 10'8"
Bed. 2	3100 x 3250	10'2" x 10'8"
Bed. 3	3100 x 3250	10'2" x 10'8"
Hall width	1600	5'3"

Construction Cost *See page 57*

ITEMS INCLUDED IN CONSTRUCTION COSTS

- Construction costs include for normal site clearance and excavation, excavating and pouring of foundations and average 900 deep blockwork from foundations to finished floor level. Sandwiched concrete insulated floors to all ground floors. External cavity, block leaf, insulated walls, rendered and skimmed internally and finished as detailed, externally. Block, rendered and skimmed internal walls throughout to all ground floors and stud walls to first floors.

- Completion of roof timbers and roof finishes including for all insulations, facias, soffits, gutters, flashings, etc. as detailed below.

- External joinery includes for all windows, glazing, external doors, etc. Internal second-fix joinery includes for all doors, frames, skirtings, architraves and fitting out of cupboards, etc., as indicated, complete with softwood staircase where required.

- Timber joists to first floor with plywood flooring.

- Electrical works to a good quality finish with external lights over all entrance doors.

- Plumbing to all bathrooms, showers, w.c.'s and sinks. Heating includes for complete system with radiators to each room with solid fuel back-boiler as standard in each house plus oil/furnace if so indicated on plan.

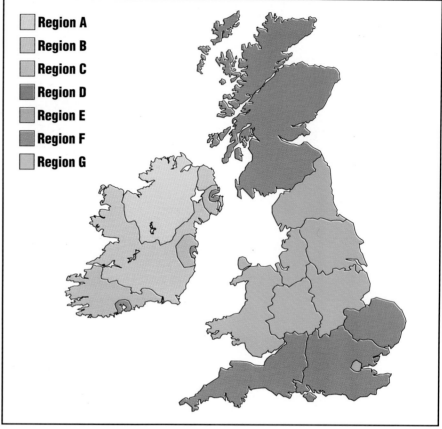

▢	**Region A**
▢	**Region B**
▢	**Region C**
▢	**Region D**
▢	**Region E**
▢	**Region F**
▢	**Region G**

- Kitchen and utility units included at approximately 6% of the overall construction cost.
- Sanitary ware throughout, good quality with standard quality fittings.

ITEMS NOT INCLUDED IN CONSTRUCTION COSTS:-

- Range or stove to kitchen. (because of the varying cost differences).
- Wardrobes
- Internal or external decoration to walls or ceilings

BRICK OR STONEWORK FINISH:

Construction cost does not include for complete stone or brick external finish to houses, as these types of finishes will be dependent on context of the house on the site.

Small feature panels in the form of quoins, or recesses, would be included.

WORK TO SITE:

Siteworks, drainage, water supply, etc. included, as outlined on attached diagram and amounts to approx. 7%-10% of the overall construction cost.

Specific to Section A

External wall finish	White roughcast, unpainted,
Roof finish	Flat concrete tiles
Facia, soffit and barge	Timber, primed and painted
Windows	Hardwood, double-glazed,
External doors	Hardwood, glazed
Internal doors	Sapelle, prefinished flush doors
Architraves and skirtings	Softwood, primed and painted
Fire surround	Tiled fire surround and hearth
Wall tiling	1200mm. high to all w.c's, bathrooms and en-suites, plus showers to ceiling, plus 3 row over all worktop areas.

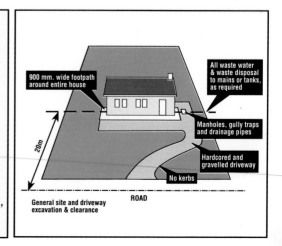

900 mm. wide footpath around entire house

All waste water & waste disposal to mains or tanks, as required

Manholes, gully traps and drainage pipes

Hardcored and gravelled driveway

No kerbs

20m

ROAD

General site and driveway excavation & clearance

DESIGN NUMBER	REGION A	REGION B	REGION C	REGION D	REGION E	REGION F	REGION G
1001	£30,958	£34,673	£39,317	£41,484	£48,295	£52,629	£58,201
1002	£37,527	£42,030	£47,659	£50,286	£58,542	£63,796	£70,551
1003	£42,168	£47,228	£53,553	£56,505	£65,782	£71,685	£79,275
1004	£36,727	£41,134	£46,644	£49,214	£57,294	£62,436	£69,047
1005	£30,662	£34,342	£38,941	£41,088	£47,833	£52,126	£57,645
1006	£44,476	£49,814	£56,485	£59,598	£69,383	£75,610	£83,616
1007	£44,544	£49,889	£56,571	£59,689	£69,488	£75,724	£83,742
1008	£37,570	£42,079	£47,714	£50,344	£58,610	£63,870	£70,632
1009	£39,918	£44,709	£50,696	£53,491	£62,273	£67,861	£75,047
1010	£43,840	£49,101	£55,677	£58,746	£68,391	£74,529	£82,420
1011	£35,894	£40,201	£45,584	£48,098	£55,994	£61,020	£67,481
1012	£44,795	£50,170	£56,889	£60,025	£69,880	£76,151	£84,214
1013	£47,546	£53,251	£60,383	£63,711	£74,171	£80,828	£89,386
1014	£39,711	£44,476	£50,432	£53,212	£61,948	£67,508	£74,656
1015	£45,776	£51,269	£58,135	£61,340	£71,410	£77,819	£86,058
1016	£40,686	£45,568	£51,671	£54,519	£63,470	£69,166	£76,490
1017	£46,576	£52,166	£59,152	£62,412	£72,659	£79,180	£87,564
1018	£41,040	£45,965	£52,121	£54,993	£64,022	£69,768	£77,155
1019	£41,017	£45,939	£52,091	£54,962	£63,986	£69,729	£77,112
1020	£43,503	£48,723	£55,248	£58,294	£67,864	£73,954	£81,785
1021	£51,738	£57,947	£65,707	£69,329	£80,711	£87,955	£97,268
1022	£46,957	£52,592	£59,635	£62,922	£73,253	£79,827	£88,279
1023	£32,846	£36,787	£41,714	£44,013	£51,239	£55,838	£61,750
1024	£46,910	£52,539	£59,576	£62,859	£73,180	£79,747	£88,191
1025	£43,081	£48,251	£54,713	£57,728	£67,206	£73,238	£80,992
1026	£43,503	£48,723	£55,248	£58,294	£67,864	£73,954	£81,785
1027	£45,941	£51,454	£58,345	£61,561	£71,668	£78,100	£86,370
1028	£56,006	£62,727	£71,128	£75,048	£87,370	£95,210	£105,291
1029	£46,159	£51,698	£58,622	£61,853	£72,008	£78,471	£86,779
1030	£47,057	£52,704	£59,762	£63,056	£73,409	£79,997	£88,467
1031	£51,179	£57,320	£64,997	£68,580	£79,839	£87,004	£96,216
1032	£45,708	£51,193	£58,050	£61,249	£71,305	£77,704	£85,932
1033	£87,209	£52,875	£59,956	£63,261	£73,647	£80,256	£88,754
1034	£45,907	£51,416	£58,302	£61,516	£71,616	£78,043	£86,306
1035	£44,461	£49,797	£56,466	£59,578	£69,360	£75,584	£83,587
1036	£34,267	£38,379	£43,519	£45,918	£53,457	£58,254	£64,422
1037	£47,581	£53,291	£60,428	£63,759	£74,227	£80,888	£89,453
1038	£43,510	£48,731	£55,258	£58,303	£67,875	£73,967	£81,799

Amounts shown are in the currency of the house location.
Prices are to be used for guideline purposes only.
Allow for variations of +/-6% depending on location, etc.
Note: in the interest of ensuring that your budget would be sufficient, we decided to use a detailed comprehensive specification and have deliberately tried not to under-estimate the construction cost shown.

A lavish 2-bedroom luxury home, complete with sun-lounge which can back up as an occasional third bedroom. The double split level in hallway is an especially attractive feature of this home and combined with garage gives you everything you could possibly want. A house of this calibre is particularly suited as a retirement home and is designed to suit a site with entrance from rear.

Construction Cost *See page 99*

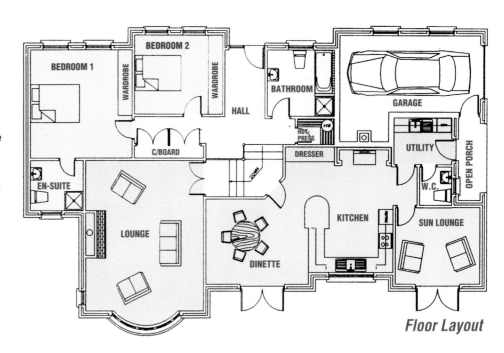

Floor Layout

DESIGN
1039

DETAILS	Metric	Imperial
Overall length	19.545 m.	64'2"
Overall width	11.570 m.	38'0"
Main body width	10.520 m.	34'6"
Floor area	154.5 sq.m.	1662 sq.ft.
Garage	19.5 sq.m.	211 sq.ft.
Kitchen	3435 x 4220	11'4" x 13'10"
Dining room	4570 x 3300	15'0" x 10'10"
Lounge	5790 x 4875	19'0" x 16'0"
Utility	2430 x 1910	8'0" x 6'2"

DETAILS	Metric	Imperial
W.C.	1525 x 1270	5'0" x 4'2"
Bathroom	2805 x 2575	9'3" x 8'5"
Bedroom 1	4060 x 4345	13'4" x 14'3"
Bedroom 2	3980 x 3150	13'0" x 10'4"
Sun Lounge	3495 x 3050	11'5" x 10'0"
Garage	5765 x 3050	18'11" x 10'0"
En-suite	2700 x 2060	8'10" x 6'9"
Main hall width	1725	

DESIGN
1040

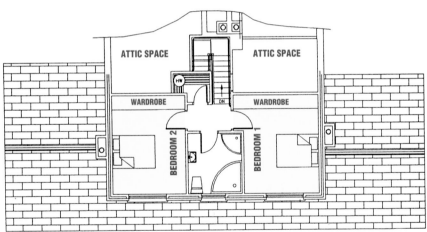

First Floor Layout

A very popular 2-storey split level home, having lengthy frontage giving the impression of a much larger house, also featuring large recessed entrance and spacious living and dining room, with attractive bays to each.

Construction Cost *See page 99*

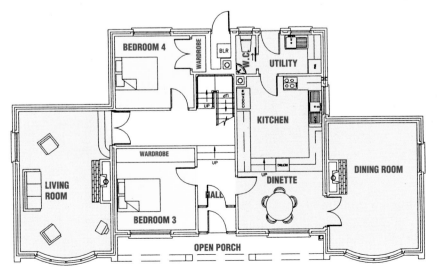

Grounf Floor Layout

DETAILS	Metric	Imperial
Overall length	18.220 m.	59'9"
Overall width	9.950 m.	32'8"
Main body width	8.850 m.	29'0"
Floor area	168 sq.m.	1806 sq.ft
Ground floor	124.5 sq.m.	1338 sq.ft.
First floor	43.5 sq.m	468 sq.ft
Kitchen	3800 x 6550	12'5" x 21'6"
Dining room	3950 x 5400	12'11" x 17'8"
Living room	3950 x 6000	12'11" x 19'8"
Bathroom	2400 x 2575	7'11" x 8'5"
W.c.	900 x 1550	3'0" x 5'1"
En-suite	2800 x 1550	9'2" x 5'1"
Bedroom 1	3350 x 4200	11'0" x 13'9"
Bedroom 2	3250 x 4200	10'8 x 13'9"
Bedroom 3	3500 x 3500	11'6" x 11'6"
Bedroom 4	3350 x 3100	11'0" x 10'2"
Hall width	1700	5'7"

DESIGN
1041

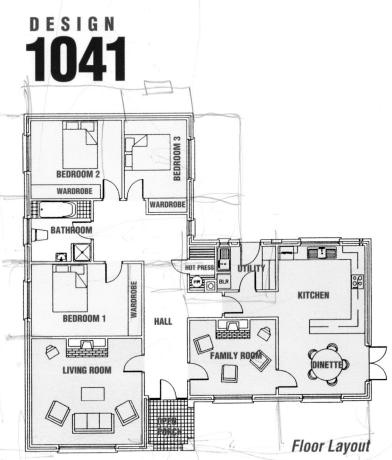

DETAILS	Metric	Imperial
Overall length	15.100 m.	49'6"
Overall width	14.300 m.	46'11"
Main body width	7.400 m.	24'3"
Floor area	138 sq.m.	1484 sq.ft.
Kitchen/dinette	3750 x 6300	12'4" x 20'8"
Family room	3800 x 3200	12'6" x 10'6"
Living room	4800 x 4500	15'9" x 14'10"
Bathroom	2600 x 2550	8'6" x 8'4"
Utility	2600 x 1850	8'6" x 6'1"
Bedroom 1	4800 x 3050	15'9" x 10'0"
Bedroom 2	3950 x 3300	13'0" x 10'10"
Bedroom 3	2750 x 3300	9'0" x 10'10"
Hot-press	1100 x 1850	3'8" x 6'1"
Hall width	1900	6'3"

A 3-bedroom home whose "T" shape gets optimum use from a narrow site. The open porch and raised quoins give this home a very attractive appearance.

Construction Cost *See page 99*

Floor Layout

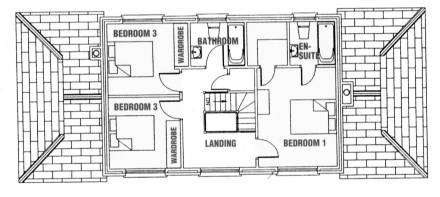

First Floor Layout

A modest 2-storey having elongated frontage on ground floor, giving the impression of a much larger home.

Construction Cost *See page 99*

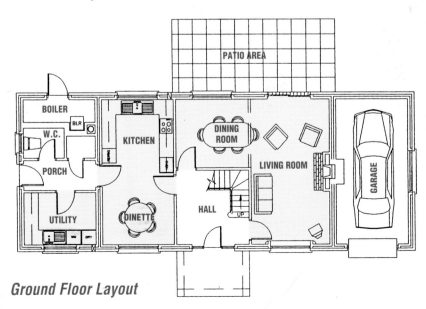

Ground Floor Layout

DETAILS	Metric	Imperial
Overall length	16710 m.	54'10"
Overall width	6410 m.	21'0"
Floor area	127 sq.m.	1368 sq.ft
Ground floor	71 sq.m.	764 sq.ft.
First floor	56 sq.m.	604 sq.ft.
Garage/boiler	20 sq.m.	216 sq.ft.
Dining room	3200 x 2750	10'6" x 9'0"
Kitchen/dinette	3000 x 5850	9'10" x 19'2"
Living room	3290 x 5850	10'9" x 19'2"
Bathroom	2300 x 1750	7'7" x 5'9"
Utility	3000 x 2100	9'10" x 6'10"
W.C.	1225 x 1700	4'0" x 5'7"
En-suite	1980 x 1750	6'6" x 5'9"
Bedroom 1	3290 x 4000	10'9" x 13'1"
Bedroom 2	3000 x 2875	9'10" x 9'5"
Bedroom 3	3400 x 2875	11'1" x 9'5"
Hall width	3100 x 3000	10'2" x 9'10"
Garage	3000 x 5850	9'10" x 19'2"

DESIGN
1043

An unusual 4-bedroomed bungalow, with interesting split level offset to right side. This home includes and exceptionally large main bedroom with adjoining en-suite. Externally raised barges and gables along with twin windows all combine to produce a pleasant mix of contemporary design with traditional method.

Construction Cost
See page 99

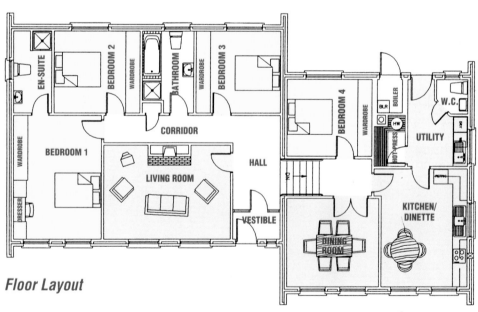

Floor Layout

DETAILS	Metric	Imperial	DETAILS	Metric	Imperial
Overall length	19.600 m.	64'4"	Utility	2000 x 2400	6'7" x 7'10"
Overall width	9.850 m.	32'4"	W.C.	1300 x 1400	4'3" x 4'7"
Main body width	8.960 m.	29'4"	En-suite	1600 x 3300	5'3" x 10'10"
Floor area	157 sq.m.	1687 sq.ft.	Bedroom 1	3650 x 5000	12'0" x 16'5"
Kitchen	3600 x 4800	11'10" x 15'9"	Bedroom 2	3550 x 3300	11'8" x 10'10"
Dining room	3900 x 3600	12'9" x 11'10"	Bedroom 3	3550 x 3300	11'8" x 10'10"
Living room	5500 x 3800	18'1" x 12'5"	Bedroom 4	3600 x 3100	11'10" x 10'2"
Bathroom	2150 x 3300	7'0"x 10'10"	Hall width	1800	6'0"

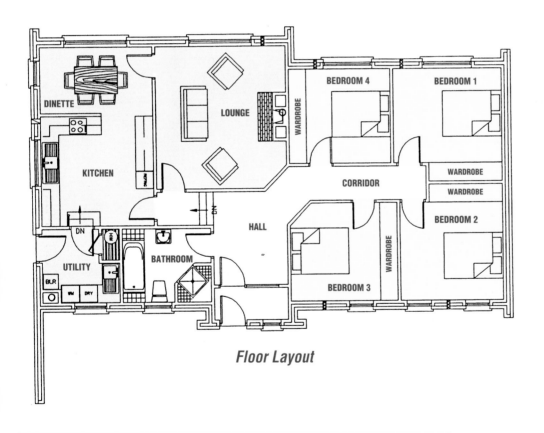

Floor Layout

DESIGN
1044

Spacious 4 bedroomed split level holiday cottage, also ideal as family home, having traditional raised barges and projecting gables externally.

Construction Cost
See page 99

DETAILS	Metric	Imperial
Overall length	16.320 m.	53'6"
Overall width	9.600 m.	31'6"
Main body width	8.820 m.	28'11"
Floor area	127 sq.m.	1365 sq.ft.
Kitchen/Din.	3800 x 5880	12'5" x 12'3"
Lounge	3900 x 4680	12'9" x 15'4"

DETAILS	Metric	Imperial
Bathroom	3000 x 2400	9'10 x 7'10"
Utility	2600 x 2400	8'6" x 7'10"
Bedroom 1	3700 x 3100	12'2" x 10'2"
Bedroom 2	3500 x 3200	11'6" x 10'6"
Bedroom3	3700 x 3200	12'2" x 10'6"
Hall width	2500	8'2"

DESIGN 1045

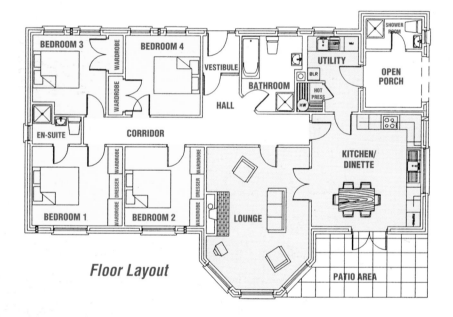

Floor Layout

DETAILS	Metric	Imperial
Overall length	16.850 m.	55'3"
Overall width	11.555 m.	37'11"
Main body width	8.300 m.	27'3"
Floor area	136 sq.m.	1465 sq.ft.
Kitchen/din	4600 x 4550	15'1" x 14'11"
Lounge	4350 x 5770	14'3" x 18'11"
Bathroom	2575 x 3050	8'5" x 10'0"
Utility	2150 x 1800	7'1" x 5'9"
W.c.	2350 x 1200	7'8" x 3'11"
Bedroom 1	3700 x 3200	12'2" x 10'6"
Bedroom 2	3300 x 3200	10'10 x 10'6"
Bedroom 3	3000 x 3200	9'10 x 10'6"
Bedroom 4	3100 x 3200	10'2" x 10'6"
Hall width	1550	5'1"

Rear Elevation

An attractive 4-bedroomed home, featuring large Georgian glazed projecting lounge and spacious double bedrooms. External shower and open porch are custom features which can be adapted to suit your personal requirements.

Construction Cost *See page 99*

Construction Cost *See pa*

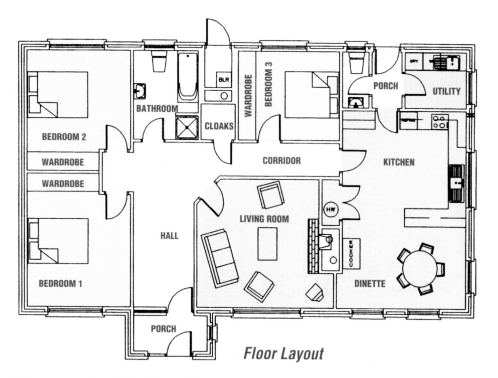

Floor Layout

An attractive traditionally styled home, with careful consideration given to room sizes to ensure that each room is adequate for it's purpose. It also provides the option of heating by either range or oil furnace.

DETAILS	Metric	Imperial
Overall length	15.200 m.	49'10"
Overall width	10.550 m.	34'8"
Main body width	9.070 m.	29'9"
Floor area	130.5 sq.m.	1405 sq.ft.
Kitchen/Din.	4250 x 6560	13'11" x 21'6"
Living room	4150 x 4250	13'8" x 13'11"
Bathroom	2190 x 2950	7'2" x 9'8"
Utility	2100 x 1850	6'9" x 6'1"
W.c.	900 x 1850	3'0" x 6'1"
Bedroom 1	3450 x 3710	11'4" x 12'2"

DETAILS	Metric	Imperial
Bedroom 2	3450 x 3300	11'4" x 10'10"
Bedroom 3	3450 x 2950	11'4" x 9'8"
Hall width	2050	6'9"
W.c.	910 x 1800	3'0" x 6'0"
En-suite	2450 x 1100	8'1" x 3'7"
Bedroom 1	4100 x 3800	13'5" x 12'5"
Bedroom 2	4150 x 3000	13'7" x 9'10"
Bedroom 3	2625 x 3000	8'8" x 9'10"
Hall width	1500	5'0"

DESIGN
1046

A large kitchen/dinette cum living room with 4 spacious bedrooms are the main layout features of this home. Externally projecting bay and hipped roof add traditional character.

Construction Cost
See page 99

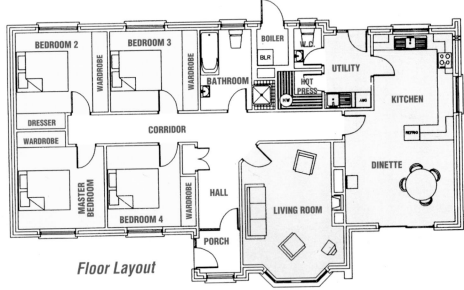

Floor Layout

DESIGN
1047

DETAILS	Metric	Imperial
Overall length	17.670 m.	57'11"
Overall width	9.820 m.	32'3"
Main body width	8.040 m.	26'4"
Floor area	135 sq.m.	1453 sq.ft.
Kitchen	3150 x 2900	10'4" x 9'6"
Dinette	4200 x 4250	13'9" x 13'11"
Living room	3950 x 4600	12'11" x 15'1"

DETAILS	Metric	Imperial
Utility	1700 x 2750	5'7" x 9'1"
W.c.	1060 x 1400	3'6" x 4'7"
Bedroom 1	3400 x 3100	11'2" x 10'2"
Bedroom 2	3600 x 3050	11'10" x 10'0"
Bedroom 3	3450 x 3050	11'4" x 10'0"
Bedroom 4	3500 x 3100	11'6" x 10'2"
Hall width	1600	5'3"

A very popular choice of 2-storey, in that the single storey element tends to give much more length to the appearance. Features include an attractive covered-in front entrance, rear return stairs with large stair window giving ample light to hallway, split level feature to kitchen/dinette, hallway and lounge, en-suite bedroom, oil heating etc.

Construction Cost
See page 99

Ground Floor Layout

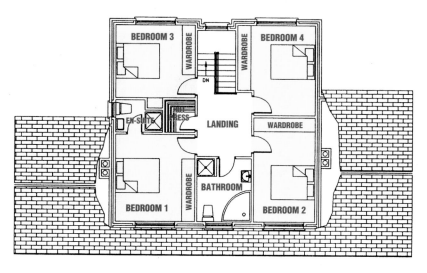

First Floor Layout

DETAILS	Metric	Imperial
Overall length	17.720 m.	58'2"
Overall width	10.310 m.	33'10"
Main body width	9.110 m.	29'11"
Floor area	177 sq.m.	1900 sq.ft.
Ground floor	103 sq.m.	1110 sq.ft.
First floor	74 sq.m.	790 sq.ft.
Gar/boiler	19 sq.m.	204 sq.ft.
Kitchen	3650 x 3400	12'0" x 11'2"
Dinette	3650 x 3200	12'0" x 10'6"
Lounge	3700 x 6300	12'2" x 20'8"
Family room	3550 x 4050	11'8" x 13'3"
Bathroom	2500 x 2750	8'2" x 9'0"
Utility	1950 x 1900	6'5" x 6'3"
W.c.	1600 x 1900	5'3" x 6'3"
En-suite	2200 x 1400	7'3" x 4'7"
Bedroom 1	3650 x 3800	12'0" x 12'6"
Bedroom 2	2800 x 4450	9'2" x 14'11"
Bedroom 3	3650 x 3150	12'0" x 10'4"
Bedroom 4	2800 x 3900	9'2" x 12'10"
Bedroom 5	3550 x 3150	11'8" x 10'2"
Hall width	1750	5'9"

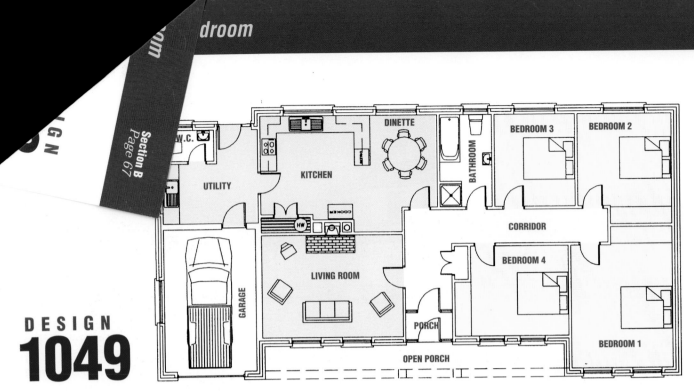

Floor Layout

DESIGN
1049

An appealing hip roofed home with recessed entrance, offering a very practical layout with no frills attached, together with direct access to garage from the utility.

Construction Cost
See page 99

DETAILS	Metric	Imperial
Overall length	19.460 m.	63'10"
Overall width	9.700 m.	31'10"
Floor area	157 sq.m.	1687 sq.ft.
Kitchen/Din.	6545 x 3600	21'5" x 11'10"
Living room	5200 x 3655	17'1" x 12'0"
Bathroom	1950 x 3400	6'5" x 11'2"
Utility	3380 x 2130	11'1" x 7'0"

DETAILS	Metric	Imperial
W.c.	1900 x 1120	6'3" x 3'8"
Bedroom 1	3780 x 4400	12'5" x 14'5"
Bedroom 2	3500 x 3400	11'5" x 11'2"
Bedroom 3	3000 x 3400	9'10 x 11'2"
Bedroom 4	4260 x 3150	14'0" x 10'4"
Hall width	1755	5'9"

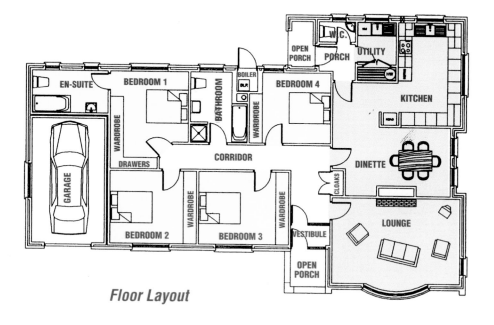

Floor Layout

DESIGN
1050

This design is particularly suited to a westerly facing site, so that the kitchen gable might avail of most of the sun, with it decending onto the living room in the evening.

Construction Cost
See page 99

DETAILS	Metric	Imperial	DETAILS	Metric	Imperial
Overall length	20.100 m.	65'11"	Utiltiy	1700 x 1900	5'7" x 6'3"
Overall width	12.450 m.	40'10"	W.c.	1650 x 900	5'5" x 3'0"
Main body width	8.250 m.	27'1"	En-suite	3300 x 1900	10'10 x 6'3"
Floor area	153 sq.m.	1651 sq.ft.	Bedroom 1	3550 x 3850	11'8" x 12'8"
Garage	18 sq.m.	197 sq.ft.	Bedroom 2	3950 x 3250	13'0" x 10'8"
Kitchen	2850 x 4600	9'4" x 15'3"	Bedroom 3	4150 x 3250	13'8" x 10'8"
Dinette	4750 x 3050	15'7" x 10'0"	Bedroom 4	3150 x 3150	10'4" x 10'4"
Lounge	5800 x 3850	19'0" x 12'8"	Hall width	1800	5'11
Bathroom	1900 x 3150	6'3" x 10'4"	Garage	3300 x 5550	10'10 x 18'2"

DESIGN
1051

DETAILS	Metric	Imperial
Overall length	17.350 m.	56'11"
Overall width	12.850 m.	42'2"
Main body width	10.050 m.	33'0"
Floor area	156 sq.m.	1679 sq.ft.
Kitchen/Din.	4900 x 6000	16'1" x 19'8"
Dining room	4800 x 3485	15'9" x 11'5"
Living room	4800 x 3775	15'9" x 12'4"
Bathroom	2500 x 3250	8'3" x 10'8"

DETAILS	Metric	Imperial
Utility	2850 x 1800	9'4" x 5'11"
En-suite	1435 x 1500	4'8" x 4'11"
Master bedroom	3950 x 3750	13'0" x 12'4"
Bedroom 2	3650 x 3250	12'0" x 10'8"
Bedroom 3	3150 x 3200	10'4" x 10'6"
Bedroom 4	3600 x 3200	11'10 x 10'6"
Hall width	2150	7'1"

Floor Layout

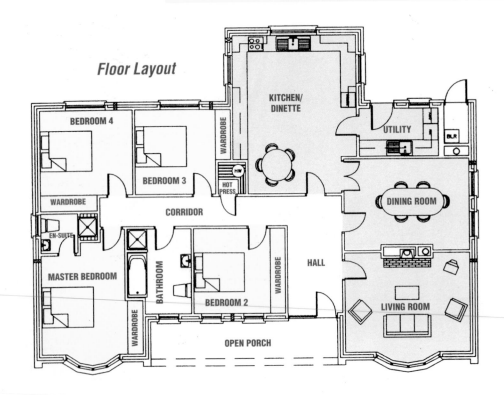

The main features of this home is it's recessed entrance porch and exceptionally large and well laid out kitchen arrangement, complemented by dining room which could in turn be converted to family room. Looks well in either white or brickwork finish, depending on it's site context.

Construction Cost
See page 99

DESIGN

1052

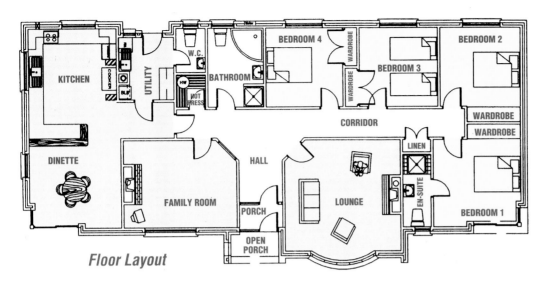

Floor Layout

(Floor plan labels: KITCHEN, UTILITY, W.C., BATHROOM, HOT PRESS, HW, DINETTE, FAMILY ROOM, HALL, PORCH, OPEN PORCH, LOUNGE, EN-SUITE, LINEN, CORRIDOR, WARDROBE, WARDROBE, BEDROOM 4, BEDROOM 3, BEDROOM 2, BEDROOM 1, WARDROBE)

DETAILS	Metric	Imperial
Overall length	20.850 m.	68'4"
Overall width	9.650 m.	31'8"
Main body width	8.600 m.	28'3"
Floor area	159.5 sq.m.	1714 sq.ft.
Kitchen/Din.	3600 x 8000	11'10" x 26'3"
Family room	4700 x 3500	15'5" x 11'6"
Lounge	4800 x 4450	15'9" x 14'7"
Bathroom	2300 x 3150	7'7" x 10'4"

DETAILS	Metric	Imperial
Utility	2300 x 2500	7'7" x 8'3"
W.c.	1200 x 1750	4'0" x 5'9"
En-suite	1150 x 2900	3'10" x 9'6"
Bedroom 1	3600 x 3500	11'10" x 11'6"
Bedroom 2	3300 x 3150	10'10" x 10'4"
Bedroom 3	3200 x 3150	10'6" x 10'4"
Bedroom 4	3200 x 3150	10'6" x 10'4"
Hall width	1800	5'11

Superbly styled bungalow, offering all the amenities you could desire.

Construction Cost
See page 99

DESIGN
1053

An "L" shaped home, with corner in living room removed and bay added to give extra interest. This building is designed to be positioned along its diagonal and incorporates 4 good sizes bedrooms, one with adjoining en-suite.

Construction Cost *See page 99*

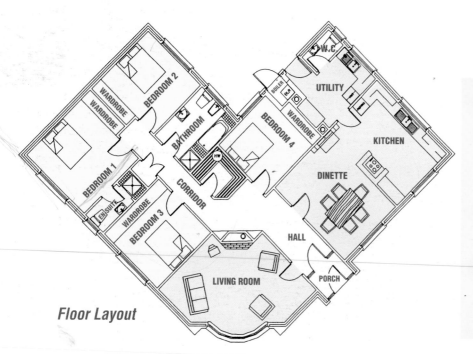

Floor Layout

DETAILS	Metric	Imperial
Overall length	14.810 m.	48'7"
Overall width	8.610 m.	28'3"
Floor area	159 sq.m.	1712 sq.ft.
Kitchen	4750 x 3350	15'7" x 11'0"
Dinette	4750 x 3500	15'7" x 11'6"
Living room	3700 x 7500	12'2" x 24'7"
Bathroom	2350 x 3150	7'9" x 10'4"
Utility	2100 x 3200	6'9" x 10'6"
W.c.	1000 x 1800	3'3" x 5'9"
En-suite	1150 x 3100	3'9" x 10'4"
Bedroom 1	3800 x 3800	12'6" x 12'6"
Bedroom 2	3150 x 3500	10'4" x 11'6"
Bedroom 3	3800 x 3500	12'6" x 11'6"
Bedroom 4	3200 x 3200	10'6" x 10'6"
Hall width	1750	5'9"

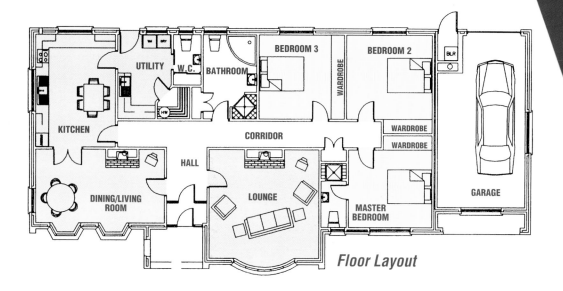

Floor Layout

This most attractive and elegant, hipped roof house, has basically all the features you could desire, including garage, sheltered porch-way, bay windows etc. - just take time and browse around it.

Construction Cost
See page 99

DETAILS	Metric	Imperial	DETAILS	Metric	Imperial
Overall length	22.740 m.	74'8"	Bathroom	2400 x 3700	7'10" x 12'2"
Overall width	10.590 m.	34'9"	Utility	2400 x 3700	7'10" x 12'2"
Main body width	9.060 m.	29'9"	W.c.	1230 x 2200	4'1" x 7'2"
Floor area	157.5 sq.m.	1695 sq.ft.	En-suite	1150 x 2850	3'9" x 9'4"
Gar/boiler	29.8 sq.m.	319 sq.ft.	Bedroom 1	3800 x 3450	12'5" x 11'4"
Kitchen	3600 x 4950	11'10" x 16'3"	Bedroom 2	3900 x 3700	12'9" x 12'2"
Din/living room	5800 x 3270	19'1" x 10'9"	Bedroom 3	3900 x 3700	12'9" x 12'2"
Lounge	4980 x 4800	16'4" x 15'9"	Hall width	1800	5'11"

Along with bedrooms (one en-suite) this home has a large lounge, family room and good sized "L" shaped kitchen/dinette. The recessed entrance, projecting bay and hipped roof returns add extra character.

Construction Cost
See page 99

DETAILS	Metric	Imperial	DETAILS	Metric	Imperial
Overall length	17.300 m.	56'9"	Utility	2150 x 1600	7'0" x 5'3"
Overall width	9.350 m.	30'8"	W.c.	1000 x 1700	3'4" x 5'7"
Floor area	142 sq.m.	1528 sq.ft.	En-suite	2050 x 1100	6'9" x 3'7"
Kitchen/Din.	2500 x 4550	8'3" x 14'11"	Bedroom 1	3950 x 4400	13'0" x 14'6"
Family room	4800 x 4100	15'9" x 13'6"	Bedroom 2	3800 x 3050	12'6" x 10'0"
Lounge	5500 x 3850	18'0" x 12'8"	Bedroom 3	3250 x 3050	10'8" x 10'0"
Bathroom	2300 x 3050	7'7" x 10'0"	Hall width	2150	7'0"

DESIGN
1055

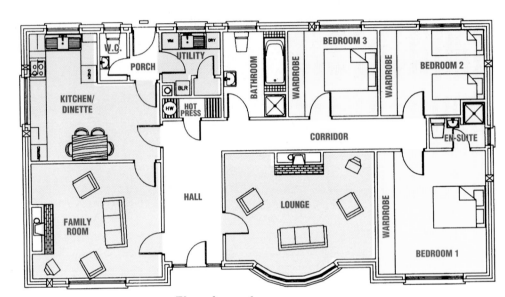

Floor Layout

DESIGN
1056

DETAILS	Metric	Imperial
Overall length	10.770 m.	35'4"
Overall width	9.020 m.	29'7"
Main body width	7.820 m.	25'8"
Floor area	152 sq.m.	1634 sq.ft.
Ground floor	76 sq.m.	817 sq.ft.
First floor	76 sq.m.	817 sq.ft.
Kitchen	3800 x 2900	12'5" x 9'6"
Dinette	2800 x 2900	9'2" x 9'6"
Living room	3800 x 3500	12'5" x 11'6"

DETAILS	Metric	Imperial
Lounge	3800 x 4750	12'5" x 15'7"
Bathroom	2700 x 1800	8'10 x 5'11"
Utility	2175 x 2400	7'2" x 7'10"
W.c.	1050 x 1500	3'6" x 4'11"
Bedroom 1	3800 x 3550	12'5" x 11'8"
Bedroom 2	3325 x 3550	10'11" x 11'8"
Bedroom 3	3800 x 3600	12'5" x 11'10"
Bedroom 4	3800 x 3500	12'5" x 11'6"
Hall width	2350	7'9"

A simple traditional and practical 2-storey home with use of vertical windows, porch and quoin stones to give that lasting appearance. Practically laid out internally, with plenty of everything.

Construction Cost
See page 99

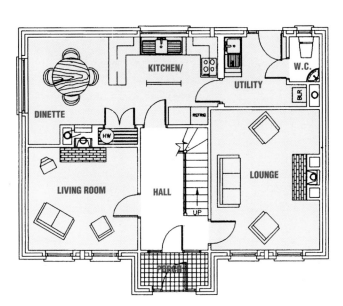

Ground Floor Layout

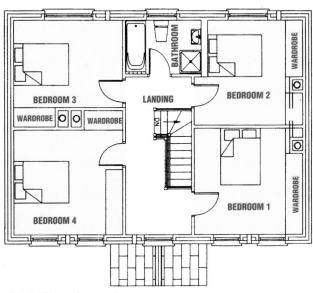

First Floor Layout

DESIGN
1057

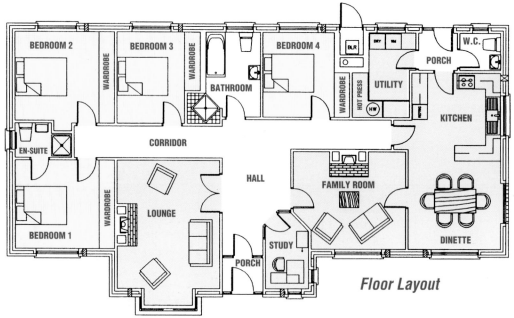

Floor Layout

Extremely practically laid out family home, complete with small study or office. The hip roofed styling adds elegance and looks well in either white or brick finish, depending on it's context.

Construction Cost
See page 99

DETAILS	Metric	Imperial
Overall length	19.600 m.	64'4"
Overall width	10.350 m.	34'0"
Main body width	8.800 m.	28'11"
Floor area	169 sq.m.	1818 sq.ft.
Kit/din.	3600 x 6700	11'10" x 22'0"
Family room	3650 x 3700	12'0" x 12'2"
Lounge	4050 x 4900	13'4" x 16'1"
Bathroom	2140 x 3200	7'0 x 10'6"
Utility	1800 x 2100	5'11" x 6'11"

DETAILS	Metric	Imperial
W.c.	1600 x 1400	5'3" x 4'7"
En-suite	2210 x 1300	7'3" x 4'3"
Bed. 1	3900 x 3350	12'10" x 11'0"
Bed. 2	3900 x 3350	12'10" x 11'0"
Bed. 3	2685 x 3450	8'9" x 11'4"
Bed. 4	2800 x 3200	9'2" x 10'6"
Study	1700 x 2900	5'7" x 9'6"
Hall width	1600	5'3"

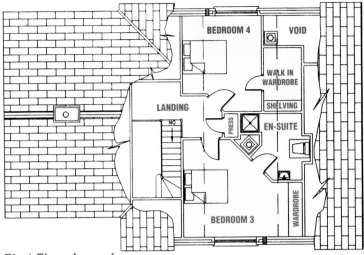

First Floor Layout

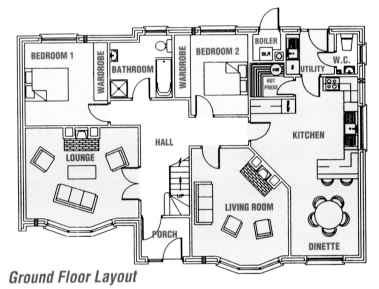

Ground Floor Layout

DETAILS	Metric	Imperial
Overall length	15.020 m.	49'3"
Overall width	9.920 m.	32'6"
Main body width	8.250 m.	27'1"
Floor area	175 sq.m.	1883 sq.f.t
Ground floor	122 sq.m.	1313 sq.ft.
First floor	53 sq.m.	570 sq.ft.
Kitchen	4600 x 4000	15'1" x 13'2"
Dinette	3200 x 2900	10'6" x 9'6"
Living room	4200 x 4500	13'9" x 14'9"
Lounge	4900 x 4900	16'1" x 16'1"
Bathroom	2700 x 2350	8'10" x 7'9"
Utility	2050 x 1700	6'9" x 5'7"
W.c.	900 x 1700	2'11" x 5'7"
En-suite	1720 x 2800	5'8" x 9'2"
Bedroom 1	3600 x 3500	11'10" x 11'6"
Bedroom 2	2600 x 3400	8'6" x 11'2"
Bedroom 3	5150 x 3050	16'10" x 10'0"
Bedroom 4	3425 x 3250	11'3" x 10'8"
Walk-in-wardrobe	1690 x 2650	5'7" x 8'8"
Hall width	2100	6'9"

Good sized 4-bedroom dormer, having en-suite to bedroom 3 and walk in wardrobe adjoining bedroom 4. Also included are kitchen with raised dinette and attractive bays off living room and lounge.

Construction Cost *See page 99*

DESIGN
1058

DESIGN
1059

A spin-off from our previous edition proving very popular because of it's compactness, appearance, and economy in the 4-bedroom dormer range.

Construction Cost *See page 99*

DETAILS	Metric	Imperial
Overall length	12.620 m.	41'5"
Overall width	9.070 m.	29'9"
Main body width	8.170 m.	26'10"
Floor area	169 sq.m.	1821 sq.ft.
Ground floor	96 sq.m.	1038 sq.ft.
First floor	73 sq.m.	783 sq.ft.
Kitchen/Din.	7050 x 3700	23'2" x 12'2"
Living room	5300 x 4550	17'4" x 14'11"
Bathroom	3000 x 3000	9'10 x 9'10"
Utility	3150 x 2100	10'4" x 6'9"
W.c.	1600 x 1400	5'3" x 4'7"
En-suite	1950 x 1570	6'4" x 5'2"
Bedroom 1	3900 x 4060	12'9" x 13'4"
Bedroom 2	3355 x 3950	11'0" x 12'11"
Bedroom 3	2950 x 3280	9'8" x 10'9"
Bedroom 4	3900 x 3750	12'9" x 12'3"
Hall width	2600	8'6"

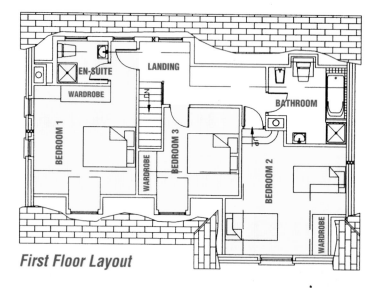

First Floor Layout

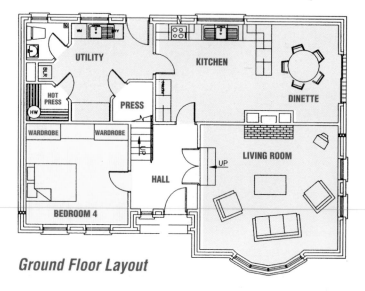

Ground Floor Layout

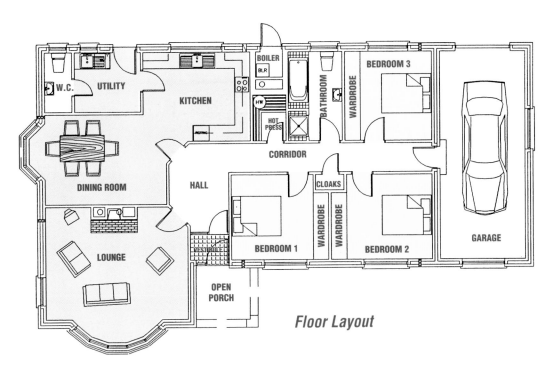

DESIGN
1060

Floor Layout

A spacious 3-bedroom home with attractive open porch in brickwork, which along with bays and half hips, lend this dwelling a special individual look.

Construction Cost *See page 99*

DETAILS	Metric	Imperial
Overall length	19.280 m.	63'3"
Overall width	10.770 m.	35'4"
Floor area	132 sq.m.	1418 sq.ft.
Gar/boiler	29 sq.m.	298 sq.ft.
Kitchen	4150 x 3350	13'7" x 11'0"
Dining	4685 x 3400	15'4" x 11'2"
Lounge	5500 x 4300	18'0" x 14'1"
Bathroom	2100 x 3350	6'11" x 11'0"

DETAILS	Metric	Imperial
Utility	2550 x 2250	8'4" x 7'4"
W.c.	1050 x 2250	3'6" x 7'4"
Bedroom 1	3800 x 3250	12'5" x 10'8"
Bedroom 2	3900 x 3250	12'10" x 10'8"
Bedroom 3	3350 x 3750	11'0" x 11'0"
Garage	3750 x 7900	11'0" x 25'11"
Hall width	1500	4'11"

DESIGN
1061

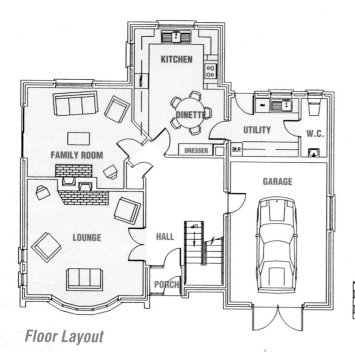

Floor Layout

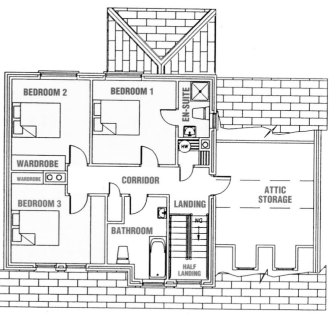

Floor Layout

A 3-bedroom, two storey home, with kitchen/dinette projecting from rear, and single storey garage to side, with storage or possibly fourth bedroom over. Monopitch roof across frontage gives length and elegance.

Construction Cost *See page 99*

DETAILS	Metric	Imperial
Overall length	13.120 m.	43'1"
Overall width	11.280 m.	37'0"
Main body width	8.880 m.	29'2"
Floor area	145.5 sq.m.	1565 sq.ft.
Ground floor	86.0 sq.m.	927.0 sq.ft.
First floor	59.5 sq.m.	638.0 sq.ft.
Storage	40.0 sq.m.	431.5 sq.ft.
Kitchen/Din.	3500 x 5100	11'6" x 16'9"
Family room	4300 x 3650	14'2" x 12'0"
Lounge	4800 x 4225	15'9" x 13'10"

DETAILS	Metric	Imperial
Bathroom	2480 x 2720	8'2" x 8'11"
Utility	2900 x 2395	9'6" x 7'10"
W.c	1100 x 2395	3'7" x 7'10"
En-suite	1300 x 2250	4'3" x 7'4"
Bedroom 1	3480 x 3350	11'5" x 11'0"
Bedroom 2	3200 x 3650	10'6" x 12'0"
Bedroom 3	3850 x 3250	12'8" x 10'8"
Attic storage	4100 x 4100	13'5" x 13'5"
Hall width	3280	10'9"

DETAILS	Metric	Imperial
Overall length	16.130 m.	52'11"
Overall width	9.700 m.	31'10"
Floor area	143 sq.m.	1539 sq.ft.
Kitchen	4270 x 4060	14'0" x 13'4"
Dining	4270 x 3200	14'0" x 10'6"
Living room	4570 x 3945	15'0" x 12'9"
Bathroom	2395 x 3200	7'10" x 10'6"

DETAILS	Metric	Imperial
Utility	4230 x 1685	13'10" x 5'6"
W.C.	1210 x 1685	13'10" x 5'6"
En-suite	1050 x 3050	3'6 x 10'0"
Bedroom 1	4690 x 3480	15'4" x 11'5"
Bedroom 2	3060 x 4410	10'0" x 14'6"
Bedroom 3	3550 x 3200	11'8" x 10'6"
Hall width	1680	5'6"

DESIGN
1062

A spacious and practical design incorporating a large bay effect to kitchen, which also features a bricked cooker housing. Externally stone quoins, hipped roof and bays serve to give this home a very attractive appearance while inside, all modern requirements are catered for with en-suite, cloakroom, walk-in-hotpress and second toilet.

Construction Cost
See page 99

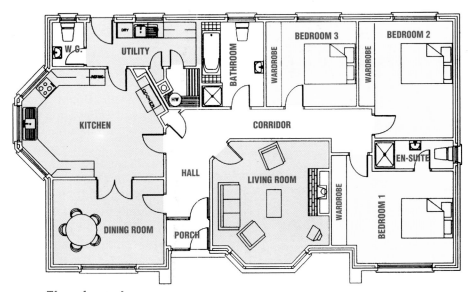

Floor Layout

DESIGN
1063

DETAILS	Metric	Imperial
Overall length	16.270 m.	53'4"
Overall width	8.570 m.	28'2"
Floor area	132.5 sq.m.	1426 sq.ft.
Gar/boiler	57 sq.m.	613.5 sq.ft.
Kitchen	3650 x 3400	12'0" x 11'2"
Dining room	3650 x 3600	12'0" x 11'10"
Lounge	5600 x 3600	18'4" x 11'10"
Bathroom	2150 x 3350	7'1" x 11'0"
Utility	2200 x 1700	7'3" x 5'7"
Bedroom 1	3250 x 3600	10'8" x 11'10"
Bedroom 2	3300 x 3600	10'10" x 11'10"
Bedroom 3	3200 x 3400	10'6" x 11'2"
Bedroom 4	3700 x 3400	10'10" x 11'2"
Hall width	1700	5'7"
Garage	8050 x 3400	27'0" x 11'2"
Store	8050 x 3150	27'0" x 10'4"

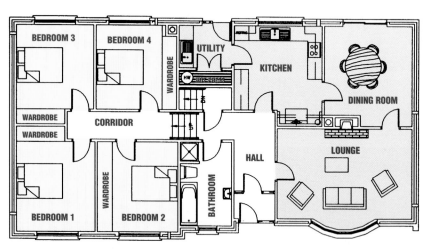

Floor Layout

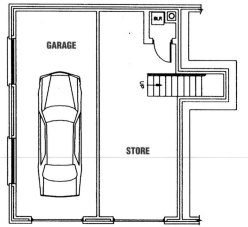

Basement Layout

Design obviously suited to a sloping site. Double garage underneath which again would be suitable for conversion, either during construction or at a later date. A choice of site for this design would be highly important in that the degree of strip level could be adjusted to suit most sites.

Construction Cost *See page 99*

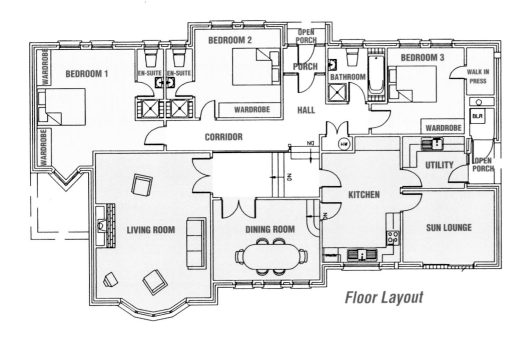

Floor Layout

DESIGN
1064

Stepped frontage with gables bays and orial window, all serve to make this home particularly attractive. Internally the layout is on three levels and includes 3-bedrooms (two with en-suite), large living room and a sun lounge which may double as occasional bedroom. A design best suited to site with rear entry and declining towards front.

Construction Cost
See page 99

DETAILS	Metric	Imperial
Overall length	19.685 m.	64'7"
Overall width	11.450 m.	37'7"
Main body width	9.260 m.	30'4"
Floor area	166 sq.m.	1783 sq.ft.
Kitchen	3300 x 4450	10'10" x 14'7"
Dining room	4500 x 3290	14'9" x 10'9"
Living room	4800 x 5900	15'9" x 19'4"

DETAILS	Metric	Imperial
Sun lounge	3800 x 2900	12'5" x 9'6"
Bathroom	2400 x 2190	7'10" x 7'2"
Bedroom 1	4100 x 4125	13'5" x 13'6"
Bedroom 2	3590 x 3600	11'9" x 11'9"
Bedroom 3	3200 x 3500	10'6" x 11'5"
Hall width	1810	5'11"

DESIGN
1065

A design incorporating four decent sized bedrooms with en-suite to first floor, with more than ample living accommodation on ground floor, complete with study and garage to complement the overall design. An elegant, traditionally styled facade, helps to enhance this choice.

Construction Cost *See page 99*

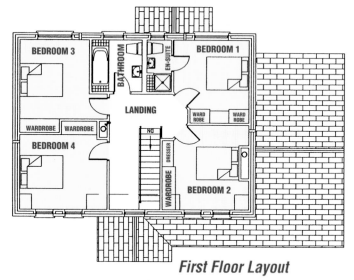

First Floor Layout

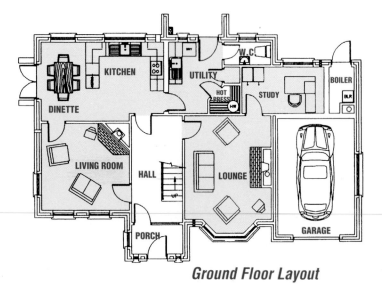

Ground Floor Layout

DETAILS	Metric	Imperial
Overall length	14.700 m.	48'3"
Overall width	10.700 m.	35'1"
Main body width	7.900 m.	25'11"
Floor area	159 sq.m.	1707 sq.ft.
Ground floor	87 sq.m.	933 sq.ft.
First floor	72 sq.m.	774 sq.ft.
Gar/boiler	21 sq.m.	222 sq.ft.
Kitchen/Din.	5475 x 3400	18'0" x 11'2"
Living room	3900 x 3800	12'10 x 12'6"
Lounge	3900 x 4500	12'10 x 14'10"
Bathroom	2275 x 2200	7'6" x 7'3"
Utility	2400 x 3000	7'11 x 9'10"
W.c.	2100 x 950	6'11 x 3'2"
En-suite	1100 x 2200	3'8" x 7'3"
Bedroom 1	3400 x 3550	11'2" x 11'8"
Bedroom 2	3900 x 3650	12'10 x 12'0"
Bedroom 3	3100 x 3400	10'2" x 11'2"
Bedroom 4	3900 x 3200	12'10 x 10'6"
Study	3735 x 2000	12'3" x 6'6"
Hall width	2300	7'7"
Garage	3500 x 5075	11'5" x 16'7"

DESIGN
1066

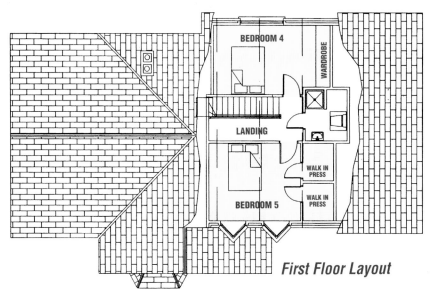

First Floor Layout

Very spacious 5-bedroom home, with facility for completing ground floor initially and doing attic conversion later. Included also, are attractive oriel windows at future first floor level.

Construction Cost *See page 99*

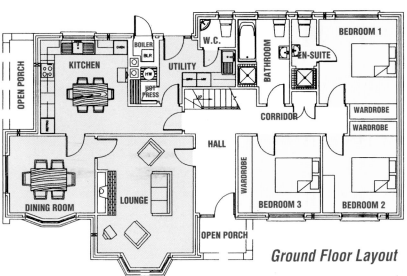

Ground Floor Layout

DETAILS	Metric	Imperial
Overall length	17.080 m.	56'1"
Overall width	10.200 m.	33'5"
Main body width	8.550 m.	28'1"
Floor area	164 sq.m.	1772 sq.ft.
Ground floor	125 sq.m.	1345 sq.ft.
First floor	39 sq.m.	427 sq.ft.
Kitchen	3750 x 3850	12'4" x 12'8"
Dining room	3900 x 3150	12'9" x 10'4"
Lounge	4130 x 4800	13'6" x 15'9"
Bathroom	2200 x 2700	7'3" x 8'10"
Utility	1650 x 2650	5'5" x 8'8"
W.c.	1500 x 1150	4'11" x 3'9"
En-suite	1050 x 2900	3'5" x 9'6"
Bedroom 1	3300 x 3500	10'10 x 11'6"
Bedroom 2	3150 x 3150	10'4" x 10'4"
Bedroom 3	3500 x 3150	11'6" x 10'4"
Bedroom 4	4950 x 2500	16'3" x 8'3"
Bedroom 5	3900 x 3150	12'10 x 10'4"
Shower room	1780 x 2100	5'10 x 6'9"
Hall width	1700	5'7"

DESIGN
1067

Floor Layout

A 4-bedroom home, with projecting porch and garage to rear giving interesting three dimensional effect. Large projecting bay feature to lounge and hipped roof give extra character.

Construction Cost *See page 99*

DETAILS	Metric	Imperial
Overall length	19.820 m.	65'1"
Overall width	18.100 m.	59'4"
Main body width	8.920 m.	29'3"
Floor area	171 sq.m.	1844 sq.ft.
Gar/boiler	24.5 sq.m.	264 sq.ft.
Kitchen	3350 x 2550	11'0" x 8'4"
Dinette	4250 x 3650	13'11 x 12'0"
Living room	4250 x 3650	13'11 x 12'0"
Lounge	4550 x 5950	14'11 x 19'6"
Bathroom	2750 x 3350	9'0" x 11'0"

DETAILS	Metric	Imperial
Utility	3350 x 2000	11'0" x 6'7"
W.c.	1550 x 1250	5'1" x 4'1"
En-suite	2050 x 1100	6'9" x 3'7"
Bedroom 1	3950 x 3450	12'11 x 11'4"
Bedroom 2	3200 x 2700	10'6" x 8'10"
Bedroom 3	3200 x 3350	10'6" x 11'0"
Bedroom 4	3250 x 3350	10'8" x 11'0"
Hall width	1800	5'9"
Garage	5700 x 3950	18'9" x 12'11"

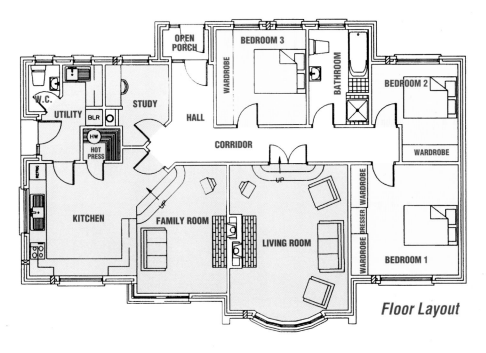

Floor Layout

DESIGN
1068

An interesting 3-bedroom split level home, with varying hipped roof profiles all combining to give an elegant luxurious design.

Construction Cost
See page 99

DETAILS	Metric	Imperial
Overall length	16.060 m.	52'8"
Overall width	10.850 m.	35'7"
Main body width	7.860 m.	25'9"
Floor area	129 sq.m.	1390 sq.ft.
Kitchen	4000 x 3900	13'2" x 12'9"
Family room	3150 x 4200	10'4" x 13'10"
Living room	4760 x 5300	15'8" x 17'4"
Bathroom	2100 x 3275	6'10 x 10'9"

DETAILS	Metric	Imperial
Utility	1400 x 1885	4'7" x 6'2"
W.c.	1100 x 1600	3'8" x 5'3"
Bedroom 1	3900 x 3825	12'9" x 12'6"
Bedroom 2	3150 x 3375	10'4" x 11'1"
Bedroom 3	3200 x 3275	10'6" x 10'9"
Study	2450 x 2000	8'0" x 6'6"
Hall width	1500	4'11

DESIGN
1069

An "L" shaped 4-bedroom home, with spacious kitchen and living room. Gables over front bedroom windows add extra character and appeal.

Construction Cost *See page 99*

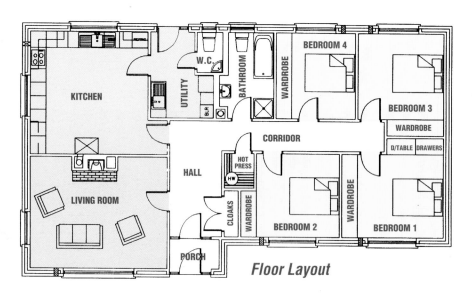

Floor Layout

DETAILS	Metric	Imperial	DETAILS	Metric	Imperial
Overall length	16.520 m.	54'2"	Utility	1700 x 3200	5'7" x 10'6"
Overall width	9.470 m.	31'1"	W.c.	975 x 1500	3'2" x 4'1"
Main body width	8.270 m.	27'2"	Bedroom 1	3850 x 3150	12'8" x 10'4"
Floor area	130.5 sq.m.	1405 sq.ft.	Bedroom 2	3800 x 3150	12'5" x 10'4"
Kitchen	4550 x 4585	14'7" x 15'1"	Bedroom 3	3250 x 3200	10'8" x 10'6"
Living room	5300 x 4185	17'4" x 13'9"	Bedroom 4	3050 x 3200	10'0" x 10'6"
Bathroom	1750 x 3200	5'9" x 10'6"	Hall width	1900	6'3"

DESIGN
1070

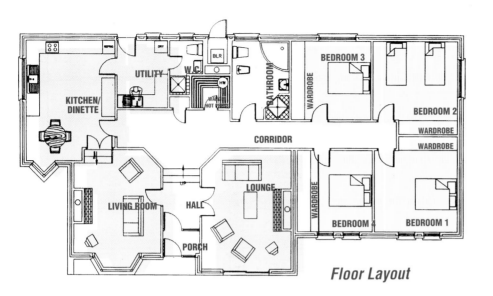

Floor Layout

DETAILS	Metric	Imperial
Overall length	20.210 m.	66'4"
Overall width	10.760 m.	35'4"
Main body width	9.060 m.	29'9"
Floor area	173 sq.m.	1860 sq.ft.
Kitchen/Din.	4000 x 4750	13'2" x 15'7"
Living room	3960 x 4650	13'0" x 15'3"
Lounge	4100 x 5350	13'6" x 17'7"
Bathroom	2600 x 3500	8'6" x 11'6"

DETAILS	Metric	Imperial
Utility	2325 x 3000	7'8" x 9'10"
W.c.	1510 x 1400	5'0" x 4'7"
Bedroom 1	3750 x 3650	12'4" x 12'0"
Bedroom 2	3850 x 3500	12'8" x 11'6"
Bedroom 3	3600 x 3500	11'10" x 11'6"
Bedroom 4	3400 x 3650	11'2" x 12'0"
Hall width	1690	5'7"

An elegant bungalow, with split level features to hallway and living room. Front view from kitchen through an attractively styled window. Dwelling is enhanced by rear toilet, oil heating, large bathroom and small fourth bedroom.

Construction Cost *See page 99*

DETAILS	Metric	Imperial
Overall length	14.500 m.	47'7"
Overall width	8.400 m.	27'7"
Floor area	168.5 sq.m.	1815 sq.ft.
Ground floor	107 sq.m.	1155 sq.ft.
First floor	61.5 sq.m.	660 sq.ft.
Kitchen/Din.	3400 x 4850	11'2" x 15'11"
Lounge	5000 x 3150	16'5" x 10'4"
Bathroom	1900 x 2600	6'3" x 8'6"
Utility	1600 x 2600	5'3" x 8'6"
W.c.	1500 x 1200	4'11" x 3'11"
En-suite	1800 x 1600	5'9" x 5'3"
Bedroom 1	3400 x 3800	11'2" x 12'5"
Bedroom 2	3400 x 2900	11'2" x 9'6"
Bedroom 3	3300 x 2900	10'10" x 9'6"
Bedroom 4	3400 x 4410	11'2" x 14'5"
Bedroom 5	3400 x 4410	11'2" x 14'5"
Shower room	1900 x 2510	6'3" x 8'3"
Study	3000 x 2510	9'10" x 8'3"
Hall width	1500	4'11

A 5-bedroom dormer home, having 2-bedrooms located at first floor level. Raised barges on gable, and cut stone to recesses, combine to give a pleasant traditional effect.

Construction Cost *See page 99*

DESIGN
1071

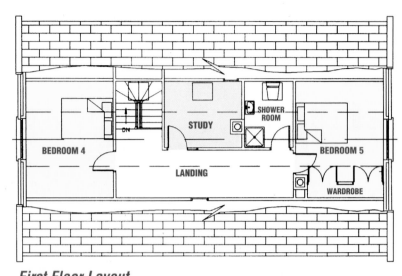

First Floor Layout

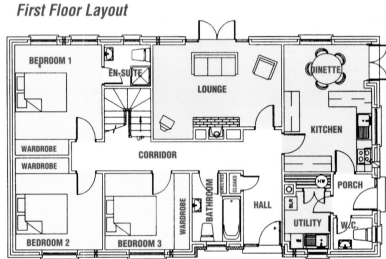

Ground Floor Layout

DETAILS	Metric	Imperial
Overall length	18.100 m.	59'5"
Overall width	11.200 m.	36'9"
Main body width	9.300 m.	30'6"
Floor area	151 sq.m.	1625 sq.ft.
Kitchen	4300 x 3700	14'1" x 12'2"
Dinette	4000 x 3100	13'2" x 10'2"
Lounge	5100 x 3500	16'9" x 11'6"
Bathroom	2100 x 3200	6'11" x 10'6"
Utility	2100 x 2600	6'11" x 8'7"

DETAILS	Metric	Imperial
W.c.	1100 x 2200	3'8" x 7'3"
En-suite	1500 x 1850	4'11" x 6'1"
Bedroom 1	4000 x 4200	13'2" x 13'9"
Bedroom 2	3000 x 4200	9'10" x 13'9"
Bedroom 3	3400 x 3850	11'2" x 12'8"
Bedroom 4	3150 x 3200	10'4" x 10'6"
Walk-in-wardrobe	1500 x 1800	4'11" x 5'11"
Hall width	2800	9'2"

Split levelled, 4-bedroom bungalow, suited to a inclining, easterly facing site. Split levelled kitchen/family room/lounge enhance it's internal appearance.

Construction Cost
See page 99

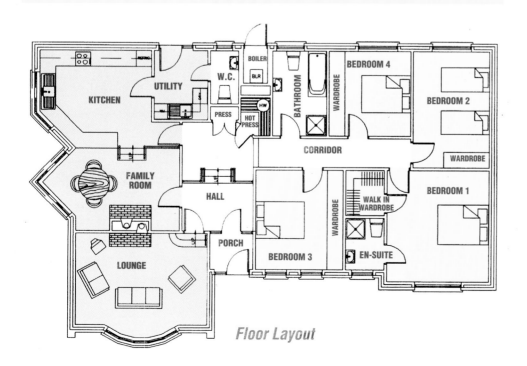

Floor Layout

DESIGN
1072

DESIGN
1073

An extremely practical and popular dormer choice, ideally suited to a narrow westerly facing site with view to south. No wasted space, with good through layout from kitchen to lounge.

Construction Cost *See page 99*

DETAILS	Metric	Imperial	DETAILS	Metric	Imperial
Overall length	11.840 m.	38'10"	Bathroom	2540 x 3100	8'4" x 10'2"
Overall width	15.500 m.	50'10"	Utility	2110 x 2200	7'0" x 7'3"
Main body width	9.010 m.	29'7"	W.c.	2310 x 1000	7'7" x 3'3"
Floor area	169 sq.m.	1819 sq.ft.	En-suite	1900 x 1320	6'3" x 4'4"
Ground floor	113 sq.m.	1216 sq.ft.	Bed. 1	3960 x 3655	13'0" x 12'0"
First floor	56 sq.m.	603 sq.ft.	Bed. 2	3960 x 3250	13'0" x 10'8"
Kitchen	3960 x 3200	13'0" x 10'6"	Bed. 3	3960 x 4875	13'0" x 16'0"
Living room	4270 x 3810	14'0" x 12'6"	Bed. 4	3500 x 4875	11'6" x 16'0"
Lounge/sitting	4875 x 4115	16'0" x 13'6"	Hall width	2200	7'3"

First Floor Layout

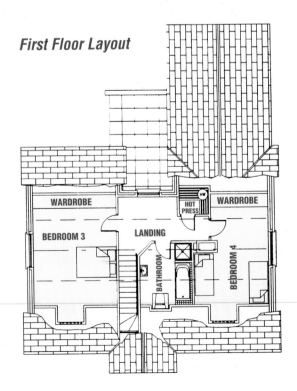

Ground Floor Layout

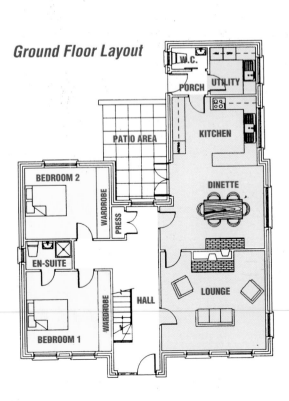

A particularly attractive and interesting design featuring an elaborate split level entrance, and spacious kitchen incorporating an arched entry to adjoining sunken dining room. 3 bedrooms are located to the rear allowing 1 master bedroom, and main living areas maximum advantage of sun and view. Consequently this home is best suited to a south facing site with slope and views to front.

Construction Cost *See page 99*

DESIGN
1074

Floor Layout

DETAILS	Metric	Imperial
Overall length	19.160 m.	62'10"
Overall width	19.600 m.	64'4"
Main body width	8.160 m.	26'9"
Floor area	160.5 sq.m.	1726
Gar/boiler	34.5 sq.m.	371.5 sq.ft.
Kitchen	4400 x 4250	14'5" x 13'11"
Dining room	3550 x 3890	11'8" x 12'9"

DETAILS	Metric	Imperial
Lounge	4220 x 4950	13'10 x 16'3"
Bathroom	2500 x 3050	8'2" x 10'0"
Utility	5000 x 1700	16'5" x 5'7"
W.c.	1450 x 1300	4'9" x 4'3"
En-suite	1450 x 3050	4'9" x 10'0"
Bedroom 1	3760 x 4450	12'4" x 14'7"
Bedroom 2	3250 x 3050	10'8" x 10'0"

DETAILS	Metric	Imperial
Bedroom 3	3050 x 3050	10'0" x 10'0"
Bedroom 4	2850 x 3050	9'4" x 10'0"
Study	2370 x 3050	7'9" x 10'0"
Hall width	1800	6'0"
Garage	5800 x 5200	19'0" x 17'0"

DESIGN
1075

DETAILS	Metric	Imperial
Overall length	16.070 m.	52'9"
Overall width	9.870 m.	32'4"
Main body width	8.220 m.	26'11"
Floor area	139 sq.m.	1397 sq.ft.
Kitchen	2750 x 4200	9'0" x 13'9"
Dinette	3400 x 4350	11'2" x 14'3"
Living room	4950 x 4250	16'3" x 13'11"

DETAILS	Metric	Imperial
Bathroom	1875 x 3150	6'2" x 10'4"
Utility	2825 x 2500	9'3" x 8'2"
W.c.	1000 x 1650	3'3" x 5'5"
Bedroom 1	4100 x 3150	13'5" x 10'4"
Bedroom 2	3350 x 3150	11'0" x 10'4"
Bedroom 3	3150 x 3150	10'4" x 10'4"
Hall width	1750	5'9"

Spacious kitchen/dinette and living room are main internal features of this 3-bedroom split level home. Projecting entrance with bay to living room, and optional flower beds give a pleasant interesting appearance externally.

Construction Cost
See page 99

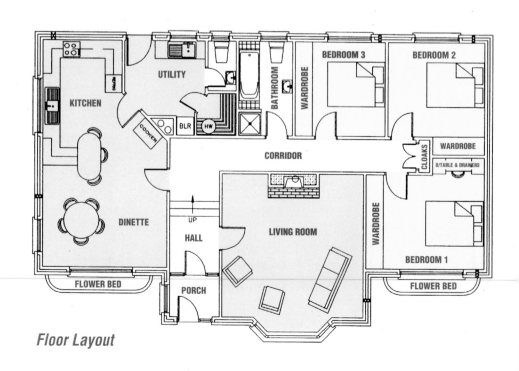

Floor Layout

DESIGN
1076

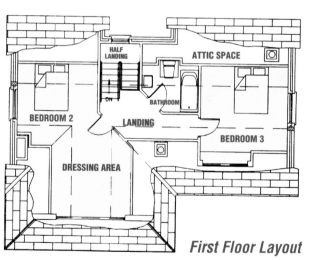

First Floor Layout

DETAILS	Metric	Imperial
Overall length	12.050 m.	39'6"
Overall width	9.280 m.	30'5"
Main body width	6.900 m.	22'8"
Floor area	127 sq.m.	1369 sq.ft.
Ground floor	78.5 sq.m.	845 sq.ft.
First floor	48.5 sq.m.	524 sq.ft.
Kitchen	2025 x 5050	6'8" x 16'7"
Dinette	3000 x 3450	9'10 x 11'4"
Living room	4300 x 4500	14'2 x 14'9"
Bathroom	2410 x 1800	7'11 x 5'9"
Utility	1900 x 2750	6'3" x 9'0"
W.c.	1550 x 1150	5'1" x 3'9"
Bedroom 1	3375 x 3880	11'1" x 12'9"
Bedroom 2	3375 x 2730	11'1" x 8'11"
Dressing area	3160 x 2910	10'4" x 9'6"
Bedroom 3	3660 x 3250	12'0" x 10'8"
Shower room	1400 x 2150	4'7" x 7'1"
Hall width	1900	6'3"

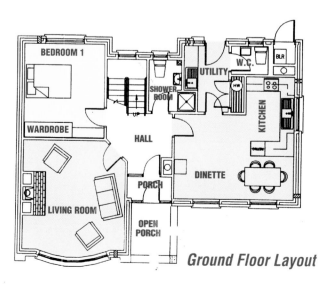

Ground Floor Layout

A spacious 3-bedroom dormer, with a large dressing area off bedroom 2. Kitchen/dinette offers family living facilities with back-up of large living room. The rear return stairs with stair window ensure ample light to hallway and landing.

Construction Cost *See page 99*

DESIGN
1077

DETAILS	Metric	Imperial
Overall length	12.200 m.	40'0"
Overall width	11.150 m.	36'2"
Main body width	10.050 m.	33'0"
Floor area	185 sq.m.	1991 sq.ft.
Ground floor	112 sq.m.	1205 sq.ft.
First floor	73 sq.m.	786 sq.ft.
Kitchen	4600 x 4350	15'3" x 14'3"
Dinette	3100 x 3900	10'2" x 12'10"
Family room	3800 x 4100	12'6" x 13'6"

DETAILS	Metric	Imperial
Lounge	3800 x 5250	12'6" x 17'3"
Bathroom	2200 x 2550	7'3" x 8'4"
W.c.	1545 x 1150	5'1" x 3'9"
Bedroom 1	3400 x 3800	11'2" x 12'6"
Bedroom 2	3300 x 3800	10'10" x 12'6"
Bedroom 3	3300 x 3800	10'10" x 12'6"
Bedroom 4	3600 x 3750	11'10" x 12'4"
Hall width	3800	12'6"

An economical to construct, 2-storey dwelling, with a large and featured foyer and landing, well lighted by means of an attractive stair window.

Construction Cost *See page 99*

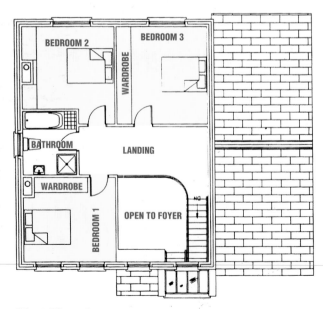

First Floor Layout

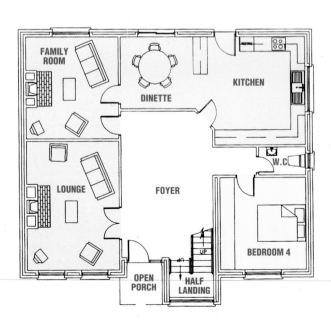

Ground Floor Layout

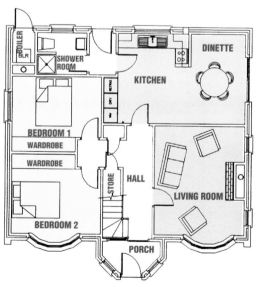

Ground Floor Layout

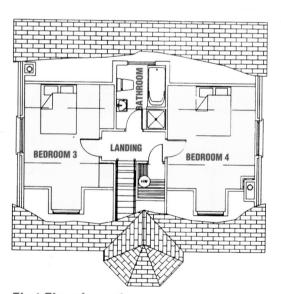

First Floor Layout

DESIGN
1078

DETAILS	Metric	Imperial
Overall length	10.400 m.	34'2"
Overall width	10.020 m.	32'10"
Main body width	9.060 m.	29'9"
Floor area	130 sq.m.	1401 sq.ft.
Ground floor	85 sq.m.	918 sq.ft.
First floor	45 sq.m.	483 sq.ft.
Kitchen/Din.	5390 x 3700	17'8" x 12'2"
Living room	3800 x 4500	12'5" x 14'9"

DETAILS	Metric	Imperial
Bathroom	2090 x 2600	6'10 x 8'6"
Shower room	2100 x 1700	6'11 x 5'7"
Bedroom 1	3450 x 2500	11'4" x 8'2"
Bedroom 2	3450 x 2700	11'4" x 8'10"
Bedroom 3	3750 x 4200	12'4" x 13'9"
Bedroom 4	3800 x 4200	12'6" x 13'9"
Hall width	1200	3'11

A standard dormer layout but with an exceptionally appealing facade, using a combination of bay windows and diagonal entrance porch.

Construction Cost
SEE PAGE 99

ITEMS INCLUDED IN CONSTRUCTION COSTS

- Construction costs include for normal site clearance and excavation, excavating and pouring of foundations and average 900 deep blockwork from foundations to finished floor level. Sandwiched concrete insulated floors to all ground floors. External cavity, block leaf, insulated walls, rendered and skimmed internally and finished as detailed, externally. Block, rendered and skimmed internal walls throughout to all ground floors area's and stud walls to first floors.

- Completion of roof timbers and roof finishes including for all insulations, facias, soffits, gutters, flashings, etc. as outlined below.

- External joinery includes for all windows, glazing, external doors, etc. Internal second-fix joinery includes for all doors, frames, skirtings, architraves and fitting out of cupboards, etc., as indicated, complete with staircase where required.

- Timber joists to first floor with plywood flooring.

- Electrical works to a good quality finish with external lights over all entrance doors.

- Plumbing to all bathrooms, showers, w.c.'s and sinks. Heating includes for complete system with radiators to each room with solid fuel back-boiler as standard in each house plus oil/furnace if so indicated on plan.

Region A
Region B
Region C
Region D
Region E
Region F
Region G

- Kitchen and utility units included at approximately 6% of the overall construction cost.

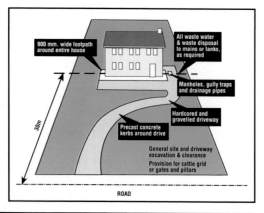

900 mm. wide footpath around entire house

All waste water & waste disposal to mains or tanks, as required

Manholes, gully traps and drainage pipes

Hardcored and gravelled driveway

Precast concrete kerbs around drive

30m

General site and driveway excavation & clearance
Provision for cattle grid or gates and pillars

ROAD

- Sanitary ware throughout, good quality with standard quality fittings.

ITEMS NOT INCLUDED IN CONSTRUCTION COSTS:-

- Range or stove to kitchen areas (because of the varying cost differences).
- Wardrobes
- Internal decoration to walls or ceilings

BRICK OR STONEWORK FINISH:

Construction cost does not include for complete stone or brick external finish to houses, as these types of finishes will be dependent on context of the house on the site. Small feature panels in the form of quoins, or recesses, would be included.

WORK TO SITE:

Siteworks, drainage, water supply etc., included, as outlined on attached diagram, and amounts to approx. 7%-10% of the overall Construction cost.

SPECIFIC TO SECTION B

External wall finish.................. smooth rendered with 3-cts. masonry paint
Roof finish................................. flat concrete tiles
Facia, soffit and barge.............. in upvc or aluminium finish
Windows.................................... upvc, double-glazed
External doors .... upvc, double-glazed
Internal doors........................... white "Regency" six-panelled door
.... (for painting)
Architrave and skirtings.......... softwood, primed and painted
Stairs & railings....................... Hardwood thru' out with softwwod treads & risers
Fire surround .... Tiled fire surround and hearth
Wall tiling................................. 1200mm. high to all w.c's, bathrooms and en
.... suites, plus showers to ceiling, plus 3 row over all
.... worktop areas.

DESIGN NUMBER	REGION A	REGION B	REGION C	REGION D	REGION E	REGION F	REGION G
1039	£66,191	£74,134	£84,063	£88,696	£103,258	£112,525	£124,439
1040	£44,951	£50,345	£57,088	£60,234	£70,124	£76,417	£84,508
1041	£49,211	£55,117	£62,498	£65,943	£76,770	£83,659	£92,517
1042	£56,708	£63,513	£72,019	£75,988	£88,464	£96,403	£106,610
1043	£59,027	£66,110	£74,964	£79,096	£92,082	£100,346	£110,971
1044	£44,343	£49,665	£56,316	£59,420	£69,176	£75,384	£83,366
1045	£50,280	£56,314	£63,856	£67,375	£78,437	£85,476	£94,527
1046	£49,427	£55,358	£62,772	£66,232	£77,106	£84,025	£92,922
1047	£48,125	£53,900	£61,119	£64,488	£75,075	£81,813	£90.476
1048	£70,162	£78,581	£89,105	£94,016	£109,452	£119,275	£131,904
1049	£55,998	£62,718	£71,117	£75,037	£87,357	£95,196	£105,276
1050	£60,98	£67,309	£76,324	£80,531	£93,752	£102,166	£112,984
1051	£56,934	£63,766	£72,306	£76,292	£88,817	£96,788	£107,036
1052	£57,328	£64,208	£72,807	£76,820	£89,432	£97,458	£107,778
1053	£57,421	£64,312	£72,925	£76,944	£89,577	£97,616	£107,952
1054	£66,792	£74,807	£84,826	£89,502	£104,196	£113,547	£125,570
1055	£54,556	£61,103	£69,286	£73,105	£85,107	£92,745	£102,565
1056	£53,452	£59,867	£67,884	£71,626	£83,386	£90,869	£100,490
1057	£59,560	£66,707	£75,641	£79,810	£92,913	£101,251	£111,972
1058	£63,808	£71,465	£81,036	£85,502	£99,540	£108,473	£119,959
1059	£50,301	£66,418	£75,313	£79,664	£92,510	£110,813	£111,487
1060	£58,973	£66,050	£74,896	£79,024	£91,998	£110,254	£110,869
1061	£74,615	£83,569	£94,761	£99,984	£116,399	£126,845	£140,276
1062	£51,492	£57,671	£65,395	£69,000	£80,328	£87,537	£96,806
1063	£62,737	£70,266	£79,677	£84,068	£97,870	£106,654	£117,946
1064	£60,312	£67,550	£76,597	£80,819	£94,087	£102,531	£113,387
1065	£71,631	£80,227	£90,972	£95,986	£111,745	£121,773	£134,667
1066	£65,879	£73,784	£83,666	£88,277	£102,771	£111,994	£123,852
1067	£75,028	£84,032	£95,286	£100,538	£117,044	£127,548	£141,053
1068	£47,756	£53,486	£60,650	£63,993	£74,499	£81,185	£89,781
1069	£47,650	£53,368	£60,515	£63,850	£74,333	£81,004	£89,581
1070	£60,877	£68,182	£77,313	£81,575	£94,968	£103,490	£114,448
1071	£61,898	£69,325	£78,610	£82,943	£96,560	£105,226	£116,368
1072	£54,218	£60,724	£68,857	£72,652	£84,580	£92,171	£101,930
1073	£61,225	£68,572	£77,755	£82,041	£95,510	£104,082	£115,102
1074	£70,322	£78,761	£89,309	£94,231	£109,702	£119,547	£132,205
1075	£50,753	£56,844	£64,457	£68,010	£79,175	£86,281	£95,416
1076	£51,541	£57,726	£65,458	£69,066	£80,405	£87,620	£96,898
1077	£65,618	£73,492	£83,335	£87,928	£102,364	£111,551	£123,362
1078	£50,969	£57,085	£64,730	£68,298	£79,511	£86,647	£95,821

Amounts shown are in the currency of the house location.

Prices are to be used for guideline purposes only.

Allow for variations of +/-6% depending on location, etc.

Note: in the interest of ensuring that your budget would be sufficient, we decided to use a detailed comprehensive specification and have deliberately tried not to under-estimate the construction cost shown.

A large yet very practical two-storey, providing five large bedrooms and bathroom on first floor. Quite suited to a large family, in that, living room and lounge are of an equal size, complemented by the large and spacious kitchen/dinette. The proposed winding staircase adds a touch of elegance to the spacious foyer.

Construction Cost
See page 143

DETAILS	Metric	Imperial	DETAILS	Metric	Imperial
Overall length	12.700 m.	41'8"	Utility	3350 x 2600	11'0" x 8'7"
Overall width	13.550 m.	44'6"	Shower room	1650 x 2100	5'5" x 6'11"
Main body width	7.400 m.	24'3"	En-suite	2200 x 2100	7'3" x 6'11"
Floor area	232 sq.m.	2498 sq.ft.	Master bedroom	4250 x 4600	13'11 x 15'3"
Ground floor	116 sq.m.	1249 sq.ft.	Bedroom 2	4250 x 3350	13'11 x 11'0"
First floor	116 sq.m.	1249 sq.ft.	Bedroom 3	4250 x 3350	13'11 x 11'0"
Kitchen/Din.	6800 x 3500	22'4" x 11'6"	Bedroom 4	3350 x 3350	11'0" x 11'0"
Living room	4250 x 5900	13'11 x 19'5"	Bedroom 5	3350 x 3150	11'0" x 10'4"
Lounge	4250 x 5900	13'11 x 19'5"	Walk-in-wardrobe	1950 x 2100	6'5" x 6'11"
Bathroom	3350 x 2150	11'0" x 7'5"	Hall width	3400	11'2"

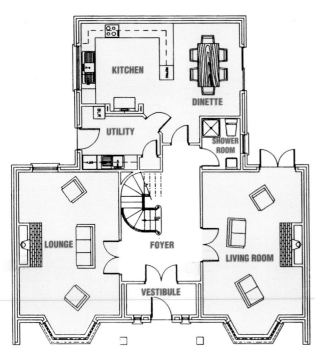

Ground Floor Layout

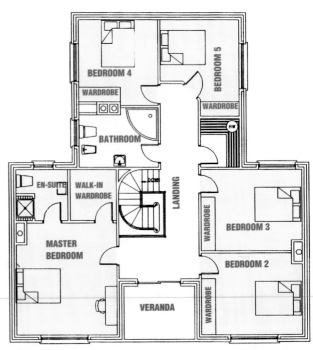

First Floor Layout

DESIGN
1080

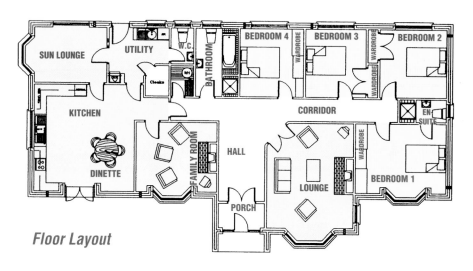

Floor Layout

A spacious and very attractive 4-bedroom home, with emphasis on the living quarters. This design boasts a large kitchen/dinette with a family room off and complemented with large lounge and sun lounge. Design suited to an easterly or westerly facing site depending on hand

Construction Cost
See page 143

DETAILS	Metric	Imperial	DETAILS	Metric	Imperial
Overall length	21.450 m.	70'4"	W.C.	1150 x 1750	3'9" x 5'9"
Overall width	10.400 m.	34'1"	En-suite	2340 x 1100	7'8" x 3'8"
Main body width	8.750 m.	28'8"	Bedroom 1	4550 x 3500	14'11 x 11'6"
Floor area	176.5 sq.m.	1900 sq.ft.	Bedroom 2	3350 x 3350	11'0" x 11'0"
Kitchen/Din.	5050 x 5350	16'7" x 17'7"	Bedroom 3	3050 x 3350	10'0" x 11'0"
Family room	4100 x 3500	13'6" x 11'6"	Bedroom 4	3250 x 3350	10'8" x 11'0"
Lounge	4400 x 5250	14'5" x 17'3"	Sun lounge	3650 x 2700	12'0" x 8'11"
Bathroom	2150 x 3350	7'0" x 11'0"	Hall width	2350	7'8"
Utility	3050 x 1750	10'0" x 5'9"			

DESIGN
1081

A popular dormer choice, with three exceptionally spacious first floor bedrooms, large split levelled accommodation on ground floor, with two double bedrooms. Additional en-suites could be provided to rooms if desired.

Construction Cost
See page 143

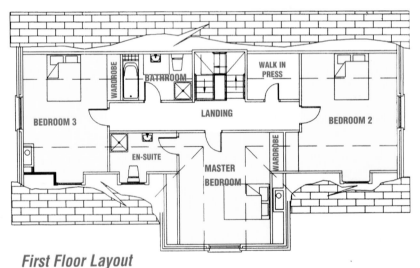

First Floor Layout

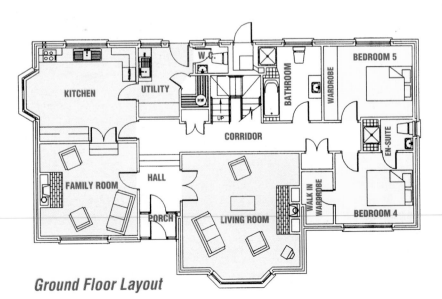

Ground Floor Layout

DETAILS	Metric	Imperial
Overall length	17.060 m.	56'0"
Overall width	10.060 m.	33'0"
Main body width	8.660 m.	28'5"
Floor area	237.5 sq.m.	2500 sq.ft.
Ground floor	140.5 sq.m.	1511 sq.ft.
First floor	97 sq.m.	989 sq.ft.
Kitchen	4300 x 4000	14'1" x 13'2"
Living room	5200 x 4900	17'1" x 16'1"
Family room	4300 x 4000	14'1" x 13'2"
Bathroom 1	2750 x 3100	9'0" x 10'2"
Bathroom 2	3070 x 2000	10'0" x 6'6"
Utility	1800 x 3000	5'11" x 9'10"
W.C.	1600 x 1125	5'3" x 3'8"
En-suite 1	2200 x 1320	7'3" x 4'4"
En-suite 2	2980 x 1655	9'9" x 5'5"
Bedroom 1	4030 x 4800	13'3" x 15'9"
Bedroom 2	4180 x 5060	13'9" x 16'8"
Bedroom 3	3710 x 5060	12'2" x 16'8"
Bedroom 4	3600 x 3050	11'10 x 10'0"
Bedroom 5	3900 x 3080	12'10 x 10'1"
Hall width	1800	5'11

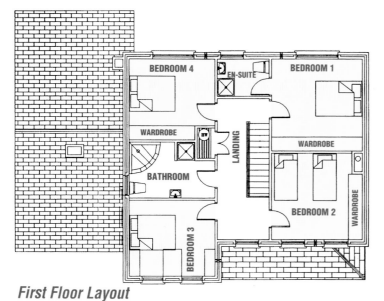

First Floor Layout

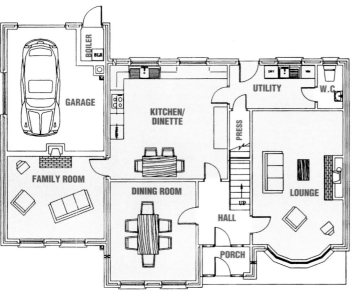

Ground Floor Layout

DESIGN
1082

An extremely attractive 2-storey, available in a variety of finishes to suit it's own personal setting. Spacious living accommodation and ground floor by elimination of unnecessary hallway and corridor space, combined with 4 ample sized bedrooms, en-suite etc.

Construction Cost
See page 143

DETAILS	Metric	Imperial
Overall length	15.350 m.	50'6"
Overall width	11.700 m.	38'5"
Main body width	8.350 m.	27'6"
Floor area	190.5 sq.m.	2054 sq.ft.
Ground floor	105.5 sq.m.	1136 sq.ft.
First floor	85 sq.m.	918 sq.ft.
Gar/boiler	22 sq.m.	241 sq.ft.
Kitchen	5200 x 4950	17'1" x 16'3"
Dining room	3800 x 4250	12'6" x 13'11"
Family room	4250 x 3550	13'11 x 11'8"
Lounge	3950 x 5750	13'0" x 18'10"
Bathroom	2900 x 2400	9'6" x 7'11"
Utility	3750 x 1900	12'4" x 6'3"
W.C.	1100 x 1900	3'8" x 6'3"
En-suite	2300 x 1600	7'7" x 5'3"
Bedroom 1	3950 x 3930	13'0" x 13'0"
Bedroom 2	3950 x 3725	13'0" x 12'3"
Bedroom 3	3800 x 3250	12'6" x 10'8"
Bedroom 4	3800 x 3450	12'6" x 11'4"
Garage	4250 x 5275	13'11 x 17'4"
Hall width	2300	7'7"

DESIGN
1083

An extremely elegant dormer suitable for wide, short site. This design does not require a rear door but one can be provided off utility if necessary.
En-suite bedroom to ground floor with large master bedroom complete with veranda on first floor. Ideally suited to a south or west facing site.

Construction Cost
See page 143

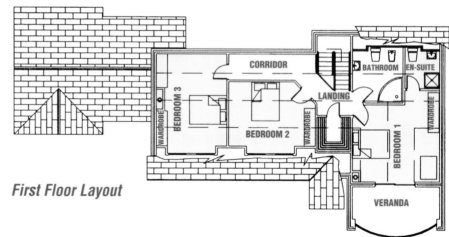

First Floor Layout

DETAILS	Metric	Imperial
Overall length	23.015 m.	75'6"
Overall width	11.430 m.	37'6"
Main body width	6.760 m.	22'2"
Floor area	213.5 sq.m.	2299 sq.ft.
Ground floor	126.0 sq.m.	1356 sq.ft.
First floor	87.5 sq.m.	943 sq.ft.
Gar/boiler	21.5 sq.m.	232.0 sq.ft.
Kitchen	4300 x 6200	14'2" x 20'4"
Dining room	4200 x 4250	13'9" x 13'11"
Lounge	4650 x 4900	15'3" x 16'1"
Bathroom	2700 x 2700	8'10 x 8'10"
Utility	2900 x 1960	9'6" x 6'5"
W.C.	1200 x 1650	3'9" x 6'5"
En-suite 1	1175 x 2725	3'10 x 9'0"
En-suite 2	1850 x 1965	6'1" x 6'5"
Bedroom 1	4650 x 4050	15'3" x 13'3"
Bedroom 2	4700 x 3350	15'5" x 11'0"
Bedroom 3	3800 x 4800	12'5" x 15'9"
Bedroom 4	3375 x 4350	11'1" x 14'3"
Garage	3800 x 6200	12'5" x 20'4"
Hall width	1800	5'11

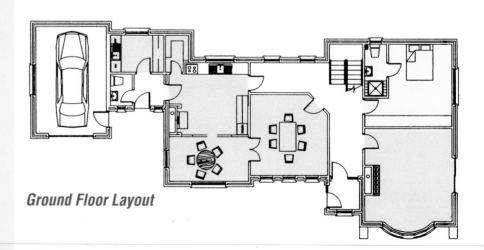

Ground Floor Layout

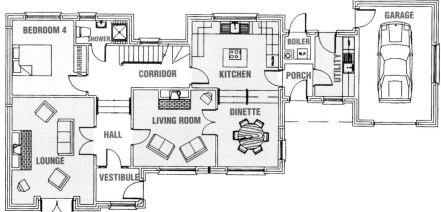

First Floor

Ground Floor

DESIGN
1084

DETAILS	Metric	Imperial
Overall length	21.350 m.	70'1"
Overall width	9.350 m.	30'8"
Main body width	7.650 m.	25'1"
Floor area	182 sq.m.	1955 sq.ft.
Ground floor	108 sq.m.	1163 sq.ft.
First floor	74 sq.m.	792 sq.ft.
Gar/boiler	21.5 sq.m.	228 sq.ft.
Kitchen	4300 x 3150	14'1" x 10'4"
Dinette	3000 x 3010	9'10 x 9'10"
Living room	4100 x 3150	13'5" x 10'4"
Lounge	4000 x 5200	13'1" x 17'1"
Bathroom	3400 x 2300	11'2" x 7'6"
Utility	1950 x 2875	6'4" x 9'5"
Shower room	2500 x 1100	8'3" x 3'8"
En-suite	1600 x 2300	5'3" x 7'6"
Bedroom 1	4295 x 3950	14'1" x 13'1"
Bedroom 2	3450 x 4400	14'7" x 14'5"
Bedroom 3	3200 x 3650	10'6" x 12'0"
Bedroom 4	3000 x 3600	9'10 x 11'10"
Hall width	1700	5'7"
Garage	5400 x 3500	18' x 11'9"

A beautifully designed and eye catching home, complete with split levels, separate utility, garge, two en-suite rooms - would prove to be an excellent choice!

Construction Cost
See page 143

This contemporary style dormer with it's bay window features and kitchen extended to the rear is best suited to a narrow westerly facing site, indeed it is not unlike design 1073. The split level kitchen/living room is optional, and angled fireplace in lounge adds an extra exclusive feature.

Construction Cost
See page 102

DETAILS	Metric	Imperial
Overall length	14.330 m.	47'0"
Overall width	15.045 m.	49'4"
Main body width	8.995 m.	29'6"
Floor area	196 sq. m.	2143 sq. ft.
Ground floor	125 sq. m.	1346 sq. ft.
First floor	71 sq. m.	797' sq. ft.
Kitchen	4200 x 3700	13'9" x 12'2"
Living room	4800 x 3400	15'9" x 11'2"
Lounge	5250 x 3900	17'3" x 12'9"

DETAILS	Metric	Imperial
Bathroom	4050 x 3125	13'3" x10'3"
Utility	2450 x2250	8'0" x 7'4"
W.C.	1650 x 1010	5'5" x 3'3"
En-suite	1885 x 2200	6'2" x 7'4"
Bedroom 1	4100 x 3120	13'5" x 10'3"
Bedroom 2	3600 x 4495	11'10" x 14'9"
Bedroom 3	3800 x 4275	12'6" x 14'0"
Bedroom 4	4460 x 3225	14'8" x 10'7"
Hall width	1800	5'11"

First Floor Layout

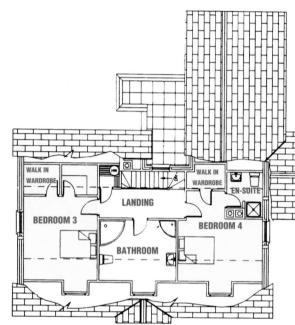

First Floor Layout

DESIGN
1085

DESIGN
1086

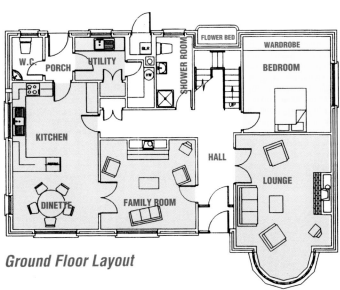

Ground Floor Layout

A simple and spacious 4-bedroom dormer, with large attractive bay to front. Designed with shower room to ground floor and main bathroom on first floor with ample built-in cupboard space, utility, etc. Winding staircase with light from same adequately lighting hallway and landing.

Construction Cost
See page 143

DETAILS	Metric	Imperial
Overall length	14.710 m.	48'3"
Overall width	9.660 m.	31'8"
Main body width	8.950 m.	29'4"
Floor area	198.6 sq.m.	2134 sq.ft.
Ground floor	119.8 sq.m.	1289 sq.ft.
First floor	78.8 sq.m.	845 sq.ft.
Kitchen/Din.	3750 x 6700	12'4" x 22'0"
Family room	4250 x 3900	14'0" x 12'9"
Lounge	4250 x 4850	14'0" x 15'11"
Bathroom	2520 x 3090	8'3" x 10'2"
Utility	2220 x 1850	7'3" x 6'1"
W.c.	1350 x 1850	4'6" x 6'1"
En-suite	2450 x 1445	8'0" x 4'9"
Bedroom 1	3890 x 3995	12'9" x 13'2"
Bedroom 2	3500 x 5450	11'6" x 17'10"
Bedroom 3	3930 x 3150	12'10" x 10'4"
Bedroom 4	3900 x 4150	12'9" x 10'8"
Shower room	1600 x 3050	5'3" x 10'0"
Hall width	1600	5'3"

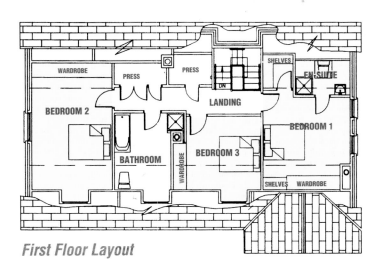

First Floor Layout

DESIGN
1087

An appealing home, having
5-bedrooms and substantial living areas. Recessed porch, Georgian windows and bays to sitting and family room give added character.

Construction Cost
See page 143

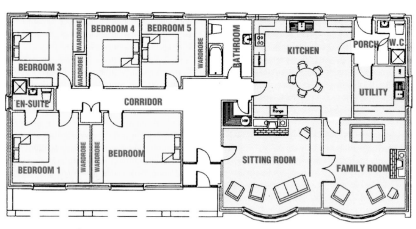

Floor Layout

DETAILS	Metric	Imperial
Overall length	21.160 m.	69'5"
Overall width	10.300 m.	33'9"
Floor area	184.5 sq.m.	1986 sq.ft.
Kitchen	5200 x 4950	17'1" x 16'3"
Family room	4300 x 4500	14'1" x 14'9"
Sitting room	5200 x 4050	17'1" x 13'3"
Bathroom	2300 x 2900	7'6" x 9'6"
Utility	2700 x 2650	8'10 x 8'8"
W.C.	1500 x 2200	4'11 x 7'3"

DETAILS	Metric	Imperial
En-suite	1100 x 2200	3'5" x 7'3"
Bedroom 1	4100 x 3600	13'5" x 11'10"
Bedroom 2	4600 x 3600	15'1" x 11'10"
Bedroom 3	3200 x 3000	10'6" x 9'10"
Bedroom 4	2750 x 3400	9'0" x 11'2"
Bedroom 5	3350 x 2900	11'9" x 9'6"
Hall width	2000	6'7"

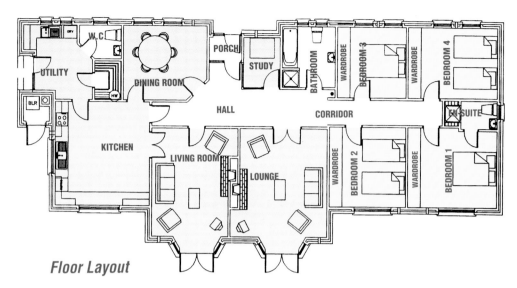

Floor Layout

DESIGN
1088

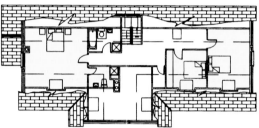

Optional First Floor Layout

DETAILS	Metric	Imperial
Overall length	22.180 m.	72'9"
Overall width	10.100 m.	33'2"
Main body width	8.700 m.	28'7"
Floor area	182 sq.m.	1959 sq.ft.
Kitchen	4220 x 4500	13'10" x 14'9"
Dining room	3800 x 3350	12'5" x 11'0"
Living room	3500 x 4900	11'6" x 16'1"
Lounge	4500 x 4900	14'9" x 16'1"
Bathroom	2450 x 2750	8'1" x 9'0"

DETAILS	Metric	Imperial
Utility	2480 x 3350	8'2" x 11'0"
W.C.	1900 x 1510	6'3" x 4'11"
En-suite	1350 x 1400	4'5" x 4'7"
Bedroom 1	3850 x 3450	12'7" x 11'4"
Bedroom 2	3550 x 3450	11'8" x 11'4"
Bedroom 3	3200 x 3200	10'6" x 10'6"
Bedroom 4	3850 x 3200	12'8" x 10'6"
Study	1700 x 2250	5'7" x 7'4"
Hall width	1500	4'11"

This large bungalow styled home can be designed with high pitched roof for attic conversion later, in which case the stairway would replace the study on the ground floor. With all main living quarters to the front it is ideally suited to a southerly facing site with view and rear entry, and the French styled doors off living room and lounge give ease of access to garden. An optional first floor layout is shown for your consideration.

Construction Cost
See page 143

DESIGN
1089

An unusual 2-storey with large entrance foyer, and optional split level lounge. 4 spacious bedrooms (one en-suite) leave ground floor free for very generous living quarters. Externally varying roof profiles, large stair window and bay, all combine to make this a very attractive home inside and out.

Construction Cost
See page 143

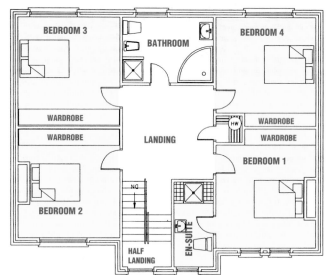

First Floor Layout

Ground Floor Layout

DETAILS	Metric	Imperial
Overall length	12.110 m.	39'9"
Overall width	11.860 m.	38'11"
Main body width	8.860 m.	29'1"
Floor area	210.5 sq.m.	2264 sq.ft.
Ground floor	114.0 sq.m.	1226 sq.ft.
First floor	96.5 sq.m.	1038 sq.ft.
Kitchen	4200 x 4000	13'9" x 13'2"
Dining room	3850 x 4100	12'8" x 13'5"
Family room	3950 x 4100	12'11 x 13'5"
Lounge	3850 x 6000	12'8" x 19'8"
Bathroom	3550 x 2450	11'8" x 8'0"
Utility	2700 x 2400	8'10" x 7'10"
W.c.	1270 x 1600	4'2" x 5,3"
En-suite	1520 x 3200	5'0" x 10'6"
Bedroom 1	3850 x 4500	12'8" x 14'9"
Bedroom 2	3950 x 4100	13'0" x 13'5"
Bedroom 3	3950 x 4100	13'0" x 13'5"
Bedroom 4	3850 x 3500	12'8" x 11'6"
Hall width	1520	5'0"

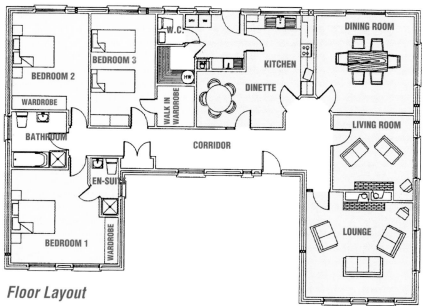

Floor Layout

DESIGN
1090

This cottage layout gives a courtyard entrance and is best suited to flat, westerly facing site. Room sizes can be be easily adjusted to suit requirements.

Construction Cost *See page 143*

DETAILS	Metric	Imperial	DETAILS	Metric	Imperial
Overall length	19.100 m.	62'8"	Bathroom	2500 x 2500	8'3" x 8'3"
Overall width	11.800 m.	38'9"	Utility	2150 x 2450	7'5" x 8'1"
Main body width	7.500 m.	24'7"	W.C.	1200 x 1350	3'11" x 4'5"
Floor area	177 sq.m.	1905 sq.ft.	En-suite	1300 x 2550	4'3" x 8'4"
Kitchen	3100 x 3540	10'2" x 11'8"	Bedroom 1	4900 x 4200	16'1" x 13'9"
Dinette	2300 x 2450	7'7" x 8'1"	Bedroom 2	3500 x 4300	11'6" x 14'1"
Living room	3700 x 3350	12'2" x 11'0"	Bedroom 3	2950 x 5000	9'8" x 16'5"
Lounge	4900 x 4350	16'12" x 14'3"	Hall width	1800	5'11"

A beautiful dormer with it's own special features. Especially suited to a narrow site in that the additional accommodation is provided towards the rear. Should incorporation of garage be a preference, then utility and kitchen layout to be altered to suit. This hand is particularly suited to a westerly facing site.

Construction Cost
See page 143

DETAILS	Metric	Imperial
Overall length	13.500 m.	44'4"
Overall width	13.070 m.	42'11"
Main body width	7.420 m.	24'10"
Floor area	190 sq.m.	2040 sq.ft.
Ground floor	118 sq.m.	1271 sq.ft.
First floor	72 sq.m.	769 sq.ft.
Kitchen/Din.	3600 x 6100	11'10" x 20'0"
Living room	3600 x 4100	11'10" x 13'6"
Lounge	3800 x 4850	12'6" x 15'11"
Bathroom	3000 x 2150	9'10" x 7'1"

DETAILS	Metric	Imperial
Utility	2600 x 2300	8'7" x 7'7"
W.c.	1150 x 1850	3'10" x 6'1"
En-suite	1700 x 2300	5'7" x 7'7"
Master bedroom	3800 x 4850	12'6" x 15'11"
Bedroom 2	3600 x 4500	11'10" x 14'10"
Bedroom 3	3500 x 4500	11'6" x 14'10"
Bedroom 4	3600 x 3350	11'10" x 11'0"
Study	1575 x 2150	5'2" x 7'1"
Hall width	1500	5'0"

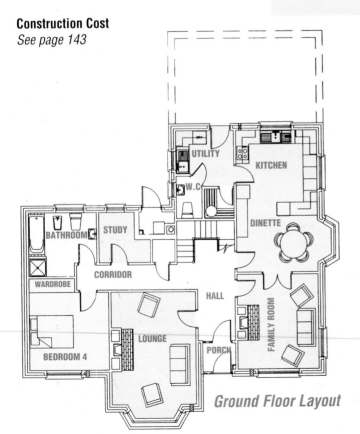

Ground Floor Layout

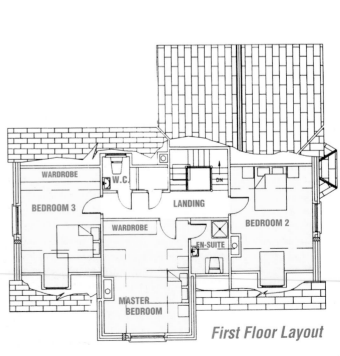

First Floor Layout

DETAILS	Metric	Imperial
Overall length	21.450 m.	70'6"
Overall width	11.350 m.	37'3"
Main body width	8.700 m.	28'6"
Floor area	180 sq.m.	1940 sq.ft.
Kitchen	3800 x 4550	12'6" x 14'11"
Dining room	3550 x 3400	11'8" x 11'2"
Family room	3400 x 3500	11'2" x 11'6"
Lounge	4200 x 5300	13'10 x 17'5"
Bathroom	2500 x 2650	8'3" x 8'8"

DETAILS	Metric	Imperial
Utility	2350 x 2250	7'9" x 7'5"
Shower room	2350 x 1300	7'9" x 4'3"
En-suite	1350 x 2250	4'5" x 8'4"
Bedroom 1	3800 x 3600	12'6" x 11'10"
Bedroom 2	3350 x 3200	11'0" x 10'6"
Bedroom 3	3300 x 3200	10'10 x 10'6"
Bedroom 4	3800 x 3250	12'6" x 10'8"
Bedroom 5	3550 x 3200	11'8" x 10'6"
Hall width	1650	5'5"

DESIGN
1092

5-bedroomed home, with interesting split level layout giving rooms on 3 different levels. Ample kitchen and dining space, with large projecting lounge incorporating bay window, are just some of it's many features.

Construction Cost
See page 143

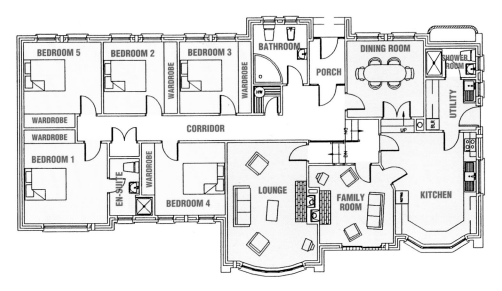

Floor Layout

DESIGN 1093

This home has been designed to suit a declining site, with the resulting attractive features to the foyer of steps and railings. Dining room is located at mid level with lounge and kitchen at alternative levels to same. Owing to the availability of height, featured ceilings can be incorporated to kitchen and dining room.

Construction Cost *See page 143*

DETAILS	Metric	Imperial
Overall length	14.100 m.	46'3"
Overall width	10.550 m.	34'8"
Main body width	9.100 m.	29'10"
Floor area	209 sq.m.	2248 sq.ft.
Ground floor	121 sq.m.	1302 sq.ft.
First floor	88 sq.m.	946 sq.ft.
Kitchen/Din.	5400 x 3800	17'9" x 12'5"

DETAILS	Metric	Imperial
Dining room	3900 x 3300	12'9" x 10'10"
Lounge	4400 x 4900	14'5" x 16'1"
Bathroom	2100 x 3500	6'10 x 11'5"
Utility	2550 x 2800	8'4" x 9'2"
W.c.	1350 x 1500	4'5" x 4'9"
En-suite 1	2600 x 1700	8'6" x 5'7"
En-sutie 2	1200 x 3050	4'0" x 10'10"

DETAILS	Metric	Imperial
Bedroom 1	4000 x 3450	13'2 x 11'4"
Bedroom 2	3900 x 4260	12'9" x 14'0"
Bedroom 3	3200 x 3500	10'6" x 11'6"
Bedroom 4	4000 x 3900	13'2" x 12'9"
Hall width	1700	5'7"

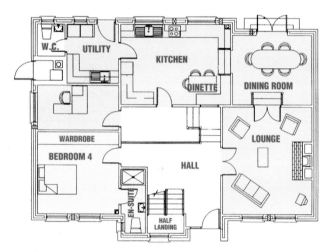

Ground Floor Layout

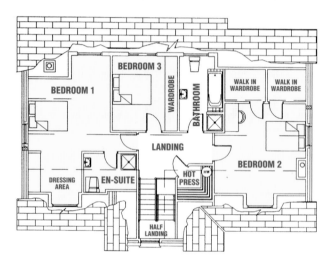

First Floor Layout

DESIGN
1094

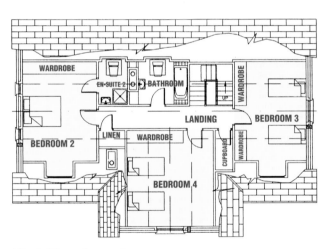

First Floor Layout

A simply designed dormer home, with emphasis on spacious living area. A large roomy kitchen, ample for both cooking and eating, with dining room off, also suitable for conversion to family room if required. Rear w.c. on ground floor with main bathroom on first floor. This design boasts two en-suite bedrooms with ground floor study which could easily be converted to bedroom or office as required.

Construction Cost *See page 143*

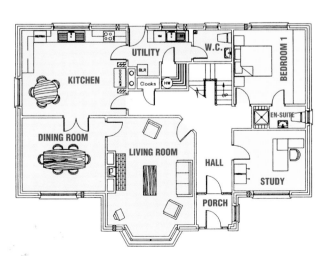

Ground Floor Layout

DETAILS	Metric	Imperial
Overall length	15.000 m.	49'3"
Overall width	10.950 m.	35'11"
Main body width	8.600 m.	28'3"
Floor area	208 sq.m.	2240 sq.ft.
Ground floor	124 sq.m.	1335 sq.ft.
First floor	84 sq.m.	905 sq.ft.
Kitchen	5300 x 4250	17'5" x 14'0"
Dining room	4200 x 3650	13'10" x 12'0"
Living room	4500 x 5300	14'10" x 17'5"
Study	3600 x 3000	11'10" x 9'10"
Bathroom	2525 x 2100	7'3" x 6'11"
Utility	3250 x 1550	10'8" x 5'1"
W.c.	1950 x 1550	6'5" x 5'1"
En-suite 1	2600 x 1100	8'7" x 3'8"
En-suite 2	1500 x 2100	5'0" x 6'11"
Bedroom 1	3600 x 3700	11'10" x 12'2"
Bedroom 2	3700 x 4900	12'2" x 16'1"
Bedroom 3	3600 x 4900	11'10" x 16'1"
Bedroom 4	4400 x 4700	14'6" x 15'6"
Hall width	1800	6'0"

DESIGN
1095

A one-and-a-half storey dwelling, with Tudor connotations, designed for a rear entry site, with excellent characters at both front and rear of dwelling. Conservatory style living room and study, complement this 5-bedroom home.

Construction Cost
See page 143

DETAILS	Metric	Imperial
Overall length	17.400 m.	57'1"
Overall width	11.100 m.	36'5"
Main body width	7.200 m.	23'8"
Floor area	204 sq.m.	2197 sq.ft.
Ground floor	114 sq.m.	1224 sq.ft.
First floor	90 sq.m.	973 sq.ft.
Kitchen/Din.	4200 x 6150	13'9" x 20'2"
Living room	3900 x 3600	12'10 x 11'10"
Lounge	4200 x 4950	13'9" x 16'3"
Bathroom	2300 x 2850	7'7" x 9'4"
Utility	2000 x 2700	6'7" x 8'11"
W.c.	1500 x 1300	4'11 x 4'3"
En-suite	2050 x 1950	6'9" x 6'5"
Bedroom 1	4200 x 4550	13'9" x 14'11"
Bedroom 2	4200 x 3750	13'9" x 12'4"
Bedroom 3	4200 x 3250	13'9" x 10'8"
Bedroom 4	4200 x 3250	13'9" x 10'8"
Bedroom 5	4200 x 3550	13'9" x 11'8"
Study	2800 x 2950	9'2" x 9'8"
Shower room	2000 x 1800	6'7" x 5'11"
Walk-in-wardrobe	2050 x 1950	6'9" x 6'5"
Vestibule width	1600	5'3"

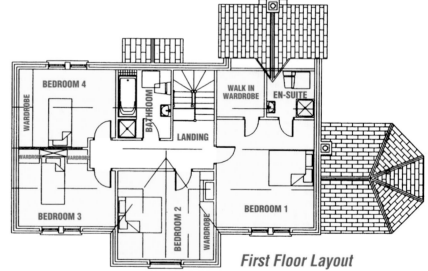

First Floor Layout

Rear Elevation

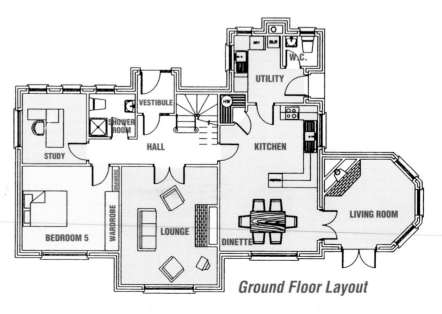

Ground Floor Layout

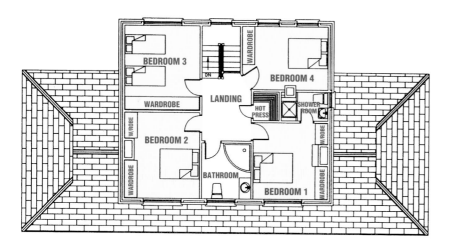

First Floor Layout

A home designed along these lines has proven to be one of the most popular choices for our previous edition, in that it tends to give length and elegance to an otherwise bland 2-storey. The design throughout is spacious and well laid out. A number of variations both in layout and size are available for this design.

Construction Cost *See page 143*

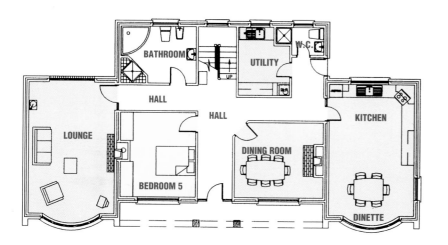

Ground Floor Layout

DETAILS	Metric	Imperial
Overall length	19.120 m.	62'9"
Overall width	9.700 m.	31'10"
Main body width	8.600 m.	28'3"
Floor area	212.5 sq.m.	2287 sq.ft.
Ground floor	133.5 sq.m.	1437 sq.ft.
First floor	79.0 sq.m.	850 sq.ft.
Kitchen/Din.	4380 x 6770	14'4" x 22'3"
Dining room	4300 x 3600	14'2" x 11'10"
Lounge	4100 x 6210	13'5" x 20'4"
Bathroom 1	3600 x 2660	11'0" x 8'9"
Bathroom 2	2400 x 2590	7'10" x 8'6"
Utility	2500 x 3200	8'2" x 11'2"
W.c.	1550 x 1300	5'1" x 4'3"
En-suite	1545 x 1350	5'1" x 4'5"
Bedroom 1	3600 x 3500	11'10" x 11'6"
Bedroom 2	3600 x 4000	11'10" x 13'2"
Bedroom 3	3600 x 3960	11'10" x 13'0"
Bedroom 4	4150 x 2950	13'8" x 9'8"
Bedroom 5	3600 x 4000	11'10" x 13'2"
Hall width	1700	5'7"

DESIGN
1097

A large attractive 4-bedroom bungalow, with exceptionally spacious living accommodation, incorporating a separate dining room and study, etc. This design is also available with hipped roofs if it's setting so requires.

Construction Cost
See page 143

DETAILS	Metric	Imperial
Overall length	21.250 m.	69'9"
Overall width	12.500 m.	41'0"
Main body width	8.600 m.	28'3"
Floor area	189 sq.m.	2039 sq.ft.
Kitchen/Din.	6150 x 4300	21'2" x 14'2"
Dining room	3550 x 4700	11'8" x 15'5"
Family room	4200 x 3700	13'9" x 12'2"
Lounge	4950 x 4800	16'3" x 15'9"
Bathroom	2150 x 3250	7'1" x 10'8"

DETAILS	Metric	Imperial
Utility	2100 x 2700	6'11 x 8'11"
W.c.	1000 x 1700	3'4" x 5'7"
En-suite	1300 x 1950	4'3" x 6'4"
Bedroom 1	3650 x 3450	12'0" x 11'4"
Bedroom 2	3550 x 3350	11'8" x 11'0"
Bedroom 3	3400 x 3250	. 11'2" x 10'8"
Bedroom 4	3650 x 2750	12'0" x 9'0"
Hall width	1800	5'11

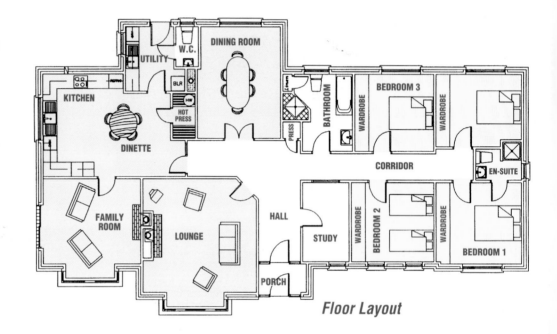

Floor Layout

DESIGN
1098

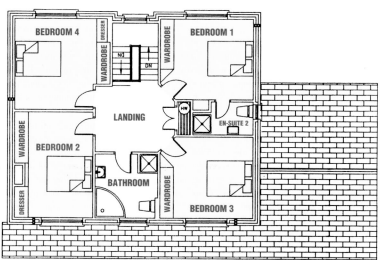

First Floor Layout

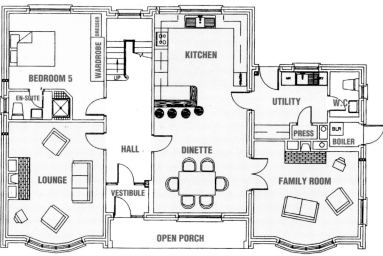

Ground Floor Layout

A winding staircase to the rear of the hallway gives a particularly attractive entrance feature, and ensures adequate light to both hall and landing. This design boasts large spacious rooms throughout and is particularly enhanced by its recessed entrance and front features.

Construction Cost *See page 143*

DETAILS	Metric	Imperial
Overall length	16.050 m.	52'8"
Overall width	10.350 m.	34'0"
Floor area	220 sq.m.	2366 sq.ft.
Ground floor	130 sq.m.	1400 sq.ft.
First floor	90 sq.m.	966 sq.ft.
Kitchen/Din.	8550 x 4100	29'0" x 13'6"
Family room	4600 x 3650	15'3" x 12'0"
Lounge	4200 x 4900	13'10 x 16'1"
Bathroom	2800 x 2750	9'2" x 9'0"
Utility	3200 x 2200	10'6" x 7'3"
W.c.	1300 x 1950	4'3" x 6'4"
En-suite 1	2700 x 1200	8'10 x 3'11"
En-suite 2	2650 x 1400	8'8" x 4'7"
Bedroom 1	4100 x 3450	13'6" x 11'4"
Bedroom 2	3450 x 4550	11'4" x 14'11"
Bedroom 3	4100 x 3500	13'6" x 11'6"
Bedroom 4	3500 x 3900	11'6" x 12'10"
Bedroom 5	4200 x 3250	13'10 x 10'8"
Hall width	2050	6'9"

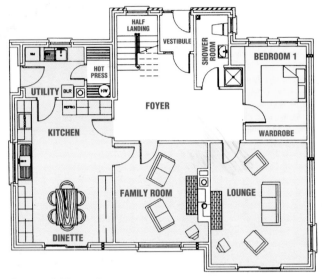

Ground Floor Layout

First Floor Layout

DESIGN
1099

A reasonably compact, yet more than adequate, 4-bedroom dormer particularly suited to a site with rear entry in that all the living quarters are located on opposite side to entrance door to avail of both sunlight and view.

DETAILS	Metric	Imperial
Overall length	12.970 m.	42'7"
Overall width	10.900 m.	35'9"
Main body width	8.700 m.	28'6"
Floor area	186 sq.m.	2000 sq.ft.
Ground floor	109 sq.m.	1175 sq.ft.
First floor	77 sq.m.	825 sq.ft.
Kitchen/Din.	5900 x 4000	19'5" x 13'2"
Family room	4000 x 4100	13'2" x 13'6"
Lounge	4150 x 5000	13'8" x 16'5"

DETAILS	Metric	Imperial
Bathroom	2950 x 2850	9'8" x 9'4"
Utility	2500 x 2100	8'3" x 6'11"
Shower room	1400 x 3000	4'7" x 9'10"
Bedroom 1	2700 x 3900	8'11" x 12'10"
Bedroom 2	4150 x 4800	13'8" x 15'9"
Bedroom 3	3850 x 3300	12'8" x 10'10"
Bedroom 4	4150 x 4800	13'8" x 15'9"
Hall width	1750	5'9"

Construction Cost
See page 143

DESIGN
1100

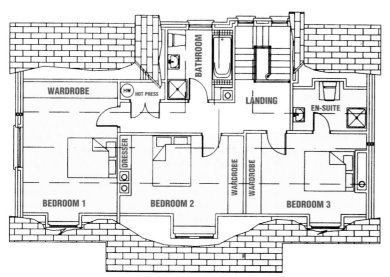

First Floor Layout

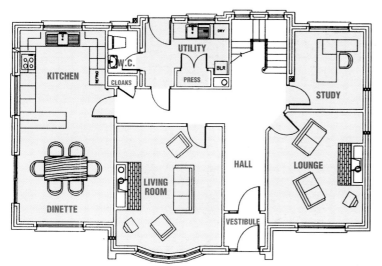

Ground Floor Layout

A simple design and easy to construct dormer home, providing large living accommodation on ground floor with study. The separate roofing over the stair also provides an elegant feature to the rear. Design is particularly suited to a southerly facing site.

Construction Cost *See page 143*

DESIGN	Metric	Imperial
Overall length	13.970 m.	45'10"
Overall width	10.770 m.	35'4"
Main body width	9.870 m.	32'4"
Floor area	182 sq.m.	1956.5 sq.ft.
Ground floor	104.5 sq.m.	1120.5 sq.ft.
First floor	77.5 sq.m.	836.0 sq.ft.
Kitchen	3300 x 3700	10'10" x 12'2"
Dinette	3650 x 3800	12'0" x 12'5"
Living room	4150 x 4550	13'8" x 14'11"
Lounge	3650 x 4200	12'0" x 13'9"
Bathroom	2550 x 2650	8'4" x 8'8"
Utility	3300 x 1700	10'10" x 5'7"
W.c.	1150 x 1600	3'9" x 5'3"
En-suite	2850 x 1580	9'4" x 5'2"
Bedroom 1	3650 x 4940	12'0" x 16'3"
Bedroom 2	4400 x 2940	14'5" x 9'8"
Bedroom 3	4650 x 3045	15'3" x 10'0"
Study	2650 x 2950	8'8" x 9'8"
Hall width	1600	5'3"

DETAILS	Metric	Imperial
Overall length	18.700 m.	61'4"
Overall width	8.400 m.	27'7"
Floor area	212.5 sq.m.	2285 sq.ft.
Ground floor	128.5 sq.m.	1380 sq.ft.
First floor	84 sq.m.	905 sq.ft.
Kitchen	3800 x 7600	12'5" x 24'11"
Dining room	4100 x 5300	13'5" x 17'4"
Lounge	4400 x 6400	14'5" x 21'0"
Bathroom	4375 x 2500	14'4" x 8'3"
Utility	2900 x 2700	9'6" x 8'10"
W.c.	1100 x 2700	3'8" x 8'10"
Bedroom 1	3670 x 5465	12'1" x 17'11"
Bedroom 2	3585 x 5465	12'1" x 17'11"
Bedroom 3	2950 x 3920	9'8" x 12'10"
Bedroom 4	3800 x 3600	12'5 x 11'10"
Shower room	2200 x 2400	7'3" x 7'10"
Hall width	2085	6'10"

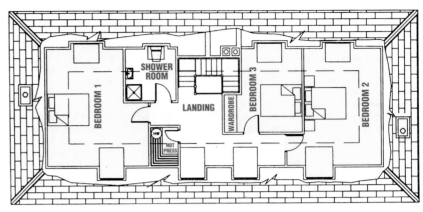

First Floor Layout

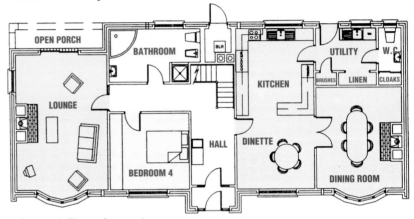

Ground Floor Layout

DESIGN
1101

This dormer home has a very appealing facade with combination of dormer windows, porch and bay windows all blending together to give it that desirable character, complete with 4-bedrooms separate dining room and all mod cons.

Construction Cost *See page 143*

First Floor Layout

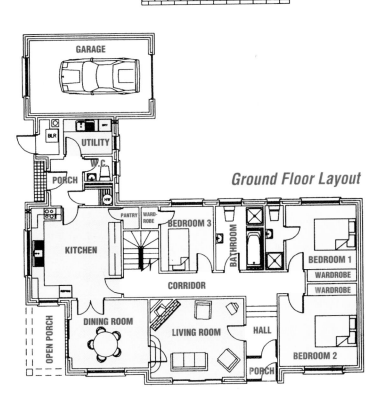

Ground Floor Layout

D E S I G N
1102

With 6-bedrooms this home is deceivingly large, due to maximum use being made of roof space, which gains natural light from Velux windows incorporated within slope of roof. Projecting utility area, with abutting garage give added interest. Design can be modified to suit conversion of roof space as a second stage of works.

Construction Cost *See page 143*

DETAILS	Metric	Imperial
Overall length	16.400 m.	53'10"
Overall width	16.643 m.	54'8"
Main body width	8.200 m.	26'11"
Floor area	208 sq.m.	2239 sq.ft.
Ground floor	128 sq.m.	1381 sq.ft.
First floor	80 sq.m.	858 sq.ft.
Gar/boiler	22 sq.m.	237 sq.ft.
Kitchen	4350 x 4270	14'3" x 14'0"
Dining room	3750 x 3250	12'4" x 10'8"
Living room	4590 x 3750	15'1" x 12'4"
Bathroom 1	2300 x 3050	7'7" x 10'0"
Bathroom 2	2200 x 2300	7'3" x 7'6"
Utility	2350 x 1850	7'9" x 6'1"
W.c.	1150 x 1350	3'10 x 4'5"
En-suite	900 x 3050	3'0" x 10'0"
Bedroom 1	3400 x 3050	11'2" x 10'0"
Bedroom 2	3750 x 3350	12'4" x 11'0"
Bedroom 3	2800 x 3050	9'2" x 10'0"
Bedroom 4	4350 x 4865	14'3" x 16'0"
Bedroom 5	3750 x 4865	12'4" x 16'0"
Bedroom 6	3350 x 3200	11'0" x 10'6"
Hall width	1510	5'0"
Garage	5800 x 3500	19'0" x 11'6"

DESIGN
1103

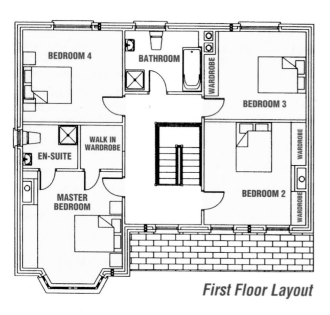

First Floor Layout

DETAILS	Metric	Imperial
Overall length	12.000 m.	39'5"
Overall width	10.400 m.	34'1"
Main body width	9.100 m.	29'10"
Floor area	189.5 sq.m.	1986.5 sq.ft.
Ground floor	97 sq.m.	1042 sq.ft.
First floor	92.5 sq.m.	994.5 sq.ft.
Kitchen/Din.	7050 x 4300	23'1" x 14'1"
Living room	4000 x 4800	13'2" x 15'9"
Lounge	4100 x 4900	13'6" x 16'1"
Bathroom	3100 x 2300	10'2" x 7'7"
Utility	2250 x 2500	7'5" x 8'3"
W.c.	1300 x 1400	4'3" x 4'7"
En-suite	2200 x 1700	7'3" x 5'7"
Master bedroom	4000 x 3750	13'2" x 12'4"
Bedroom 2	4100 x 4000	13'6" x 13'2"
Bedroom 3	4100 x 3400	13'6" x 11'4"
Bedroom 4	4000 x 3550	13'2" x 11'8"
Hall width	3100	10'2"

Ground Floor Layout

Beautiful mock Tudor styled home, which also looks good in plain white plaster depending on it's environmental setting. The arched, recessed entrance complete with large foyer and winding staircase give very good first impressions of this home. A large kitchen with provision for "Aga" oil range adacant to units, complemented with spacious utility and rear w.c. Two large living rooms and four large bedrooms, make this a very desirable choice.

Construction Cost *See page 143*

DESIGN
1104

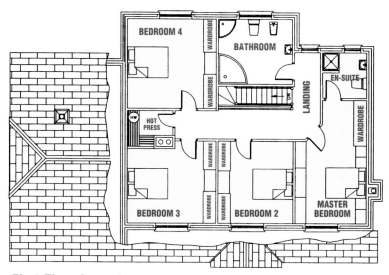

First Floor Layout

Elegant frontal features, together with attached garage, are some of the features offered in this home. Also a central foyer serving all living quarters with direct access to garage through utility. A large master bedroom and bathroom with lighted landing, are the main features to the first floor.

Construction Cost *See page 143*

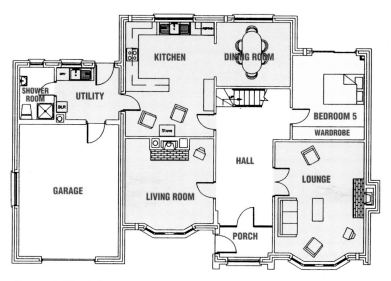

Ground Floor Layout

DETAILS	Metric	Imperial
Overall length	16.859 m.	55'4"
Overall width	11.500 m.	37'9"
Main body width	8.650 m.	28'4"
Floor area	222 sq.m.	2391 sq.ft.
Ground floor	122 sq.m.	1315 sq.ft.
First floor	100 sq.m.	1076 sq.ft.
Gar/boiler	28 sq.m.	302 sq.ft.
Kitchen	4200 x 5300	13'10" x 17'5"
Dining room	3500 x 2950	11'6" x 9'8"
Living room	4200 x 3900	13'10" x 12'10"
Lounge	4200 x 5150	13'10" x 16'11"
Bathroom	3500 x 2950	11'6" x 9'8"
Utility	2900 x 2440	9'6" x 8'0"
Shower room	1600 x 2440	5'3" x 8'0"
En-suite	2050 x 2050	6'9" x 6'9"
Bedroom 1	3350 x 3650	11'0" x 12'0"
Bedroom 2	3550 x 3750	11'8" x 12'4"
Bedroom 3	4200 x 3400	13'10" x 11'2"
Bedroom 4	4200 x 4050	13'10" x 13'4"
Bedroom 5	3400 x 3900	11'2" x 12'10"
Hall width	2500	8'3"
Garage	4600 x 6100	15'3" x 20'0"

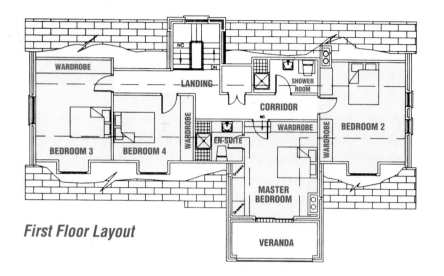

First Floor Layout

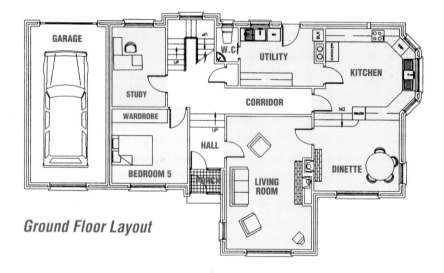

Ground Floor Layout

DETAILS	Metric	Imperial
Overall length	18.010 m.	59'1"
Overall width	11.735 m.	38'5"
Main body width	7.750 m.	25'5"
Floor area	206 sq.m.	2216 sq.ft.
Ground floor	115 sq.m.	1237 sq.ft.
First floor	91 sq.m.	979 sq.ft.
Garage	25 sq.m.	270 sq.ft.
Kitchen	3500 x 3800	11'6" x 12'6"
Dinette	4050 x 3750	13'4" x 12'4"
Living room	4100 x 6125	13'6" x 20'1"
Study	2500 x 3650	8'3" x 12'0"
Utility	4000 x 2650	13'2" x 8'8"
W.c.	1050 x 1550	3'6" x 5'1"
En-suite	2250 x 1850	7'4" x 6'1"
Master bedroom	4100 x 4350	13'6" x 14'3"
Bedroom 2	4050 x 4550	13'4" x 14'11"
Bedroom 3	3500 x 4550	11'6" x 14'11"
Bedroom 4	3750 x 3000	12'4" x 9'10"
Bedroom 5	3550 x 3450	11'8" x 11'4"
Shower room	3000 x 1500	9'10" x 4'11"
Veranda	4100 x 1500	13'5" x 4'11"
Garage	3500 x 7200	11'6" x 23'8"
Hall width	1650	5'5"

This dormer styling, complete with garage and veranda adds both length and elegance to this fine home which is well equipped throughout, including split level features off hallway and dinette.

Construction Cost
See page 143

D E S I G N
1105

DESIGN
1106

This design which was conceived in our previous edition has been exceptionally popular and this is a completely different and practical layout using the same appealing appearance of it's predecessors.

Construction Cost *See page 143*

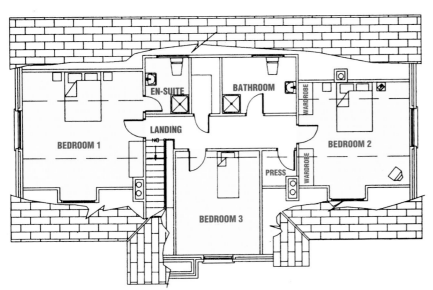

First Floor Layout

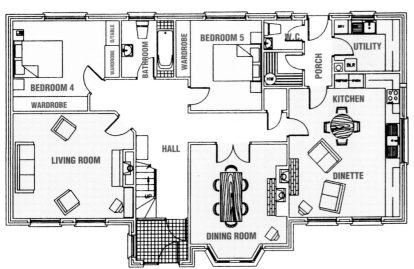

Ground Floor Layout

DETAILS	Metric	Imperial
Overall length	16.760 m.	55'0"
Overall width	9.760 m.	32'1"
Main body width	8.660 m.	28'5"
Floor area	230 sq.m.	2479 sq.ft.
Ground floor	140.5 sq.m.	1513 sq.ft.
First floor	89.5 sq.m.	966 sq.ft.
Kitchen/Din.	4650 x 5900	15'3" x 19'4"
Dining room	4050 x 4100	13'3" x 13'5"
Living room	5000 x 4300	16'5" x 14'2"
Bathroom	2200 x 2300	7'3" x 7'7"
Utility	2750 x 2100	9'1" x 6'11"
W.c.	1600 x 1200	5'3" x 3'11"
En-suite	1850 x 2300	6'1" x 7'7"
Bedroom 1	5000 x 4695	16'5" x 15'5"
Bedroom 2	4650 x 4200	15'3" x 13'10"
Bedroom 3	3540 x 4245	11'8" x 13'11"
Bedroom 4	4400 x 3700	14'5" x 12'2"
Bedroom 5	3000 x 3700	9'10" x 12'2"
Shower room	3570 x 2300	11'9" x 7'7"
Hall width	2200	7'3"

DESIGN 1107

A somewhat similar design to this attracted great attention in our previous edition. A roomy home yet reasonably economical to construct giving an excellent appearance.

Construction Cost *See page 143*

First Floor Layout

DETAILS	Metric	Imperial
Overall length	14.920 m.	48'11"
Overall width	9.970 m.	32'9"
Main body width	8.770 m.	28'9"
Floor area	205 sq.m.	2209 sq.ft.
Ground floor	115 sq.m.	1237 sq.ft.
First floor	90 sq.m.	972 sq.ft.
Kitchen	3750 x 2900	12'4" x 9'6"
Dinette	3000 x 3550	9'10 x 11'8"
Living room	5200 x 4650	17'1" x 15'3"
Bathroom	2450 x 2140	8'0" x 7'0"
Utility	3175 x 1600	10'5" x 5'3"
En-suite	1925 x 2190	6'4" x 7'2"
Bedroom 1	3825 x 4075	12'6" x 13'4"
Bedroom 2	3825 x 3975	12'6" x 13'1"
Bedroom 3	4195 x 5100	13'9" x 16'9"
Bedroom 4	3825 x 5200	12'6" x 17'1"
Bedroom 5	4000 x 4100	13'2" x 13'5"
Shower room	3530 x 2140	11'6" x 7'1"
Hall width	1975	6'6"

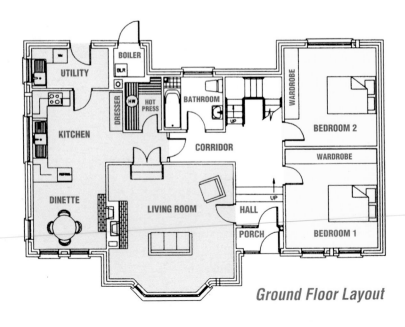

Ground Floor Layout

DESIGN
1108

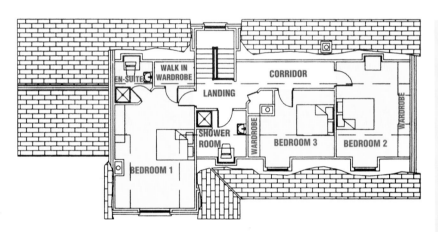

First Floor Layout

DETAILS	Metric	Imperial
Overall length	19.830 m.	65'1"
Overall width	9.320 m.	30'7"
Main body width	8.320 m.	27'3"
Floor area	197 sq.m.	2127 sq.ft.
Ground floor	118 sq.m.	1272 sq.ft.
First floor	79 sq.m.	855 sq.ft.
Gar/boiler	23 sq.m.	250 sq.ft.
Kitchen	4500 x 4000	14'9" x 13'2"
Family room	4200 x 4000	13'9" x 13'2"
Lounge	4000 x 5000	13'2" x 16'5"
Bathroom	3500 x 1900	11'6" x 6'3"
Utility	1800 x 2100	5'9" x 6'11"
En-suite	1900 x 2000	6'3" x 6'6"
Bedroom 1	4000 x 5100	13'2" x 16'9"
Bedroom 2	3700 x 4650	12'2" x 15'3"
Bedroom 3	4400 x 3250	14'5" x 10'8"
Shower room	2500 x 2270	8'2" x 7'5"
Hall width	1900	6'3"

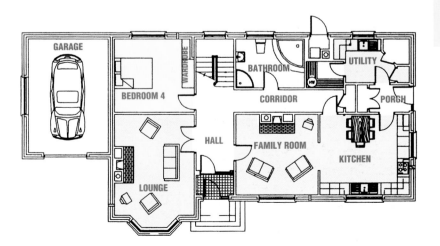

Ground Floor Layout

A home designed to capitalise on the sun and view on a south westerly facing site. The combined garage gives excellent length to this design which looks well with or without the stone cladding

Construction Cost
See page 143

DESIGN
1109

A large spacious conventional 2-storey home, with no added flair or cost. Designed for the person with a bit of space in mind.

Construction Cost
See page 143

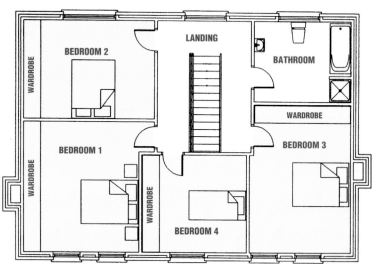

First Floor Layout

DETAILS	Metric	Imperial
Overall length	12.100 m.	39'8"
Overall width	8.490 m.	27'10"
Floor area	183 sq.m.	1970 sq.ft.
Ground floor	91.5 sq.m.	985 sq.ft.
First floor	91.5 sq.m.	985 sq.ft.
Kitchen	5770 x 3900	18'11" x 12'10"
Family room	4570 x 3950	15'0" x 13'0"
Sitting room	4570 x 5630	15'0" x 18'6"
Bathroom	3450 x 2730	14'8" x 8'11"
Utility	3920 x 1600	12'10" x 5'3"
Shower room	1650 x 2200	5'5" x 7'3"
Bedroom 1	4030 x 4480	13'3" x 14'8"
Bedroom 2	4570 x 3350	15'0" x 11'0"
Bedroom 3	3600 x 5100	11'10" x 16'9"
Bedroom 4	3710 x 3350	12'2" x 11'0"
Hall width	2200	7'3"

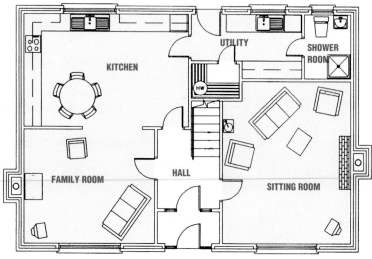

Ground Floor Layout

DESIGN
1110

First Floor Layout

Ground Floor Layout

An open planned living quarters making maximum use of all space, together with a large foyer and an economically designed first floor. Again more suited to a rear entry site with large bay window facing southwards for the view.

Construction Cost
See page 143

DETAILS	Metric	Imperial
Overall length	16.410 m.	53'10"
Overall width	11.450 m.	37'7"
Main body width	9.060 m.	29'9"
Floor area	237.5 sq.m.	2472 sq.ft.
Ground floor	146 sq.m.	1548 sq.ft.
First floor	91.5 sq.m.	924 sq.ft.
Kitchen	5100 x 4150	16'9" x 13'8"
Dining room	2870 x 3600	9'5" x 11'10"
Living room	5100 x 4250	16'9" x 13'11"
Utility	2500 x 2700	8'2" x 8'10"
En-suite 1(Bed 1)	1350 x 2400	4'5" x 7'10"
En-suite 2(Bed 3)	2000 x 3125	6'7" x 10'3"
En-suite 3 (Bed 4)	2000 x 3125	6'7" x 10'3"
Bedroom 1	4200 x 4200	13'9" x 13'9"
Bedroom 2	4200 x 4200	13'9" x 13'9"
Bedroom 3	4200 x 5330	13'9" x 17'6"
Bedroom 4	4300 x 5330	14'1" x 17'6"
Study	2950 x 3125	9'8" x 10'3"
Shower room	1750 x 2400	5'9" x 7'10"
Hall width	3800	12'6"

DESIGN
1111

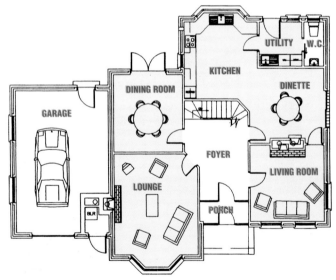

Ground Floor Layout

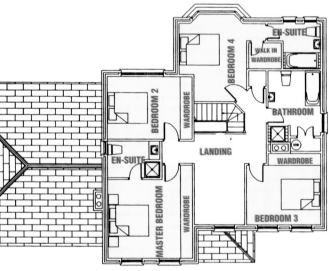

First Floor Layout

Main feature of this dwelling is the central foyer with all living rooms accessed directly off same. The winding staircase adds finishing touches to the end of the foyer while the attached garage adds length. Brick quoins as indicated are an optional feature.

Construction Cost
See page 143

DETAILS	Metric	Imperial
Overall length	15.975 m.	52'5"
Overall width	12.050 m.	39'6"
Main body width	7.810 m.	25'8"
Floor area	211 sq.m.	2271 sq.ft.
Ground floor	106 sq.m.	1141 sq.ft.
First floor	105 sq.m.	1130 sq.ft.
Gar/boiler	32.5 sq.m.	349 sq.ft.
Kitchen	3800 x 3780	12'5" x 12'4"
Dinette	3800 x 3420	12'5" x 11'3"
Dining room	3500 x 3850	11'6" x 12'8"
Living room	3800 x 3750	12'5" x 12'3"

DETAILS	Metric	Imperial
Lounge	4250 x 4950	11'11 x 16'3"
Bathroom	2690 x 3175	8'10 x 10'5"
Utility	2200 x 2170	7'3" x 7'2"
W.C.	1000 x 2170	3'3" x 7'2"
En-suite (Mas Bed)	1900 x 2190	6'3" x 7'2"
En-suite (Bed 4)	2625 x 1800	8'8" x 5'9"
Bedroom 1	4250 x 3850	11'11 x 12'8"
Bedroom 2	4250 x 3050	11'11 x 10'0"
Bedroom 3	3850 x 2925	12'8" x 9'7"
Bedroom 4	3425 x 3780	11'3" x 12'5"
Hall width	2550	8'4"

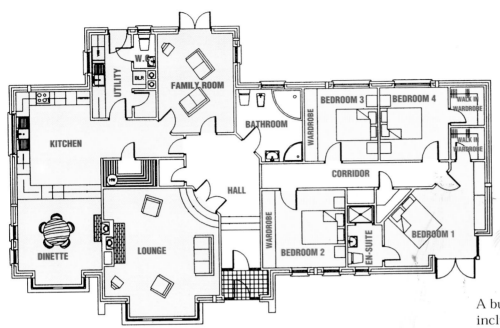

Floor Layout

DESIGN
1112

A bungalow with everything including an excellent and appealing appearance from all sides. An interestingly shaped bedroom complete with split level off hall and lounge are only some of the features.

Construction Cost
See page 143

DETAILS	Metric	Imperial		DETAILS	Metric	Imperial
Overall length	22.070 m.	72'5"		Utility	1800 x 3750	5'9" x 12'4"
Overall width	12.900 m.	42'4"		W.C.	1000 x 1500	3'3" x 4'11"
Main body width	8.620 m.	28'3"		En-suite (Bed 1)	1600 x 1850	5'3" x 6'1"
Floor area	204 sq.m.	2195.5 sq.ft.		Bedroom 1	4650 x 3450	15'3" x 11'4"
Kitchen	4800 x 3350	15'9" x 11'0"		Bedroom 2	3250 x 3450	10'8" x 11'4"
Dinette	3200 x 3350	10'6" x 11'0"		Bedroom 3	3150 x 3250	10'4" x 10'8"
Family room	3450 x 4400	11'4" x 14'5"		Bedroom 4	3400 x 3250	11'2" x 10'8"
Lounge	5250 x 4800	17'3" x 15'9"		Hall width	1800	5'9"
Bathroom	3050 x 3250	10'0" x 10'8"				

DESIGN
1113

An excellent home elegantly featured both front and rear and our decision to incorporate this on our front cover endorses that fact. Specially designed for a northerly facing site with view and sun to the rear, which in elevation is 2-storey.

Construction Cost
See page 143

DETAILS	Metric	Imperial
Overall length	18.740 m.	61'5"
Overall width	10.210 m.	33'5"
Main body width	8.300 m.	27'3"
Floor area	196 sq.m.	2108 sq.ft.
Ground floor	111 sq.m.	1193 sq.ft.
First floor	85 sq.m.	915 sq.ft.
Gar/boiler	21 sq.m.	225 sq.ft.
Kitchen/Din.	5850 x 3800	19'2" x 12'5"
Dining room	3500 x 3300	11'5" x 10'10"
Family room	3675 x 3800	12'1" x 12'5"
Lounge	4250 x 6500	13'11" x 21'4"
Bathroom	3675 x 2350	12'1" x 7'9"
Utility	3350 x 1975	11'0" x 6'6"
W.C.	1000 x 1975	3'3" x 6'6"
En-suite (Bed 1)	2840 x 2550	9'4" x 8'4"
Bedroom 1	3650 x 3850	12'0" x 12'7"
Bedroom 2	3150 x 3750	10'4" x 12'4"
Bedroom 3	3600 x 3050	12'1" x 10'0"
Bedroom 4	3100 x 3600	10'2" x 11'10"
Hall width	2200	7'3"
Garage	4630 x 4800	15'2" x 15'8

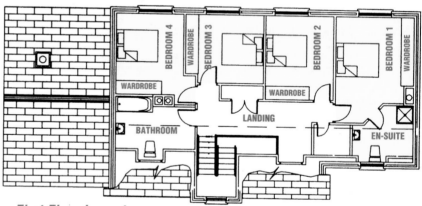

First Floor Layout

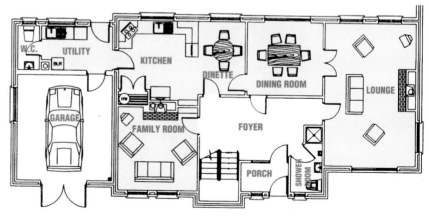

Ground Floor Layout

Rear Elevation

First Floor Layout

DESIGN
1114

Because of it's popularity in choice it differs in layout to design 1113. The rear elevation has been reduced to a storey and a half, which gives it a much more attractive appearance and reduces ridge height which might be necessary on elevated sites. Same site orientation as previous design applies.

Construction Cost
See page 143

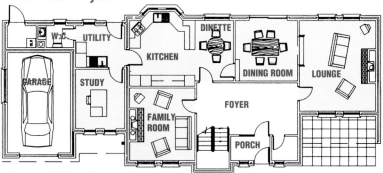

Ground Floor Layout

DETAILS	Metric	Imperial
Overall length	21.120 m.	69'3"
Overall width	9.100 m.	29'10"
Main body width	8.260 m.	27'1"
Floor area	198 sq.m.	2129.5 sq.ft.
Ground floor	115 sq.m.	1237 sq.ft.
First floor	83 sq.m.	892.5 sq.ft.
Gar/boiler	22 sq.m.	237.0 sq.ft.

DETAILS	Metric	Imperial
Kitchen/Din.	5850 x 3300	19'2" x 10'10"
Dining room	3500 x 3300	11'6" x 10'10"
Family room	3675 x 4000	12'1" x 13'2"
Lounge	4250 x 5000	13'11 x 16'5"
Bathroom	3675 x 2325	12'1" x 7'8"
Utility	2700 x 2275	8'10 x 7'6"
W.C.	1980 x 1200	6'6" x 4'0"

DETAILS	Metric	Imperial
En-suite (Bed 1)	2300 x 1100	7'6" x 3'7"
Bedroom 1	3800 x 3800	12'5" x 12'5"
Bedroom 2	3000 x 3850	9'10 x 12'8"
Bedroom 3	3600 x 3050	11'10 x 10'0"
Bedroom 4	3100 x 3050	10'2" x 10'0"
Study	2700 x 3300	8'10 x 10'10"
Hall width	2200	7'3"

DESIGN
1115

This split level dormer is best suited to a slightly side sloping site. The large study can have alternative use as bedroom and master bedroom occupies prime position on first floor.

Construction Cost
See page 143

DETAILS	Metric	Imperial
Overall length	20.550 m.	67'5"
Overall width	11.750 m.	38'7"
Main body width	8.950 m.	29'4"
Floor area	232 sq.m.	2500 sq.ft.
Ground floor	132 sq.m.	1424 sq.ft.
First floor	100 sq.m.	1076 sq.ft.
Garage	20 sq.m.	212 sq.ft.
Kitchen/Din.	3700 x 6900	12'2" x 22'8"
Dining room	3600 x 3500	11'10" x 11'6"
Living room	4000 x 6000	13'2" x 19'8"
Study	3500 x 3700	11'6" x 12'2"
Bathroom 1	2500 x 2000	8'3" x 6'7"
Bathroom 2	2550 x 2200	8'5" x 7'3"
Utility	2550 x 2000	8'5" x 6'7"
W.C.	1100 x 2000	3'8" x 6'7"
En-suite(MasBed)	2050 x 2000	6'9" x 6'7"
Master bedroom	4000 x 6000	13'2" x 19'8"
Bedroom 2	3500 x 4450	11'6" x 14'7"
Bedroom 3	3500 x 5700	11'6" x 18'8"
Bedroom 4	3900 x 4300	12'10" x 14'2"
Hall width	2050	6'9"

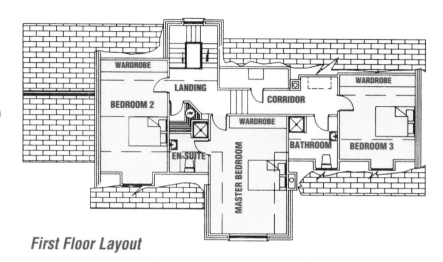

First Floor Layout

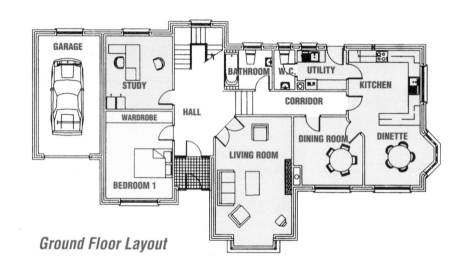

Ground Floor Layout

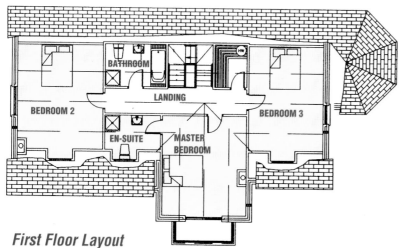

First Floor Layout

BATHROOM
LANDING
BEDROOM 2
EN-SUITE
MASTER BEDROOM
BEDROOM 3

The open veranda off master bedroom adds a touch of class to this contemporary styled dormer. Internally - split levels, with winding staircase, which lends light to the hallway, corridors and landing.

Construction Cost
See page 143

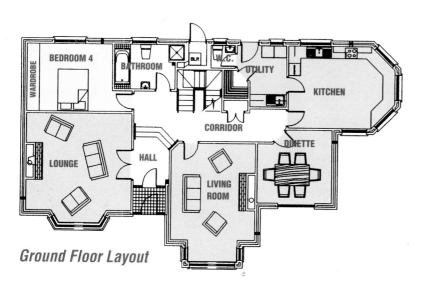

Ground Floor Layout

BEDROOM 4
WARDROBE
BATHROOM
BLR
W.C.
UTILITY
KITCHEN
CORRIDOR
LOUNGE
HALL
LIVING ROOM
DINETTE

DETAILS	Metric	Imperial
Overall length	18.900 m.	62'0"
Overall width	11.150 m.	36'7"
Main body width	8.200 m.	26'11"
Floor area	226 sq.m.	2428 sq.ft.
Ground floor	139 sq.m.	1498 sq.ft.
First floor	87 sq.m.	930 sq.ft.
Kitchen	5300 x 4000	17'5" x 13'2"
Dinette	3700 x 3550	12'2" x 11'8"
Living room	4200 x 4700	13'9" x 15'5"
Lounge	5200 x 4700	17'1" x 15'5"
Bathroom 1	3100 x 2150	10'2" x 7'1"
Bathroom 2	3050 x 1900	10'0" x 6'3"
Utility	2450 x 2950	8'1" x 9'8"
W.C.	1200 x 1125	4'0" x 3'8"
En-suite(MasBed)	2800 x 1650	9'2" x 5'5"
Master bedroom	4200 x 4800	13'9" x 15'9"
Bedroom 2	4200 x 5050	13'9" x 16'7"
Bedroom 3	3700 x 5050	12'2" x 16'7"
Bedroom 4	4200 x 3300	13'9" x 10'10"
Hall width	1800	5'11

DESIGN
1117

A Tudor/brick appearance enhances this house but the choice of finishes would obviously be dependant on it's site context. A large central foyer serves all rooms, with a similar type landing. A practical and adequate home.

Construction Cost
See page 143

DETAILS	Metric	Imperial
Overall length	17.400 m.	57'1"
Overall width	12.200 m.	40'0"
Main body width	9.710 m.	31'10"
Floor area	229 sq.m.	2463 sq.ft.
Ground floor	125.5 sq.m.	1350.5 sq.ft
First floor	103.5 sq.m.	1112.5 sq.ft.
Gar/boiler	25.5 sq.m.	274.0 sq.ft.
Kitchen/Din.	3400 x 5800	11'2" x 19'0"
Dining room	4000 x 3700	13'2" x 12'2"
Family room	4200 x 4150	13'9" x 13'8"
Lounge	4200 x 4900	13'9" x 16'1"
Bathroom	2550 x 3700	8'4" x 12'2"
Utility	2650 x 1900	8'8" x 6'3"
W.C.	1600 x 1800	5'3" x 5'9"
En-suite(Bed 1)	1350 x 2800	4'6" x 9'2"
Bedroom 1	3800 x 4450	12'6" x 14'7"
Bedroom 2	4790 x 3750	15'9" x 12'4"
Bedroom 3	3000 x 4250	9'10 x 13'11"
Bedroom 4	4400 x 2930	14'5" x 9'8"
Office	4400 x 2650	14'5" x 8'8"
Study	2400 x 2930	7'10 x 9'8"
Hall width	3000	9'10

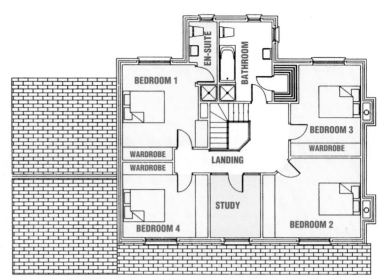

First Floor Layout

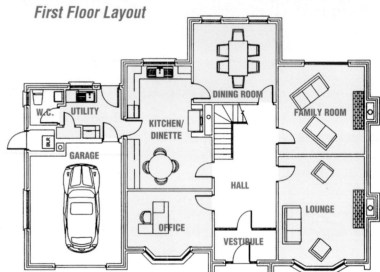

Ground Floor Layout

D E S I G N
1118

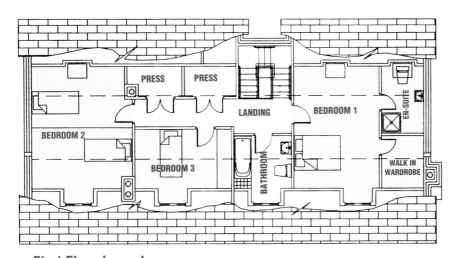

First Floor Layout

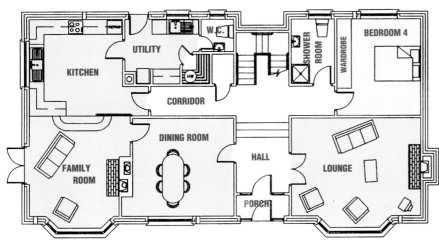

Ground Floor Layout

A simple and exceptionally appealing dormer, complete with two attractive bays. Practical layout for souterly facing site with three large and one small bedroom.

Construction Cost
See page 143

DETAILS	Metric	Imperial
Overall length	16.800 m.	55'2"
Overall width	9.100 m.	29'10"
Main body width	8.600 m.	28'2"
Floor area	214.5 sq.m.	2308 sq.ft.
Ground floor	130.5 sq.m.	1405 sq.ft.
First floor	84 sq.m.	903 sq.ft.
Kitchen	3800 x 3900	12'5" x 12'10"
Dining room	4200 x 4000	13'9" x 13'2"
Family room	3700 x 4100	12'2" x 13'6"
Lounge	5400 x 4000	17'9" x 13'2"
Shower room	1800 x 2600	5'11" x 8'6"
Bathroom	2400 x 2115	7'10" x 7'0"
Utility	3050 x 2100	10'0" x 6'10"
W.C.	1350 x 1300	4'5" x 4'3"
En-suite(Bed 1)	1750 x 2700	5'9" x 8'10"
Bedroom 1	3550 x 4900	11'8" x 16'1"
Bedroom 2	3800 x 4900	12'5" x 16'1"
Bedroom 3	4000 x 2385	13'2" x 7'10"
Bedroom 4	3500 x 3900	11'6" x 12'10"
Hall width	2200	7'3"

DESIGN
1119

A traditional style dormer with large kitchen cum living room. The use of "Velux" lights should help to reduce the cost of attic conversion which is reasonably compact yet adequate.

Construction Cost
See page 143

DETAILS	Metric	Imperial
Overall length	16.560 m.	54'4"
Overall width	9.970 m.	32'1"
Main body width	8.690 m.	28'6"
Floor area	214.5 sq.m.	2306 sq.ft.
Ground floor	132.5 sq.m.	1424.5 sq.ft.
First floor	82 sq.m.	881.5 sq.ft.
Kitchen	4100 x 4200	13'5" x 13'9"
Living room	4100 x 3950	13'5" x 13'0"
Lounge	5000 x 3950	16'5" x 13'0"
Bathroom 1	2300 x 2850	7'6" x 9'4"
Bathroom 2	1875 x 2300	6'1" x 7'6"
Utility	2350 x 1675	7'8" x 5'6"
W.C.	1650 x 1200	5'4" x 3'11"
En-suite(Bed 1)	2100 x 1380	6'10 x 4'6"
Bedroom 1	3800 x 3400	12'5" x 11'1"
Bedroom 2	3800 x 3150	12'5" x 10'4"
Bedroom 3	3950 x 5000	13'0" x 16'5"
Bedroom 4	3825 x 3610	12'6" x 11'10"
Bedroom 5	4100 x 5000	13'5" x 16'5"
Study	2000 x 2850	6'6" x 9'3"
Hall width	2200	7'2"

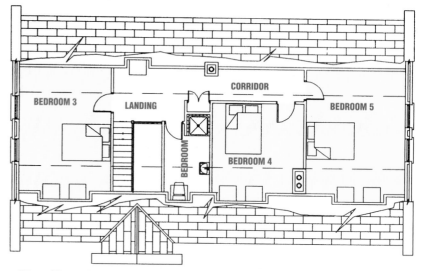

First Floor Layout

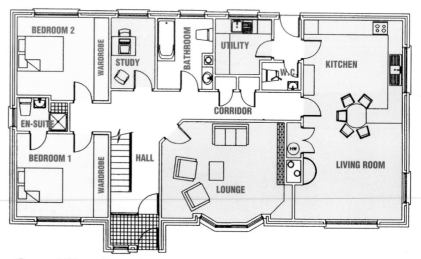

Ground Floor Layout

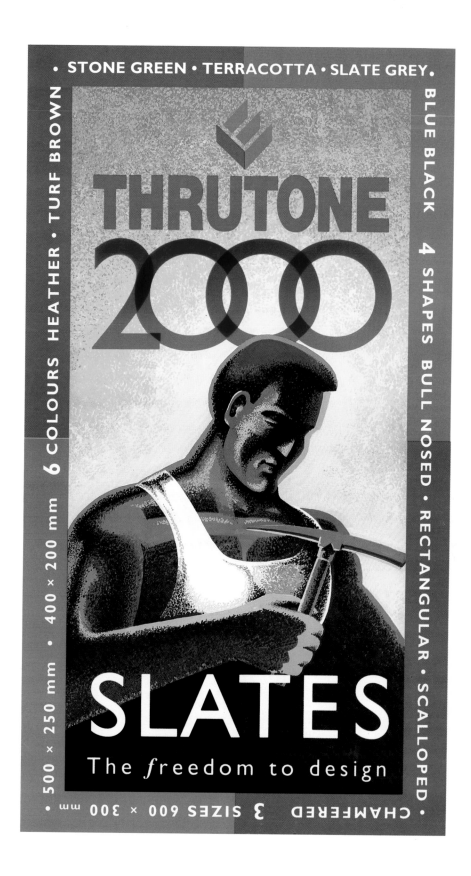

Tegral

Tegral Building Products Ltd., Athy, Co. Kildare. Tel. 0507 31316. Fax 0507 38637.
A MEMBER OF THE ETERNIT GROUP

ITEMS INCLUDED IN CONSTRUCTION COSTS

- Construction costs include for normal site clearance and excavation, excavating and pouring of foundations and average 900 deep blockwork from foundations to finished floor level. Sandwiched concrete insulated floors to all ground floors. External cavity, block leaf, insulated walls, rendered and skimmed internally and finished as detailed, externally. Block, rendered and skimmed internal walls throughout to all ground floors area's and stud walls to first floors.
- Completion of roof timbers and roof finishes including for all insulations, facias, soffits, gutters, flashings, etc. as outlined below.
- External joinery includes for all windows, glazing, external doors, etc. Internal second-fix joinery includes for all doors, frames, skirtings, architraves and

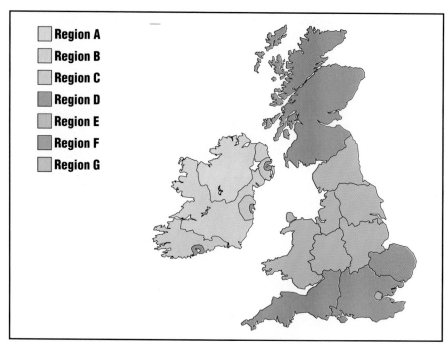

Region A
Region B
Region C
Region D
Region E
Region F
Region G

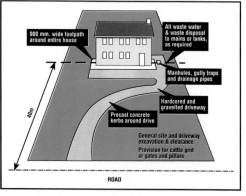

900 mm. wide footpath around entire house

All waste water & waste disposal to mains or tanks, as required

Manholes, gully traps and drainage pipes

Hardcored and gravelled driveway

Precast concrete kerbs around drive

General site and driveway excavation & clearance

Provision for cattle grid or gates and pillars

40m

ROAD

fitting out of cupboards, etc., as indicated, complete with staircase where required.
- Timber joists to first floor with plywood flooring.
- Electrical works to a good quality finish with external lights over all entrance doors.
- Plumbing to all bathrooms, showers, w.c.'s and sinks. Heating includes for complete system with radiators to each room with solid fuel back-boiler as standard in each house plus oil/furnace if so indicated on plan.
- Kitchen and utility units included at approximately 6% of the overall construction cost.
- Sanitary ware throughout, good quality with standard quality fittings.

GENERAL

Slight increase in other items such as quality of wall tiles, fireplaces, heating and electrical spec., etc.

ITEMS NOT INCLUDED IN CONSTRUCTION COSTS:-

- Range or stove to kitchen areas (because of the varying cost differences).
- Wardrobes
- Internal decoration to walls or ceilings

BRICK OR STONEWORK FINISH:

Construction cost does not include for complete stone or brick external finish to houses, as these types of finishes will be dependent on context of the house on the site.

Small feature panels in the form of quoins, or recesses, would be included.

WORK TO SITE:

Siteworks, drainage, water supply etc., included, as outlined on attached diagram, and amounts to approx. 6%-9% of the overall Construction cost.

SPECIFIC TO SECTION C

External wall finish	smooth rendered with 3-cts. masonry paint
Roof finish	fibre cement slates
Facia, soffit and barge	in upvc or aluminium finish
Windows	upvc, double-glazed
External doors	upvc, double-glazed
Internal doors	white "Regency" six-panelled door (for painting)
Architrave and skirtings	softwood, primed and painted
Stairs & railings	Hardwood thru' out with softwwod treads & risers
Fire surround	Tiled fire surround and hearth
Wall tiling	Bathroom complete, 1200mm. high to all w.c's, and en-suites, plus showers to ceiling, plus 3 row over all worktop areas.

DESIGN NUMBER	REGION A	REGION B	REGION C	REGION D	REGION E	REGION F	REGION G
1079	£79,555	£89,102	£101,035	£106,604	£124,106	£135,244	£149,564
1080	£70,966	£79,482	£90,127	£95,095	£110,708	£120,643	£133,417
1081	£80,832	£90,532	£102,657	£108,315	£126,098	£137,415	£151,964
1082	£73,386	£82,193	£93,201	£98,338	£114,483	£124,757	£137,967
1083	£87,003	£97,444	£110,494	£116,584	£135,725	£147,906	£163,566
1084	£78,480	£87,898	£96,670	£105,164	£122,429	£133,417	£147,543
1085	£74,121	£83,016	£94,134	£99,323	£115,629	£126,006	£139,348
1086	£72,057	£80,704	£91,513	£96,557	£112,409	£122,498	£135,468
1087	£70,775	£79,268	£89,884	£94,838	£110,409	£120,317	£133,057
1088	£71,879	£80,504	£91,286	£96,317	£112,131	£122,194	£135,132
1089	£75,822	£84,921	£96,294	£101,601	£118,282	£128,897	£142,545
1090	£69,769	£78,141	£88,607	£93,490	£108,840	£118,607	£131,166
1091	£72,908	£81,657	£92,593	£97,697	£113,736	£123,943	£137,067
1092	£72,623	£81,338	£92,232	£97,315	£113,292	£123,460	£136,532
1093	£76,843	£86,064	£97,591	£102,970	£119,875	£130,633	£144,465
1094	£72,704	£81,429	£92,334	£97,424	£113,419	£123,597	£136,684
1095	£80,992	£90,711	£102,860	£108,529	£126,348	£137,686	£152,265
1096	£76,000	£85,120	£96,520	£101,840	£118,560	£129,200	£142,879
1097	£72,734	£81,462	£97,372	£97,463	£113,465	£123,647	£136,739
1098	£74,868	£83,852	£95,083	£100,323	£116,794	£127,276	£140,752
1099	£67,558	£75,665	£85,799	£90,528	£105,391	£114,849	£127,009
1100	£63,140	£70,717	£80,188	£84,608	£98,499	£107,338	£118,703
1101	£76,729	£85,937	£97,446	£102,817	£119,697	£130,439	£144,251
1102	£78,710	£88,156	£99,962	£105,472	£122,788	£133,807	£147,975
1103	£67,950	£76,104	£86,297	£91,053	£106,002	£115,515	£127,746
1104	£80,784	£90,478	£102,595	£108,250	£126,023	£137,332	£151,873
1105	£86,640	£97,036	£110,032	£116,097	£135,158	£147,287	£162,882
1106	£79,768	£89,340	£101,306	£106,889	£124,438	£135,606	£149,964
1107	£73,959	£82,835	£93,928	£99,106	£115,377	£125,731	£139,044
1108	£81,379	£91,144	£103,351	£109,048	£126,951	£138,344	£152,992
1109	£57,940	£64,893	£73,584	£77,640	£90,387	£98,498	£108,928
1110	£76,835	£86,056	£97,581	£102,959	£119,863	£130,620	£144,450
1111	£82,951	£92,905	£105,348	£111,155	£129,404	£141,017	£155,948
1112	£75,680	£84,762	£96,114	£101,412	£118,061	£128,657	£142,279
1113	£84,608	£94,761	£107,452	£113,374	£131,988	£143,833	£159,062
1114	£88,762	£99,414	£112,728	£118,941	£138,469	£150,896	£166,873
1115	£85,310	£95,547	£108,344	£114,316	£133,084	£145,027	£160,383
1116	£84,671	£94,831	£107,532	£113,459	£132,087	£143,940	£159,181
1117	£80,434	£90,087	£102,152	£107,782	£125,478	£136,738	£151,217
1118	£75,650	£84,728	£96,076	£101,371	£118,015	£128,606	£142,223
1119	£69,163	£77,463	£87,838	£92,679	£107,895	£117,578	£130,027

Amounts shown are in the currency of the house location.
Prices are to be used for guideline purposes only.
Allow for variations of +/-6% depending on location, etc.
Note: in the interest of ensuring that your budget would be sufficient, we decided to use a detailed comprehensive specification and have deliberately tried not to under-estimate the construction cost shown.

DESIGN
1120

This one-and-a-half storey dwelling with dormer styled roof over living room, is a classic design, and suited to westerly facing site, so as to get maximum sunlight to kitchen/dining, with setting sun on living room and lounge. This spacious home is complemented by an elegantly shaped dining room, study and all en-suite bedrooms.

Construction Cost
See page 177

DETAILS	Metric	Imperial
Overall length	18.300 m.	60'0"
Overall width	12.100 m.	39'8"
Main body width	10.400 m.	34'1"
Floor area	262 sq.m.	2819 sq.ft.
Ground floor	142 sq.m.	1528 sq.ft.
First floor	120 sq.m.	1291 sq.ft.
Kitchen	4600 x 4300	15'3" x 14'1"
Dining room	4000 x 4200	13'2" x 13'9"
Living room	4600 x 3600	15'3" x 10'10"
Lounge	4500 x 5700	14'9" x 18'8"
Bathroom	2650 x 2700	8'8" x 8'10"
Utility	2350 x 2600	7'9" x 8'6"
W.C.	1200 x 1700	4'0" x 5'7"
Study	2300 x 2600	7'7" x 8'6"
En-suite (Bed 1)	1200 x 2600	4'0" x 8'6"
En-suite (Bed 2)	1600 x 2700	5'3" x 8'10"
En-suite (Bed 3)	2200 x 2300	7'3" x 7'7"
En-suite (Bed 4)	1750 x 2600	5'9" x 8'6"
En-suite (Bed 5)	1750 x 2600	5'9" x 8'6"
Bedroom 1	3600 x 3700	11'10 x 12'2"
Bedroom 2	3600 x 3700	11'10 x 12'2"
Bedroom 3	4500 x 4100	14'9" x 13'6"
Bedroom 4	4750 x 3000	15'7" x 9'10"
Bedroom 5	3600 x 4530	11'10 x 14'10"
Hall width	1800	5'11

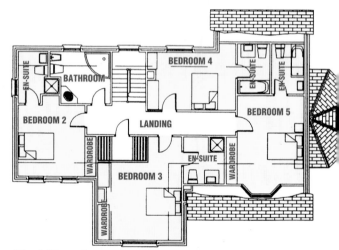

First Floor Layout

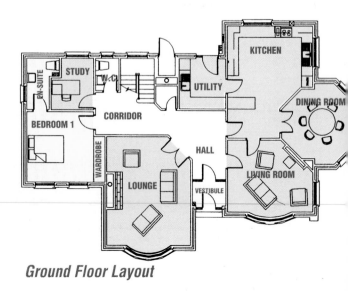

Ground Floor Layout

Ground Floor Layout

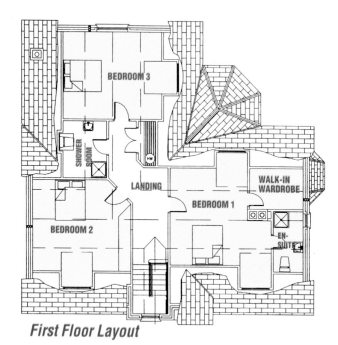

First Floor Layout

DETAILS	Metric	ImperiaL
Overall length	13.550 m.	44'6"
Overall width	14.100 m.	46'3"
Floor area	261 sq.m.	2806 sq.ft.
Ground floor	157 sq.m.	1689 sq.ft.
First floor	104 sq.m.	1117 sq.ft.
Kitchen	3900 x 4400	12'10" x 14'5"
Dinette	3500 x 2700	11'6" x 8'10"
Dining room	3390 x 2780	11'2" x 9'2"
Living room	4900 x 3700	16'1" x 12'2"
Lounge	4900 x 4200	16'1" x 13'10"
Bathroom	3100 x 2200	10'2" x 7'3"

DETAILS	Metric	Imperial
Utility	4000 x 2300	13'2" x 7'7"
W.C.	1400 x 1250	4'7" x 4'1"
En-suite	1475 x 2900	4'10" x 9'6"
Bedroom 1	5025 x 4650	16'6" x 15'5"
Bedroom 2	4900 x 4350	16'1" x 14'8"
Bedroom 3	4950 x 4150	16'3" x 13'8"
Bedroom 4	4900 x 3400	16'1" x 11'2"
Play room	4900 x 4200	16'1" x 13'10"
Shower room	2185 x 2722	7'2" x 8'11"
Walk-in-wardrobe	2650 x 1950	8'8" x 6'5"
Hall width	3500	11'6"

This home which has been designed to capture the landscaping to the rear of the house, is spacious throughout, with a nicely featured front and entrance.

Construction costs
See page 177

DESIGN
1122

An attractive storey-and-a-half layout with particular emphasis on large kitchen/ living accommodation, and two exceptionally spacious bedrooms, backed up with 2 no. standard double bedrooms, and elegant bathroom.

Construction Cost
See page 177

DETAILS	Metric	Imperial
Overall length	15.300 m.	50'2"
Overall width	11.400 m.	37'5"
Main body width	8.200 m.	26'11"
Floor area	271.5 sq.m.	2921 sq.ft.
Ground floor	146 sq.m.	1572 sq.ft.
First floor	125.5 sq.m.	1349 sq.ft.
Kitchen	4200 x 5000	13'9" x 16'5"
Dining room	4200 x 4100	13'9" x 13'5"
Family room	4200 x 4800	13'9" x 15'9"
Lounge	4200 x 7600	13'9" x 24'11"
Bathroom	3600 x 3000	11'10 x 9'10"
Utility	3650 x 2200	12'0" x 7'3"
Shower room	2350 x 2200	7'9" x 7'3"
En-suite 1	1500 x 2800	4'11 x 9'2"
En-suite 2	2100 x 1600	6'10 x 5'3"
Master bedroom	4200 x 4700	13'9" x 15'5"
Bedroom 2	4600 x 4800	15'1" x 15'9"
Bedroom 3	3200 x 5000	10'6" x 16'5"
Bedroom 4	3400 x 3800	11'2" x 12'5"
Dressing area 1	2600 x 2900	8'6" x 9'6"
Dressing area 2	2200 x 2900	7'3" x 9'6"
Hall width	3600	11'10

First Floor Layout

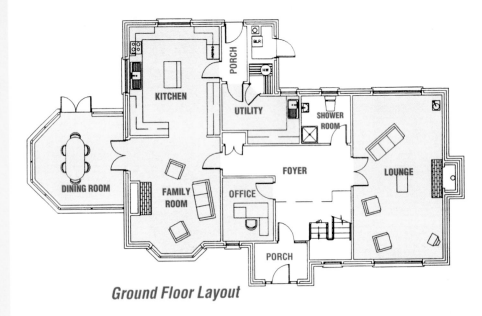

Ground Floor Layout

DESIGN
1123

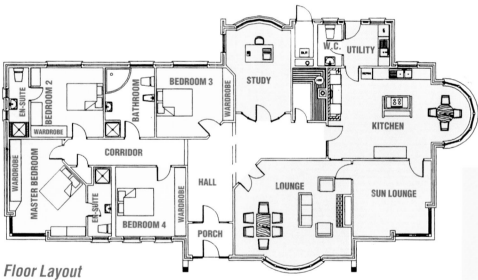

Floor Layout

One of the more elegant choices of bungalow's, complete with both small and large bays, large kitchen lending itself to numerous choice of layouts, including provision for "Aga" or range and many other features.

Construction Cost
See page 177

DETAILS	Metric	Imperial
Overall length	23.210 m.	76'2"
Overall width	12.600 m.	41'4"
Main body width	9.380 m.	30'10"
Floor area	233 sq.m.	2507 sq.ft.
Kitchen	4300 x 4750	14'1" x 15'7"
Dinette	3000 x 3000	9'10" x 9'10"
Lounge	6305 x 4965	20'8" x 16'3"
Bathroom	2590 x 3650	8'6" x 12'0"
Utility	2450 x 2240	8'1" x 7'4"
W.C.	1300 x 2240	4'3" x 7'4"
En-suite 1	1250 x 3650	4'1" x 12'0"
En-suite 2	1100 x 3650	3'8" x 12'0"
Bedroom 1	4120 x 5100	13'6" x 16'9"
Bedroom 2	3854 x 3650	12'8" x 12'0"
Bedroom 3	4140 x 3650	13'8" x 12'0"
Bedroom 4	3710 x 3650	12'2" x 12'0"
Study	3000 x 4250	9'10" x 14'0"
Sun lounge	4230 x 4000	13'11 x 12'2"
Hall width	2425	8'0"

Ground Floor Layout

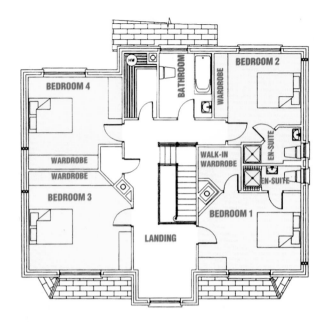

First Floor Layout

A beautiful 2-storey residence, styled on a traditional theme, with a spacious and practical layout, complete with many features including study, larder off kitchen, corner fireplaces, and two en-suites.

Construction Cost
See page 177

DETAILS	Metric	Imperial
Overall length	12.620 m.	41'5"
Overall width	12.340 m.	40'6"
Main body width	8.920 m.	29'2"
Floor area	221 sq.m.	2376 sq.ft.
Ground floor	112 sq.m.	1205 sq.ft.
First floor	109 sq.m.	1171 sq.ft.
Kitchen/Din.	4100 x 4700	13'6" x 15'5"
Living room	4500 x 4500	14'9" x 14'9"
Lounge	4500 x 5000	14'9" x 16'5"
Bathroom	2350 x 2750	7'9" x 9'0"
Utility	2250 x 2750	7'5" x 9'0"

DETAILS	Metric	Imperial
W.C.	1250 x 2750	4'2" x 9'0"
En-suite 1	1070 x 2520	3'6" x 8'3"
En-suite 2	2000 x 1425	6'7" x 4'8"
Bedroom 1	4500 x 3330	14'9" x 10'11"
Bedroom 2	3800 x 3050	12'6" x 10'0"
Bedroom 3	4500 x 4250	14'9" x 13'11"
Bedroom 4	3750 x 3950	12'4" x 13'0"
Study	4200 x 3200	13'9" x 10'6"
Walk-in-wardrobe	1850 x 1300	6'1" x 4'3"
Hall width	2800	9'2"

DESIGN
1124

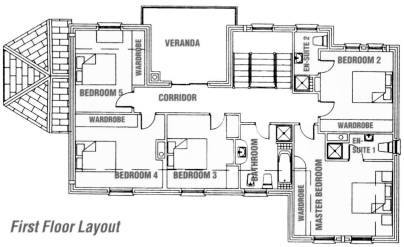

First Floor Layout

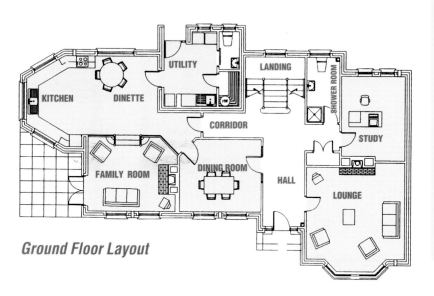

Ground Floor Layout

A classic Tudor home, with many appealing features, both internally and externally, including bay shaped kitchen, study, double flight staircase, and veranda to rear. Probably best suited to a easterly facing site.

Construction Cost
See page 177

DETAILS	Metric	Imperial
Overall length	19.560 m.	64'2"
Overall width	11.900 m.	39'1"
Main body width	8.300 m.	27'3"
Floor area	267 sq.m.	2873 sq.ft.
Ground floor	149 sq.m.	1603 sq.ft.
First floor	118 sq.m.	1270 sq.ft.
Kitchen/Din.	6550 x 3950	21'6" x 13'0"
Dining room	4150 x 3600	13'8" x 11'10"
Family room	4450 x 3700	14'7" x 12'2"
Lounge	5000 x 4500	16'5" x 14'9"
Bathroom	2660 x 3150	8'9" x 10'4"
Utility	2650 x 3100	8'9" x 10'2"
W.C.	1035 x 1875	3'5" x 6'2"
En-suite 1	2400 x 1250	7'11 x 4'1"
En-suite 2	1375 x 2850	4'6" x 9'4"
Master bedroom	5000 x 3650	16'5" x 12'0"
Bedroom 2	3650 x 3900	12'0" x 12'10"
Bedroom 3	3600 x 3600	11'10" x 11'10"
Bedroom 4	4450 x 3600	14'7" x 11'10"
Bedroom 5	2850 x 3950	9'4" x 13'0"
Study	3200 x 3900	10'6" x 12'10"
Shower room	1675 x 3200	5'6" x 10'6"
Veranda	3750 x 3600	12'6" x 11'10"
Hall width	2150	7'0"

DESIGN
1126

A large dormer, with popular porch feature. The winding stair terminating at the landing with a gallery type finish onto the front hallway. Two en-suite bedrooms and sauna off the main bathroom just to give the final finishing touches.
Note: brick finish optional.

Construction Cost
See page 177

DETAILS	Metric	Imperial
Overall length	16.860 m.	55'4"
Overall width	11.560 m.	37'11"
Main body width	8.760 m.	28'9"
Floor area	251 sq.m.	2702 sq.ft.
Ground floor	148 sq.m.	1593 sq.ft.
First floor	103 sq.m.	1109 sq.ft.
Kitchen	4000 x 4600	13'2" x 15'1"
Dinette	4200 x 3600	13'9" x 11'10"
Family room	5200 x 3500	17'1" x 11'5"
Lounge	4300 x 6100	14'2" x 20'0"
Bathroom	3210 x 3300	10'6" x 10'10"
Utility	2350 x 2900	7'9" x 9'6"
W.C.	1500 x 1300	4'9" x 4'3"
En-suite 1	2850 x 1460	9'4" x 4'9"
En-suite 2	2550 x 1300	8'4" x 4'3"
Bedroom 1	4300 x 3240	14'2" x 10'8"
Bedroom 2	4000 x 5180	13'2" x 17'0"
Bedroom 3	4300 x 4210	14'2" x 13'9"
Bedroom 4	4300 x 3780	14'2" x 12'5"
Sauna	2090 x 1840	6'9" x 6'1"
Hall width	2300	7'6"

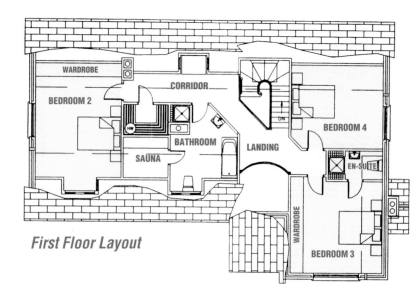

First Floor Layout

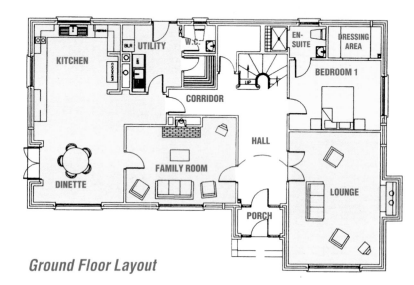

Ground Floor Layout

DESIGN
1127

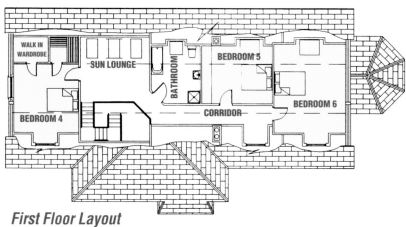

First Floor Layout

Beautifully designed contemporary dormer, with use of hips, half hips, and stone cladding to enhance it's length. Combined kitchen/dinette/ family room together with access to lounge, gives a very practical through layout. Six large bedrooms with two en-suite, completed with a sunlounge landing giving ample light to halls and landing.

Construction Cost
See page 177

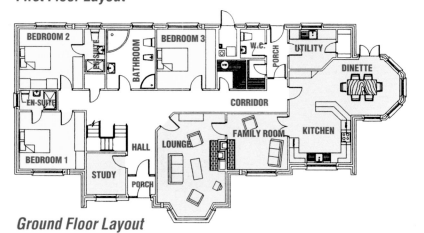

Ground Floor Layout

DETAILS	Metric	Imperial	DETAILS	Metric	Imperial	DETAILS	Metric	Imperial
Overall length	24.020 m.	78'10"	Family room	3800 x 3460	12'6" x 11'4"	Bedroom 2	3900 x 3600	12'10 12'0"
Overall width	11.120 m.	36'6"	Lounge	4200 x 5400	13'9" x 17'9"	Bedroom 3	3600 x 3600	12'0" x 12'0"
Main body width	9,120 m.	29'11"	Bathroom 1	2950 x 3600	9'8" x 11'10"	Bedroom 4	4000 x 4100	13'2" x 13'6"
Floor area	311 sq.m.	3323.5 sq.ft.	Bathroom 2	3000 x 3450	9'10 x 11'4"	Bedroom 5	4400 x 3450	14'5" x 11'4"
Ground floor	198 sq.m.	2108.5 sq.ft.	Utility	2900 x 2400	9'6" x 7'10"	Bedroom 6	4400 x 5300	14'5" x 17'4"
First floor	113 sq.m.	1215.0 sq.ft.	W.C.	1550 x 1740	5'1" x 5'9"	Sun lounge	4200 x 3800	13'9" x 12'6"
Kitchen	3800 x 2915	12'6" x 9'7"	En-suite	2260 x 1200	7'5" x 3'9"	Hall width	1700	5'7"
Dinette	4800 x 3380	15'9" x 11'1"	Bedroom 1	4000 x 3500	13'2" x 11'6"			

DESIGN
1128

This part brick, part block design, featuring extended walls, and raised parapet finish, features a mono style roof, to give it that unique look. The internal design puts emphasis on as many rooms as possible to front, and is finished off with a simple, yet spacious, veranda.

Construction Cost
See page 177

DETAILS	Metric	Imperial
Overall length	21.650 m.	71'0"
Overall width	10.000 m.	32'10"
Main body width	9.700 m.	31'10"
Floor area	266 sq.m.	2867 sq.ft.
Ground floor	131 sq.m.	1414 sq.ft.
First floor	135 sq.m.	1453 sq.ft.
Boiler	2.8 sq.m.	30 sq.ft.
Kitchen	3400 x 4500	11'2" x 14'9"
Dinette	2500 x 2900	8'2" x 9'6"
Living room	4800 x 4200	15'9" x 13'10"
Lounge	5400 x 4500	18'9" x 14'9"
Bathroom	2250 x 3300	7'5" x 10'10"
Utility	2500 x 2500	8'2" x 8'2"
En-suite 1	1200 x 2500	3'11" x 8'2"
En-suite 2	1600 x 1900	5'3" x 6'3"
Bedroom 1	5400 x 4500	18'9" x 14'9"
Bedroom 2	3600 x 5500	11'10 x 18'0"
Bedroom 3	3600 x 4200	11'10 13'10"
Bedroom 4	3400 x 4200	11'2" x 13'10"
Bedroom 5	3500 x 3300	11'0" x 10'10"
Bedroom 6	3500 x 3300	11'0" x 10'10"
Dining room	3900 x 3300	12'10 x 10'10"
Play room	3530 x 3000	11'7" x 10'10"
Shower room	1650 x 3300	5'5" x 10'10"
Hall width	2450	8'1"

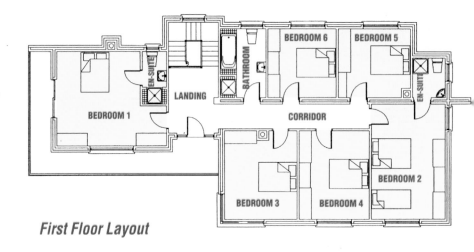

First Floor Layout

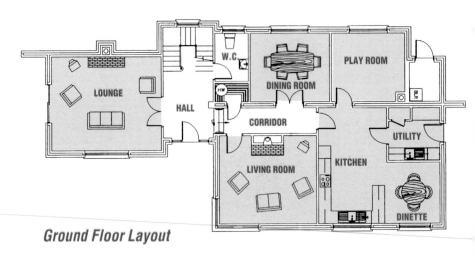

Ground Floor Layout

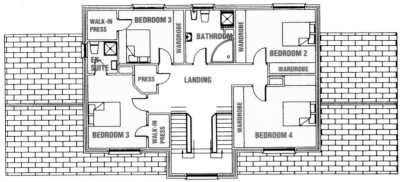

First Floor Layout

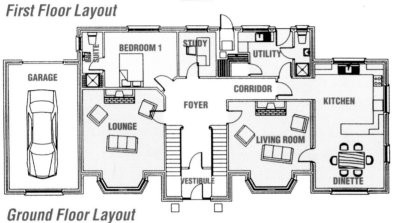

Ground Floor Layout

DESIGN
1129

Everything in a 2-storey, together with elegance, size, and layout, and our decision to feature it on our front cover bears testimony also to this fact! It's spacious foyer with winding staircase accesses most rooms, which like the foyer are spacious and appealing.

Construction Cost
See page 177

DETAILS	Metric	Imperial	DETAILS	Metric	Imperial	DETAILS	Metric	Imperial
Overall length	22.500 m.	73'10"	Lounge	4800 x 4600	15'9" x 15'1"	Bedroom 4	4800 x 3600	15'9" x 11'10"
Overall width	10.000 m.	32'10"	Bathroom	2850 x 3100	9'4" x 10'2"	Bedroom 5	3450 x 4200	11'4" x 13'9"
Main body width	8.500 m.	27'11"	Utility	2600 x 2600	8'6" x 8'6"	Walk-in-wardrobe 1	1750 x 1750	5'9" x 5'9"
Floor area	250 sq.m.	2682 sq.ft.	Shower room	900 x 2600	3'0" x 8'6"	Walk-in-wardrobe 2	1250 x 1900	4'2" x 6'3"
Ground floor	147 sq.m.	1580 sq.ft.	En-suite 1	1200 x 3200	4'0" x 10'6"	Study	2200 x 2600	7'3" x 8'6"
First floor	103 sq.m.	1102 sq.ft.	En-suite 2	1750 x 1800	5'9" x 5'11"	Hall width	3600	11'10
Garage	28 sq.m.	306 sq.ft.	Bedroom 1	4300 x 3200	14'1" x 10'6"	Garage	4000 x 7100	13'2" x 23'4"
Kitchen/Din.	4000 x 7100	13'2" x 23'4"	Bedroom 2	4650 x 3100	15'5" x 10'2"			
Living room	4800 x 3950	15'9" x 13'0"	Bedroom 3	3850 x 3100	12'8" x 10'2"			

DESIGN
1130

This is an elongated version of a very popular home featured in our third edition, and gives the added facility of playroom, and additional bedroom on first floor. A superb looking home, ideally suited to a flat site.

Construction Cost
See page 177

DETAILS	Metric	Imperial
Overall length	11.165 m.	36'8"
Overall width	14.360 m.	47'2"
Main body width	5.700 m.	18'9"
Floor area	275 sq.m.	2962 sq.ft.
Ground floor	144 sq.m.	1554 sq.ft.
First floor	131 sq.m.	1408 sq.ft.
Gar/boiler	21.5 sq.m.	232 sq.ft.
Kitchen/Din.	4000 x 5100	13'2" x 16'9"
Dining room	4200 x 3650	13'9" x 12'0"
Living room	3700 x 4350	12'2" x 14'3"
Lounge	4000 x 7600	13'2" x 25'0"
Bathroom	3600 x 2650	11'10 x 8'8"
Utility	2350 x 3500	7'9" x 11'6"
W.C.	1700 x 1500	5'7" x 4'11"
En-suite	1490 x 2000	4'10 x 6'7"
Master bedroom	4000 x 5500	13'2" x 18'0
Bedroom 2	3800 x 5500	12'5" x 18'0"
Bedroom 3	3600 x 3800	11'10 x 12'5"
Bedroom 4	3575 x 3800	11'9" x 12'5"
Bedroom 5	3500 x 3800	11'6" x 12'5"
Play room	3800 x 5700	12'5" x 18'8"
Hall width	1650	5'5"

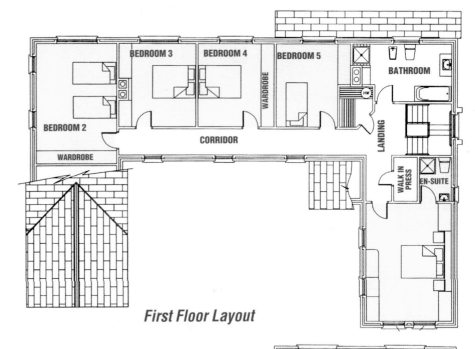

First Floor Layout

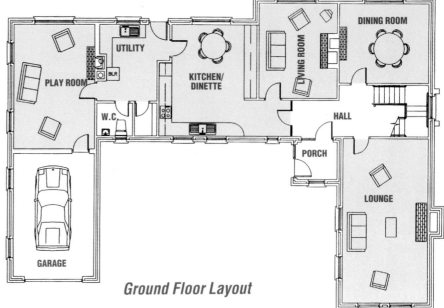

Ground Floor Layout

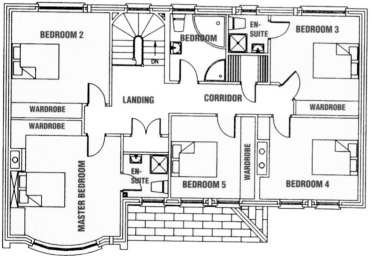

First Floor Layout

Another spacious contemporary 2-storey dwelling, with winding staircase as main feature of hallway, lots of space and cupboards throughout, with two en-suite bedrooms. Brick features to front optional depending on it's setting.

Construction Cost
See page 177

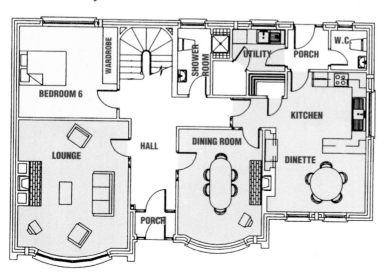

Ground Floor Layout

DETAILS	Metric	Imperial
Overall length	15.000 m.	49'3"
Overall width	9.850 m.	32'4"
Main body width	8.000 m.	26'3"
Floor area	234 sq.m.	2520 sq.ft.
Ground floor	120 sq.m.	1290 sq.ft.
First floor	114 sq.m.	1230 sq.ft.
Kitchen/Din	3300 x 5700	10'10" x 18'8"
Dining room	3500 x 4300	11'6" x 14'2"
Lounge	4500 x 5200	14'10" x 17'1"
Bathroom	2325 x 2700	7'8" x 8'11"
Utility	2200 x 1700	7'3" x 5'7"
W.C.	1500 x 1600	5'0" x 5'3"
En-suite 1	1900 x 1750	6'3" x 5'9"
En-suite 2	1650 x 1550	5'5" x 5'1"
Master bedroom	4500 x 4050	14'9" x 13'4"
Bedroom 2	4000 x 3650	13'2" x 12'0"
Bedroom 3	3700 x 3600	12'4" x 11'0"
Bedroom 4	3600 x 3600	11'10" x 10'10"
Bedroom 5	3500 x 3300	11'6" x 10'10"
Bedroom 6	4000 x 3700	13'2" x 12'2"
Shower room	1375 x 2700	4'6" x 8'11"
Hall width	1900	6'3"

DESIGN
1132

An extremely generously sized home, with double garage. Attractive facade, with stair window ensuring adequate light to foyer and landing.

Construction Cost

See page 177

DETAILS	Metric	Imperial
Overall length	18.650 m.	61'10"
Overall width	10.300 m.	33'10"
Floor area	243 sq.m.	2623 sq.ft.
Ground floor	133 sq.m.	1434 sq.ft.
First floor	110 sq.m.	1189 sq.ft.
Gar/boiler	33 sq.m.	360 sq.ft.
Kitchen	5600 x 4200	18'4" x 13'10"
Dining room	4000 x 4400	13'2" x 14'5"
Family room	4050 x 4200	13'4" x 13'10"
Lounge	4600 x 5050	15'3" x 16'7"
Bathroom	2850 x 3850	9'4" x 12'8"
Utility	4000 x 1975	13'2" x 6'6"
W.C.	1100 x 1975	3'8" x 6'6"
En-suite	1850 x 1600	6'1" x 5'3"
Bedroom 1	3350 x 4300	11'0" x 14'2"
Bedroom 2	4050 x 4100	13'4" x 13'6"
Bedroom 3	3500 x 3900	11'6" x 12'10"
Bedroom 4	3400 x 3350	11'2" x 11'0"
Bedroom 5	3050 x 3350	10'0" x 11'0"
Study	2800 x 3350	9'2" x 11'0"
Hall width	1750	5'9"
Garage	5200 x 5900	17'1" x 19'5"

First Floor Layout

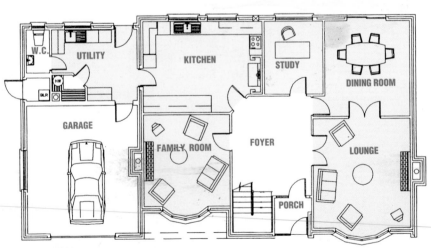

Ground Floor Layout

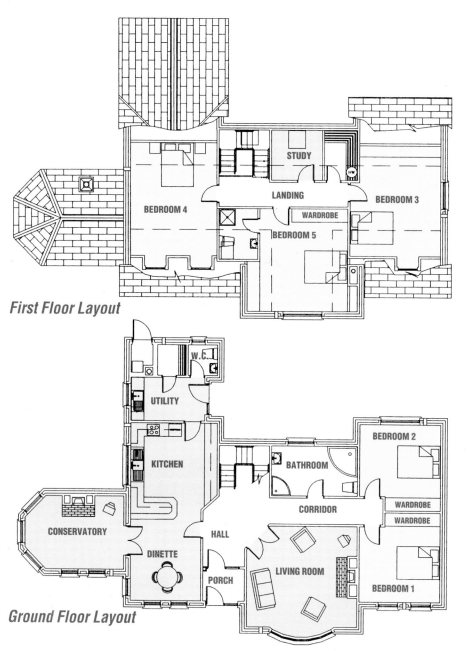

First Floor Layout

Labels: BEDROOM 4, STUDY, LANDING, WARDROBE, BEDROOM 5, BEDROOM 3, HW

Ground Floor Layout

Labels: W.C., UTILITY, KITCHEN, CONSERVATORY, DINETTE, HALL, PORCH, LIVING ROOM, BEDROOM 1, CORRIDOR, WARDROBE, WARDROBE, BATHROOM, BEDROOM 2

A beautiful house originating as a variation from our previous book. This being a more extravagant version complete with conservatory, large bathroom, utility and three excellent first floor bedrooms.

Construction Cost
See page 177

DETAILS	Metric	Imperial
Overall length	20.120 m.	66'0"
Overall width	13.570 m.	44'6"
Main body width	8.770 m.	28'9"
Floor area	240.5 sq.m.	2588 sq.ft.
Ground floor	148.5 sq.m.	1598 sq.ft.
First floor	92.0 sq.m.	990 sq.ft.
Kitchen/Din.	3300 x 8150	10'10" x 9'7"
Conservatory	4590 x 2925	15'0" x 26'9"
Living room	5200 x 4650	17'1" x 15'3"
Bathroom	4050 x 2290	13'3" x 7'6"
Utility	3450 x 2200	11'4" x 7'3"
W.C.	1385 x 1400	4'7" x 4'8"
En-suite	1825 x 2340	6'0" x 7'8"
Bedroom 1	3825 x 3450	12'6" x 11'4"
Bedroom 2	3825 x 3300	12'6" x 10'10"
Bedroom 3	4275 x 5100	14'1" x 16'9"
Bedroom 4	4050 x 5200	13'3" x 17'1"
Bedroom 5	5200 x 4750	17'1" x 15'7"
Hall width	1975	6'6"

DESIGN
1134

A generous dormer home, with three large first floor bedrooms, and three double bedrooms on ground floor. Additional en-suites could be provided at first floor levels if desired. External finishes would vary depending on context.

Construction costs
See page 177

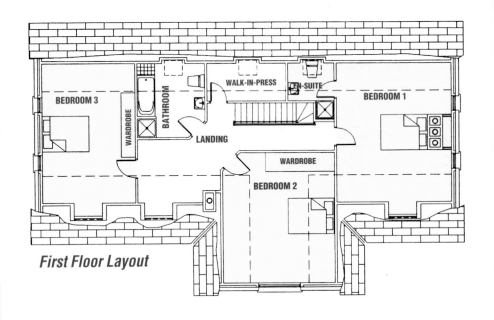

First Floor Layout

DETAILS	Metric	Imperial
Overall length	18.010 m.	59'1"
Overall width	10.560 m.	34'8"
Main body width	8.860 m.	29'1"
Floor area	258 sq.m.	2778 sq.ft.
Ground floor	150 sq.m.	1614 sq.ft.
First floor	108 sq.m.	1164 sq.ft.
Kitchen	5650 x 4400	18'6" x 14'5"
Living room	4200 x 3700	13'9" x 12'2"
Lounge	4550 x 5000	14'11" x 16'5"
Bathroom	2450 x 3600	8'1" x 11'10"
Utility	2900 x 2750	9'6" x 9'0"
W.C.	1450 x 1400	4'9" x 4'7"
En-suite	2000 x 1560	6'6" x 5'1"
Bedroom 1	4950 x 5830	16'3" x 19'2"
Bedroom 2	4840 x 4950	15'10" x 16'3"
Bedroom 3	3700 x 5830	12'2" x 19'2"
Bedroom 4	3300 x 3300	10'10" x 10'10"
Bedroom 5	3200 x 3300	10'6" x 10'10"
Bedroom 6	3100 x 3800	10'2" x 12'6"
Hall width	1700	5'7"

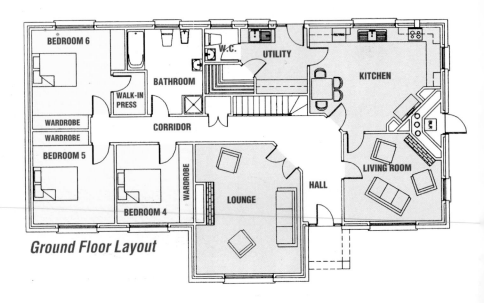

Ground Floor Layout

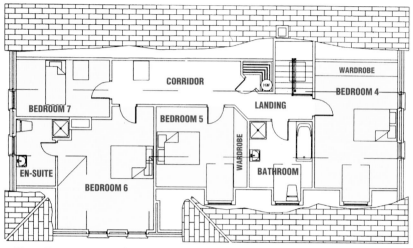

First Floor Layout

A large dormer, complete with recessed entrance and walkway. Dormer and half hips for that classic look. Best suited for a large family as bedrooms are in abundance.

Construction Cost
See page 177

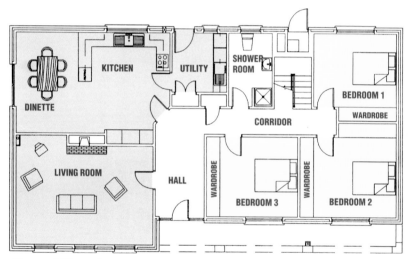

Ground Floor Layout

DETAILS	Metric	Imperial
Overall length	17.560 m.	57'8"
Overall width	9.710 m.	39'10"
Floor area	240 sq.m.	2582 sq.ft.
Ground floor	140 sq.m.	1510 sq.ft.
First floor	100 sq.m.	1072 sq.ft.
Kitchen/Din.	6900 x 4325	22'8" x 14'2"
Living room	6710 x 4250	22'0" x 13'11"
Bathroom	2800 x 2845	9'2" x 9'4"
Utility	2450 x 2550	8'0" x 8'4"
Shower room	1950 x 3150	6'4" x 10'4"
En-suite	1750 x 2870	5'9" x 9'5"
Bedroom 1	3650 x 3150	12'0" x 10'4"
Bedroom 2	4250 x 3450	14'0" x 11'4"
Bedroom 3	4100 x 3450	13'5" x 11'4"
Bedroom 4	3650 x 5440	12'0" x 17'10"
Bedroom 5	4100 x 3545	13'5" x 11'8"
Bedroom 6	4300 x 4700	14'2" x 15'5"
Bedroom 7	4175 x 2470	13'8" x 8'2"
Hall width	2200	7'2"

D E S I G N
1135

DESIGN
1136

A more contemporary choice of facades for this large dormer home. With three en-suite bedrooms, lends it very suitable for B.& B. purposes also, in which case the lounge would have to be converted for dining room facilities.

Construction Cost
See page 177

DETAILS	Metric	Imperial
Overall length	19.550 m.	64'2"
Overall width	9.900 m.	32'6"
Main body width	8.450 m.	27'9"
Floor area	253 sq.m	2705 sq.ft.
Ground floor	156 sq.m.	1666 sq.ft.
First floor	97 sq.m.	1039 sq.ft.
Kitchen	5400 x 4550	17'9" x 14'11"
Living room	3750 x 3200	12'4" x 10'6"
Lounge	4050 x 4650	13'3" x 15'3"
Bathroom	1950 x 3350	6'4" x 11'0"
Utility	2450 x 2550	8'1" x 8'4"
W.C.	1400 x 1450	4'7" x 4'9"
Bedroom 1	3750 x 3200	12'4" x 10'6"
En-suite (Bed.1)	2200 x 1100	7'3" x 3'8"
Bedroom 2	4450 x 3350	14'7" x 11'0"
Bedroom 3	3450 x 3200	11'4" x 10'6"
En-suite (Bed.3)	2500 x 1100	8'2" x 3'6"
Bedroom 4	4325 x 4420	14'2" x 14'6"
Bedroom 5	3550 x 4420	11'8" x 14'6"
En-suite (bed.5)	1100 x 2000	3'8" x 6'7"
Bedroom 6	4695 x 4695	15'5" x 15'5"
Bathroom 2	3600 x 2800	11'10 x 9'2"
Hall width	2200	7'3"

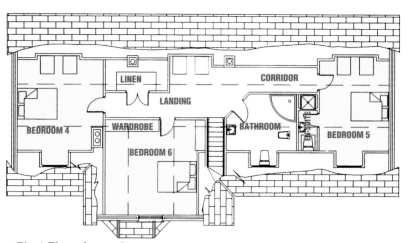

First Floor Layout

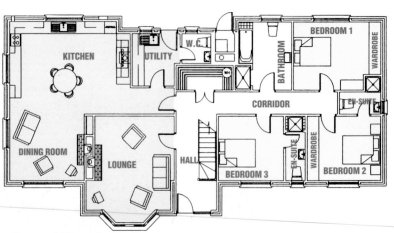

Ground Floor Layout

DESIGN
1137

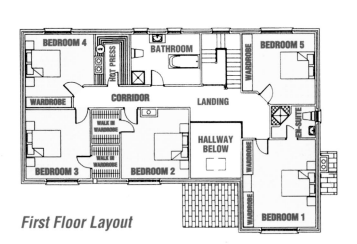

First Floor Layout

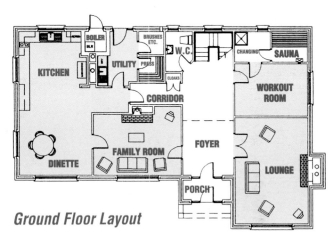

Ground Floor Layout

DETAILS	Metric	Imperial
Overall length	17.600 m.	57'9"
Overall width	11.600 m.	38'1"
Main body width	8.800 m.	28'11"
Floor area	295.5 sq.m.	3136 sq.ft.
Ground floor	154 sq.m.	1660 sq.ft.
First floor	141.5 sq.m.	1476 sq.ft.
Kitchen/Din.	3600 x 8200	11'10" x 26'11"
Family room	5200 x 3500	17'10" x 11'6"
Lounge	4300 x 6100	14'2" x 20'0"
Bathroom	4025 x 2850	13'1" x 9'4"
Utility	1600 x 3050	5'3" x 10'0"
W.c.	1600 x 2250	5'3" x 7'4"
En-suite	2575 x 1800	8'5" x 5'11"

DETAILS	Metric	Imperial
Bedroom 1	4300 x 5000	14'2" x 16'5"
Bedroom 2	3950 x 3900	13'0" x 12'10"
Bedroom 3	3750 x 3900	12'4" x 12'10"
Bedroom 4	4000 x 3450	13'2" x 11'4"
Bedroom 5	3220 x 4300	10'7" x 14'1"
Walk-in-wardrobe 1	1600 x 2000	5'3" x 6'7"
Walk-in-wardrobe 2	1600 x 1925	5'3" x 6'4"
Walk-in-wardrobe 3	1975 x 2850	6'6" x 9'4"
Sauna	2100 x 1700	6'11" x 5'7"
Shower	2100 x 1700	6'11" x 5'7"
Gym	4300 x 3000	14'1" x 9'10"
Porch	3000 x 1100	9'10" x 3'8"
Hall width	3000	9'10"

A large brick, mock Tudor house complete with work-out room for the health conscious family. Gallery type landing adds an extra touch of class to the generous hallway below. Good use made of walk-in wardrobes which are becoming evermore popular.

Construction Cost *See page 177*

DESIGN
1138

An extravent and lucrative design, offering may combining features in the front, this together with multiple split levelling, access to garage etc., would be a wonderful choice for suitably sloping site.

Construction Cost
See page 177

DETAILS	Metric	Imperial
Overall length	15.800 m.	51'10"
Overall width	10.600 m.	34'10"
Main body width	8.150 m.	26'5"
Floor area	242 sq.m.	2605 sq.ft.
Ground floor	161.5 sq.m.	1739 sq.ft.
First floor	80.5 sq.m.	866 sq.ft.
Garage	23 sq.m.	251 sq.ft.
Kitchen	3300 x 4600	10'10" x 15'3"
Dinette	3400 x 3150	12'2" x 10'4"

DETAILS	Metric	Imperial
Games room	4000 x 5325	13'2" x 17'6"
Living room	4100 x 4400	13'6" x 14'6"
Lounge	4600 x 4700	15'3" x 15'6"
Bathroom	2500 x 2800	8'3" x 9'2"
Utility	2950 x 2350	9'8" x 7'9"
W.c.	1450 x 1300	4'9" x 4'3"
En-suite 1	1600 x 2700	5'3" x 8'11"
En-suite 2	2150 x 1580	7'1" x 5'2"
Walk-in-wardrobe	1900 x 1300	6'3" x 4'3"

DETAILS	Metric	Imperial
Hotpress	2300 x 1300	7'7" x 4'3"
Bedroom 1	3200 x 3750	10'6" x 12'4"
Bedroom 2	4150 x 3740	13'8" x 12'4"
Bedroom 3	3750 x 3650	12'4" x 12'0"
Bedroom 4	3400 x 4630	11'2" x 15'4"
Office	2900 x 3600	9'6" x 11'10"
Hall width	1700	5'7"
Garage	4000 x 5300	13'1" x 17'4"

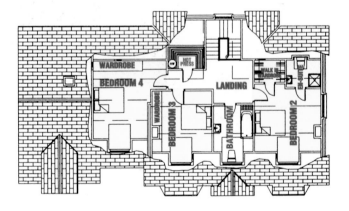

First Floor Layout

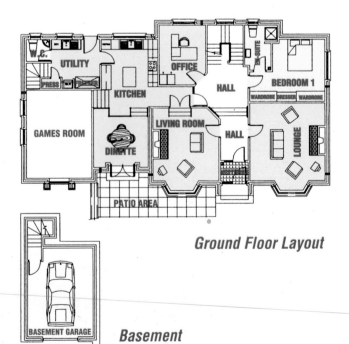

Ground Floor Layout

Basement

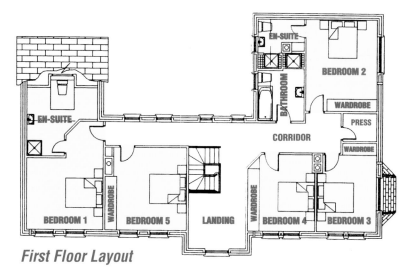

First Floor Layout

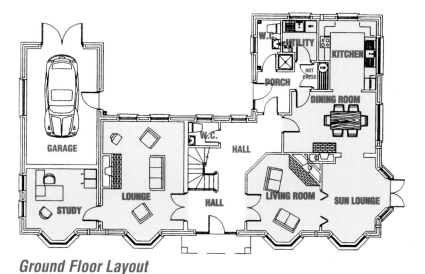

Ground Floor Layout

DETAILS	Metric	
Overall length	18.800 m.	61'8"
Overall width	11.400 m.	37'5"
Main body width	6.110 m.	20'1"
Floor area	231.5 sq.m.	2494 sq.ft.
Ground floor	121 sq.m.	1302 sq.ft.
First floor	110.5 sq.m.	1192 sq.ft.
Gar/boiler	21.5 sq.m.	231.5 sq.ft.
Kitchen	2400 x 3500	7'10" x 11'6"
Dining room	4400 x 3100	14'2" x 10'2"
Living room	3800 x 3900	12'6" x 12'10"
Lounge	4200 x 5500	13'4" x 18'1"
Utility	1800 x 2000	5'9" x 6'7"
W.c.	1575 x 1200	5'2" x 3'9"
En-suite 1	1800 x 1850	5'9" x 11'8"
En-suite 2	2400 x 1600	7'10" x 5'3"
Bedroom 1	4200 x 3560	13'4" x 11'8"
Bedroom 2	3700 x 4600	12'2" x 15'1"
Bedroom 3	3100 x 3900	10'2" x 12'10"
Bedroom 4	3500 x 3900	11'6" x 12'10"
Bedroom 5	4200 x 4200	13'4" x 13'4"
Sun lounge	2800 x 3775	9'2" x 12'4"
Shower room	1200 x 2500	3'11" x 8'1"
Study	3600 x 2800	11'10" x 9'2"
Hall width	2975	9'9"
Garage	3600 x 5500	11'10" x 18'1"

Luxurious home complete with separate dining room, sun lounge, study and everything your heart might desire. Veranda to side and front render this design suitable for southerly facing site.

Construction Cost *See page 177*

D E S I G N
1139

DESIGN
1140

This is a unique example of how a rear entry declining site can be best used. This layout, excluding the basement is also quite suitable for a flat, south-easterly facing site.

Construction Cost
See page 177

DETAILS	Metric	Imperial
Overall length	17.320 m.	56'10"
Overall width	10.520 m.	34'6"
Main body width	9.720 m.	31'11"
Floor area	226 sq.m.	2436 sq.ft.
Ground floor	130 sq.m.	1401 sq.ft.
First floor	96 sq.m.	1035 sq.ft.
Garage	31 sq.m.	336 sq.ft.
Basement	63 sq.m.	682 sq.ft.
Kitchen	3800 x 4000	12'6" x 13'2"
Dinette	3300 x 3500	10'10 x 11'6"

DETAILS	Metric	Imperial
Dining room	4200 x 3600	13'9" x 11'10"
Living room	4100 x 4000	13'6" x 13'2"
Kitchen/Liv. room	3900 x 6500	12'10 x 21'4"
Lounge	5500 x 4800	18'0" x 15'9"
Bathroom	3000 x 2500	9'10 x 8'3"
Shower room	1400 x 2800	4'7" x 9'2"
Utility	2550 x 3900	8'4" x 12'10"
W.c.	1100 x 2100	3'8" x 6'11"
Larder	1400 x 1600	4'7" x 5'3"
En-suite	1545 x 2200	5'1" x 7'3"

DETAILS	Metric	Imperial
Bedroom 1	3265 x 4800	10'8" x 15'9"
Bedroom 2	3460 x 3900	11'4" x 12'10"
Bedroom 3	3800 x 5685	12'6" x 18'7"
Bedroom 4	4000 x 4800	13'2" x 15'9"
Walk-in-wardrobe 1	1545 x 2500	5'1" x 8'3"
Walk-in-wardrobe 2	1400 x 1900	4'7" x 6'3"
Dressing area	3600 x 3300	11'10 x 10'10"
Hall width	1800	5'11
Garage	3300 x 6500	10'10 x 21'4"

Ground Floor Layout

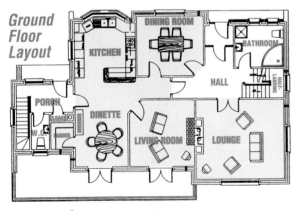

First Floor Layout

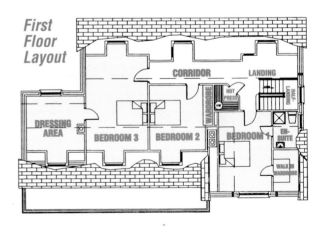

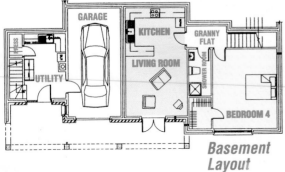

Basement Layout

Front Elevation

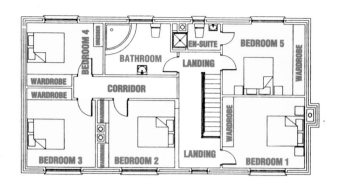

First Floor Layout

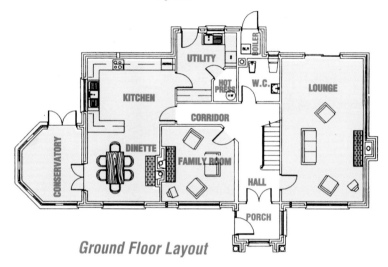

Ground Floor Layout

DETAILS	Metric	Imperial
Overall length	14.950 m.	49'1"
Overall width	11.200 m.	36'9"
Main body width	7.900 m.	25'11"
Floor area	218 sq.m.	2342 sq.ft.
Ground floor	113 sq.m.	1215 sq.ft.
First floor	105 sq.m.	1127 sq.ft.
Kitchen	4350 x 3900	14'3" x 12'10"
Dinette	3750 x 3500	12'4" x 11'6"
Family room	3785 x 3800	12'5" x 12'6"
Lounge	4250 x 7300	13'11 x 23'11"
Bathroom	3375 x 2600	11'1" x 8'6"
Utility	3100 x 3500	10'2" x 11'6"
W.c.	2110 x 2200	7'0" x 7'3"
Bedroom 1	4250 x 3600	13'11 x 11'10"
Bedroom 2	4010 x 3400	13'2" x 11'2"
Bedroom 3	3525 x 3400	11'7" x 11'2"
Bedroom 4	3925 x 2600	12'10" x 8'6"
Bedroom 5	4250 x 3600	13'11 x 11'10"
Hall width	2750	9'1"

A large contemporary styled 2-storey with through lounge and conservatory. Fireplace location in family room optional - could be fitted on opposite wall thereby eliminating fireplace to dinette.

Construction Cost *See page 177*

D E S I G N
1141

DESIGN
1142

A large Tudor style home with seven bedrooms, three of which are en-suite. Separate dining room and family room off kitchen provides a good practical layout, whereas the open viewing gallery to foyer adds it's own special touch of character.

Construction Cost *See page 177*

DETAILS	Metric	Imperial
Overall length	23.440 m.	76'11"
Overall width	13.400 m.	43'11"
Main body width	9.500 m.	31'2"
Floor area	394.5 sq.m.	4241 sq.ft.
Ground floor	207 sq.m.	2228 sq.ft.
First floor	187.5 sq.m.	2013 sq.ft.
Gar/boiler	27.5 sq.m.	296 sq.ft.
Kitchen	4600 x 4750	15'1" x 15'7"
Dinette	3350 x 4100	11'0" x 13'5"
Dining room	4050 x 4150	13'3" x 13'7"
Family room	5750 x 4100	18'10 x 13'5"
Lounge	4400 x 6100	14'5" x 20'0"
Bathroom	2300 x 4000	7'7" x 13'1"

DETAILS	Metric	Imperial
Utility	2650 x 3000	8'8" x 9'10"
W.c.	1350 x 1500	4'5" x 4'11"
En-suite 1	2200 x 2150	7'3" x 7'1"
En-suite 2	1500 x 3800	4'11 x 12'6"
Master bedroom	4400 x 4150	14'5" x 13'7"
Bedroom 2	4800 x 5000	15'9" x 16'5"
Bedroom 3	3700 x 4000	12'2" x 13'1"
Bedroom 4	3750 x 4100	12'6" x 13'5"
Bedroom 5	3800 x 5500	12'6" x 18'1"
Bedroom 6	4500 x 3300	14'9" x 10'10"
Bedroom 7	3400 x 3800	11'2" x 12'6"
Hall width	4700	15'5"

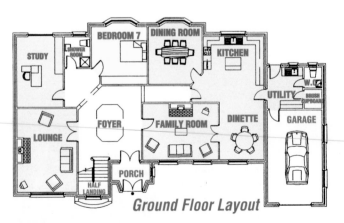

Ground Floor Layout

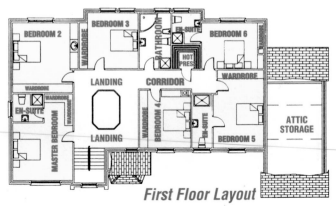

First Floor Layout

DESIGN
1143

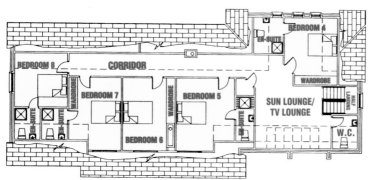

First Floor Layout

This design highlights one of the ways in which a home can be designed to suit B.& B. purposes. It consists of a 3-bedroom, self-contained house with lounge, family room, and dinette, together with 5 rooms available for B.& B. purposes on first floor. The layout is unique in that the B.& B. section is completely isolated from the main house by simply locking the kitchen/hall door.

Construction Cost *See page 177*

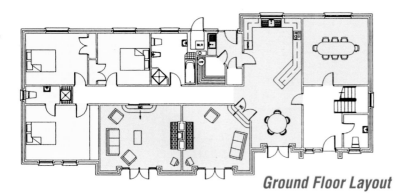

Ground Floor Layout

DETAILS	Metric	Imperial
Overall length	24.200 m.	79'5"
Overall width	10.900 m.	35'9"
Main body width	9.200 m.	30'2"
Floor area	368 sq.m.	3958 sq.ft.
Ground floor	210 sq.m.	2260 sq.ft.
First floor	158 sq.m.	1698 sq.ft.
Kitchen	4000 x 4600	13'2" x 15'4"
Dinette	3500 x 3000	11'6" x 9'8"
Dining room	4500 x 4500	14'9" x 14'9"
Family room	4600 x 4400	15'4" x 14'4"

DETAILS	Metric	Imperial
Lounge	5600 X 4400	18'0" x 14'4"
Bathroom	3000 x 3500	9'8" x 11'5"
Utility	2400 x 1500	8'0" x 5'0"
W.c. 1	1700 x 2250	5'7" x 7'6"
W.c. 2	1700 x 2250	5'7" x 7'6"
En-suite 1	3100 x 1200	10'4" x 4'0"
En-suite 2	2050 x 2435	6'9" x 8'0"
En-suite 3	1250 x 2180	4'1" x 7'2"
En-suite 4	1750 x 2100	5'9" x 6'11"
En-suite 5	1750 x 2100	5'9" x 6'11"

DETAILS	Metric	Imperial
Bedroom 1	4950 x 3700	16'3" x 12'2"
Bedroom 2	4200 x 3500	13'9" x 11'6"
Bedroom 3	3600 x 3500	12'10 x 11'6"
Bedroom 4	3650 x 4500	13'0" x 14'9"
Bedroom 5	4000 x 4590	13'2" x 16'9"
Bedroom 6	3600 x 4890	12'10 x 16'1"
Bedroom 7	3600 x 4890	12'10 x 16'1"
Bedroom 8	3600 x 3600	12'10 x 12'10"
Sun lounge	5250 x 4250	17'3" x 13'11"
Hall width	2700	8'10

DESIGN
1144

A commanding 2-storey home complete with veranda, dormer, and stair window giving it it's own individual character. Spaciously laid out internally with rooms easily accessed off central foyer and landing.

Construction Cost
See page 177

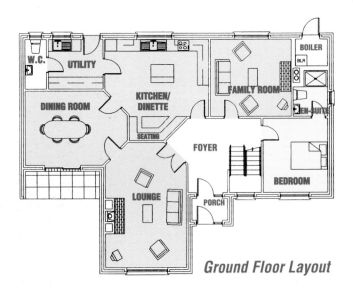

Ground Floor Layout

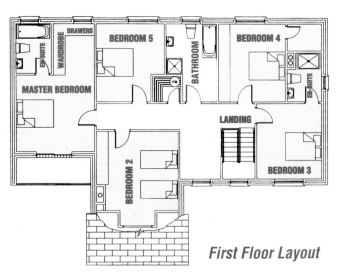

First Floor Layout

DETAILS	Metric	Imperial
Overall length	16.400 m.	53'10"
Overall width	12.200 m.	40'0"
Main body width	8.400 m.	27'6"
Floor area	260 sq.m.	2798 sq.ft.
Ground floor	135.5 sq.m.	1458 sq.ft.
First floor	124.5 sq.m.	1340 sq.ft.
Kitchen	5400 x 3900	17'8" x 12'10"
Family room	4300 x 3900	14'1" x 12'10"

DETAILS	Metric	Imperial
Dining room	5250 x 3800	17'3" x 12'6"
Lounge	4200 x 6370	13'10 x 20'11"
Bathroom	2600 x 3900	8'2" x 12'10"
Utility	2800 x 2500	9'2" x 7'10"
Shower room	2500 x 1100	7'10 x 3'7"
En-suite 1	2500 x 1800	8'2" x 5'11"
En-suite 2	1800 x 2425	5'11 x 8'0"
En-suite 3	1800 x 2425	5'11 x 8'0"

DETAILS	Metric	Imperial
Bedroom 1	4000 x 2800	13'2" x 9'2"
Bedroom 2	3400 x 3800	11'2" x 12'6"
Bedroom 3	3400 x 3800	11'2" x 12'6"
Bedroom 4	3500 x 3900	11'6" x 12'10"
Bedroom 5	3900 x 3500	12'10 x 11'6"
Bedroom 6	4200 x 4680	13'10 x 15'6"
Dressing area	2100 x 2600	6'11 x 8'6"
Foyer	3900 x 3800	12'10 x 12'6"

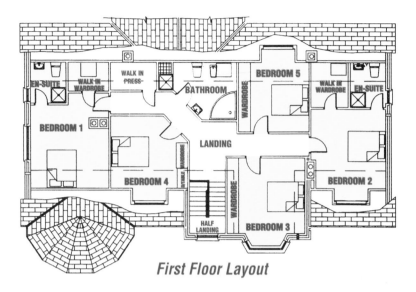

First Floor Layout

DETAILS	Metric	Imperial
Overall length	19.350 m.	63'6"
Overall width	13.000 m.	42'8"
Main body width	9.700 m.	31'10"
Floor area	317 sq.m.	3411 sq.ft.
Ground floor	187 sq.m.	2012 sq.ft.
First floor	130 sq.m.	1399 sq.ft.
Kitchen/Din.	5800 x 5000	19'0" x 16'5"
Dining room	4550 x 4150	14'11" x 13'8"
Family room	4000 x 4600	13'2" x 15'3"
Lounge	5700 x 4400	18'9" x 14'6"
Bathroom	2900 x 2800	9'6" x 9'2"
Utility	3385 x 2600	11'1" x 8'7"
W.c.	1800 x 1600	5'11" x 5'3"
En-suite 1	1800 x 2000	5'11" x 6'7"
En-suite 2	1800 x 2200	5'11" x 7'3"
Bedroom 1	3950 x 4140	13'0" x 13'8"
Bedroom 2	3800 x 3950	12'6" x 13'0"
Bedroom 3	4000 x 3800	13'2" x 12'6"
Bedroom 4	3950 x 3600	13'0" x 11'10"
Bedroom 5	3600 x 3400	11'10 x 11'2"
Study	3800 x 3750	12'6" x 12'4"
Play-room	3350 x 3550	11'0" x 11'6"
Walk-in-wardrobe 1	2050 x 1400	6'9" x 4'7"
Walk-in-wardrobe 2	1900 x 2200	6'3" x 7'3"
Hall width	2000	6'7

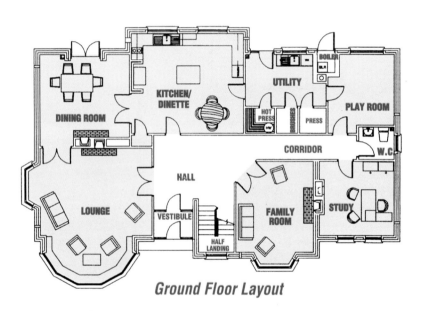

Ground Floor Layout

This is a revised version also of a design in our previous edtion. This layout gives much better use of floor space, in that it incorporates an additional bedroom on the first floor. All-in, an exceptionally spacious and desirable home.

Construction Cost *See page 177*

DESIGN
1145

DETAILS	Metric	Imperial
Overall length	27.650 m.	90'8"
Overall width	15.000 m.	49'2"
Main body width	9.100 m.	29'11"
Floor area	447 sq.m.	4813 sq.ft.
Ground floor	269 sq.m.	2896 sq.ft.
First floor	178 sq.m.	1917 sq.ft.
Kitchen/Din.	5200 x 6400	17'1" x 21'0"
Dining room	5200 x 4300	17'1" x 14'1"
Living room	5350 x 5250	17'6" x 17'2"
Utility	2900 x 2600	9'6" x 8'7"
W.c.	1700 x 1400	5'7" x 4'7"
W.c. (off Foyer)	1500 x 2600	4'11 x 8'7"
Walk-in-larder	2200 x 2600	7'3" x 8'7"
Bar	3225 x 3370	10'11" x 11'1"
Games room	5000 x 4650	16'5" x 15'5"
Steam room	1950 x 2200	6'5" x 7'3"
Jacuzzi/shower	2700 x 4500	8'11" x 4'9"
Plant room	2300 x 2300	7'7" x 7'7"
Master bedroom	4850 x 4700	15'11" x 15'6"
En-suite 1	2240 x 2720	7'4" x 8'11"
Bedroom 2	3700 x 4450	12'2" x 14'7"
En-suite 2	1200 x 3000	3'11" x 9'10"
Bedroom 3	4020 x 3400	13'2" x 11'2"
En-suite 3	1650 x 2150	5'5" x 7"1"
Bedroom 4	3900 x 3400	12'10" x 11'2"
En-suite 4	1500 x 3100	4'11" x 10'2"
Bedroom 5	3900 x 3550	12'10" x 11'8"
En-suite 5	2700 x 1800	8'11" x 5'11"
Studio	5000 x 5350	16'5" x 17'6"
Walk-in-wardrobe	2230 x 3000	7'4" x 9'10"

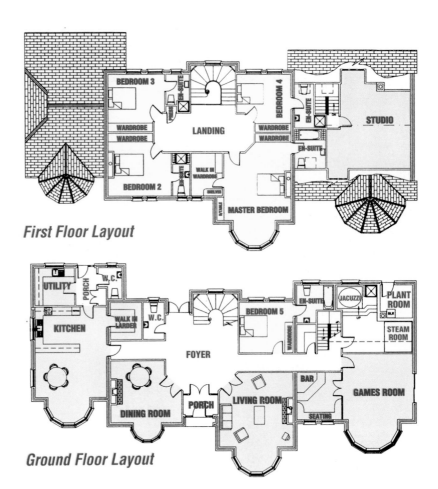

First Floor Layout

Ground Floor Layout

Featured in our special section for more than obvious reasons! Apart from having everything necessary in a home, together with internal layout and external appearance, it is complemented with a complete recreational wing, suitable for both the energetic and the laid-back occupier. It's elegance could be enhanced by use of brickwork or other external finishes, depending on it's site context.

Construction Cost *See page 177*

Construction Cost *See page 177*

DESIGN
1146

DESIGN
1147

The large open foyer with winding staircase together with many other features available from the foyer give the necessary character to this calibre of exquisite home. Rooms are more than generous throughout with exceptionally large kitchen/dinette and lounge. Probably best suited to a south-easterly facing site.

Construction Cost
See page 177

First Floor Layout

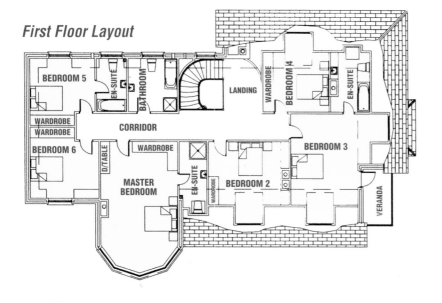

Ground Floor Layout

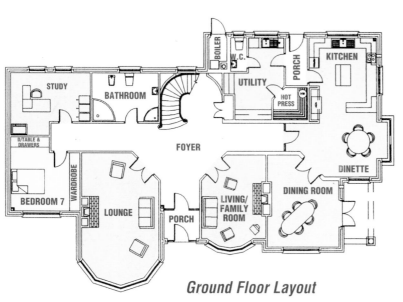

DETAILS	Metric	Imperial
Overall length	22.710 m.	74'6"
Overall width	14.950 m.	49'1"
Main body width	8.620 m.	28'3"
Floor area	417 sq.m.	4489 sq.ft.
Ground floor	228 sq.m.	2454 sq.ft.
First floor	189 sq.m.	2035 sq.ft.
Kitchen	4000 x 4350	13'2" x 14'3"
Dinette	4000 x 3750	13'2" x 12'4"
Dining room	4000 x 5285	13'2" x 17'6"
Family/living room	3800 x 4750	12'6" x 15'7"
Lounge	4500 x 5900	13'6" x 19'4"
Bathroom	3900 x 2850	12'10" x 9'4"
Bathroom	2850 x 3050	9'4" x 10'0"
Utility	2100 x 4800	6'11 x 15'9"
W.c.	950 x 2050	3'2" x 6'9"
En-suite 1	1600 x 3600	5'3" x 11'10"
En-suite 2	2300 x 3400	7'7" x 12'6"
En-suite 3	1800 x 3050	5'11 x 10'0"
Master bedroom	4500 x 5900	13'6" x 19'4"
Bedroom 2	4250 x 3600	13'11" x 11'10"
Bedroom 3	3900 x 5200	12'10 x 17'3"
Bedroom 4	3950 x 3400	13'0" x 11'2"
Bedroom 5	3800 x 3050	12'6" x 10'0"
Bedroom 6	4000 x 3250	13'2" x 10'8"
Bedroom 7	4000 x 3600	13'2" x 11'10"
Study	4600 x 2850	14'0" x 9'4"
Hall width	2090	6'10

View A

DESIGN
1148

A wonderful split level home, designed to fit onto it's own sloping site, with endless features both externally and internally. Split levelled entrance foyer with it's magnificently designed staircase, sheeted "Velux" lightwell and many other features will match any room in the house for elegance and design. Designed specifically to suit the customer's needs and site requirements, which is what we at Plan-a-Home specialise in.

Construction Cost *See page 177*

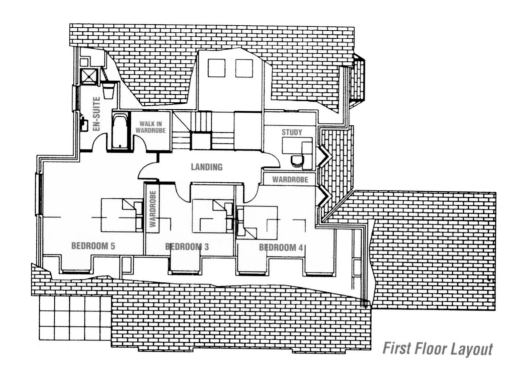

First Floor Layout

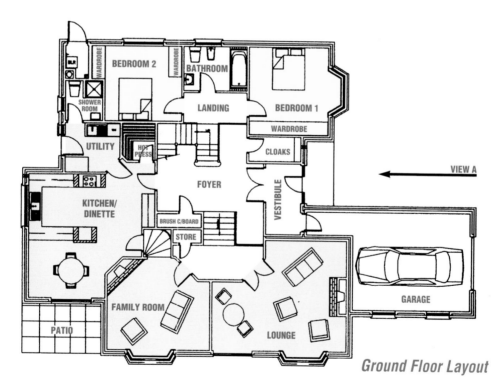

VIEW A

Ground Floor Layout

DETAILS	Metric	Imperial
Overall length	21.050 m.	69'1"
Overall width	14.300 m.	46'11"
Floor area	249 sq.m.	2679 sq.ft.
Ground floor	169 sq.m.	1818 sq.ft.
First floor	80 sq.m.	861 sq.ft.
Garage	27 sq.m.	291 sq.ft.
Kitchen/Din.	5150 x 5600	16'11" x 18'5"
Family room	4700 x 4100	15'5" x 13'6"

DETAILS	Metric	Imperial
Lounge	5300 x 5000	17'5" x 16'5"
Bathroom	2950 x 2000	9'8" x 6'7"
Utility	2500 x 2200	8'3" x 7'3"
Shower room	1800 x 1700	5'11" x 5'7"
En-suite	3000 x 1700	9'10" x 5'7"
Bedroom 1	3700 x 3950	12'2" x 13'0"
Bedroom 2	3500 x 3400	11'6" x 11'2"
Bedroom 3	3450 x 3220	11'4" x 10'6"

DETAILS	Metric	Imperial
Bedroom 4	3700 x 3820	12'2" x 12'6"
Bedroom 5	4350 x 4150	14'3" x 13'8"
Study	2420 x 2030	8'0" x 6'8"
Walk-in-wardrobe	1800 x 1750	5'11" x 5'9"
Hall width	1800	5'11"
Garage	5500 x 4450	18'0" x 14'7"

DESIGN
1149

DETAILS	Metric	Imperial
Overall length	20.100 m.	65'11"
Overall width	19.000 m.	62'4"
Floor area	224 sq.m.	2413 sq.ft.
Gar/boiler	20 sq.m.	215 sq.ft.
Kit/din.	5400 x 5000	17'9" x 16'5"
Dining room	4600 x 3800	15'3" x 12'6"
Living room	4400 x 3800	14'5" x 12'6"
Lounge	4100 x 5500	13'6" x 18'0"
Bathroom	2600 x 3600	8'7" x 11'10"
Utility	2250 x 3600	7'4" x 11'10"
W.c.	1250 x 1800	4'1" x 5'11"
En-suite	2600 x 1400	8'7" x 4'7"
Bed. 1	4300 x 4000	14'1" x 13'2"
Bed. 2	4600 x 4850	15'3" x 15'11"
Bed. 3	3600 x 5000	11'10 x 16'5"
Bed. 4	3600 x 3600	11'10 x 11'10"
Hall width	1900	6'3"
Garage	5375 x 3475	17'9" x 11'5"

Similar to the previous design in that it is designed to help straddle a sloping landscape and yet capture the views off to the left hand side of a site. Internally, the house would lend itself to a number of optional layouts, yet holding the appealing external appearance.

Construction Cost *See page 177*

Floor Layout

DESIGN
1150

DETAILS	Metric	Imperial
Overall length	17.450 m.	57'3"
Overall width	14.800 m.	48'7"
Main body width	6.400 m.	21'0"
Floor area	215 sq.m.	2315 sq.ft.
Ground floor	158 sq.m.	1700 sq.ft.
First floor	57 sq.m.	615 sq.ft.
Kitchen/Din.	4500 x 4900	14'9" x 16'1"
Living room	4550 x 3400	14'11 x 11'2"
Lounge	5500 diametre	18'0"
Bathroom	2700 x 3300	8'11 x 10'10"
Utility	2500 x 1900	8'3" x 6'3"

DETAILS	Metric	Imperial
W.c.	1500 x 1900	4'11 x 6'3"
En-suite	1700 x 1600	5'7" x 5'3"
Bedroom 1	4500 x 3500	14'9" x 11'6"
Bedroom 2	4500 x 3500	14'9" x 11'6"
Bedroom 3	4500 x 3500	14'9" x 11'6"
Bedroom 4	4500 x 3500	14'9" x 11'6"
Bedroom 5	3300 x 3500	10'10 x 11'6"
Shower room	3300 x 1800	10'10 x 5'11"
Walk-in-wardrobe	1500 x 1600	4'11 x 5'3"
Foyer	7150 x 3200	23'6" x 10'6"

Just to finish on a touch of class, this castle-like home design offers many elegant features internally and externally, including conical roofs, slim window design, large foyer cum seating or play area, complete with fireplace, together with rounded lounge, etc. Hope it gives you some insight into our versatility in design and layout!

Construction Cost *See page 177*

Ground Floor Layout

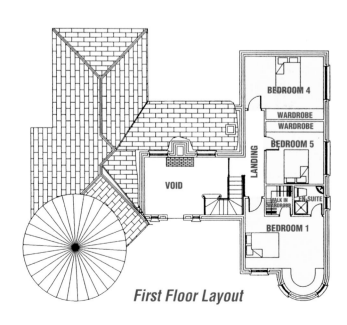

First Floor Layout

ITEMS INCLUDED IN CONSTRUCTION COSTS

- Construction costs include for normal site clearance and excavation, excavating and pouring of foundations and average 900 deep blockwork from foundations to finished floor level. Sandwiched concrete insulated floors to all ground floors. External cavity, block leaf, insulated walls, rendered and skimmed internally and finished as detailed, externally. Block, rendered and skimmed internal walls throughout to all ground floors area's and stud walls to first floors.
- Completion of roof timbers and roof finishes including for all insulations, facias, soffits, gutters, flashings, etc. as outlined below.
- External joinery includes for all windows, glazing, external doors, etc. Internal second-fix joinery includes for all doors, frames, skirtings, architraves and fitting out of cupboards, etc., as indicated, complete with staircase where required.
- Timber joists to first floor with plywood flooring.
- Electrical works to a good quality finish with external lights over all entrance doors.
- Plumbing to all bathrooms, showers, w.c.'s and sinks. Heating includes for complete system with radiators to each room with solid fuel back-boiler as standard in each house plus oil/furnace if so indicated on plan.
- Kitchen and utility units included at approximately 6% of the overall construction cost.
- Sanitary ware throughout, good quality with standard quality fittings.

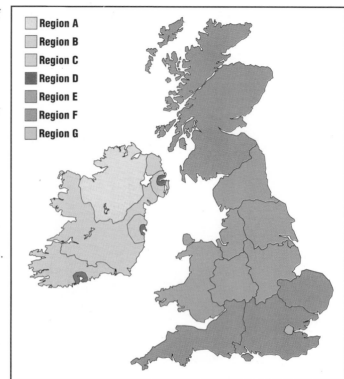

Region A
Region B
Region C
Region D
Region E
Region F
Region G

GENERAL

Slight increase over Section C.

ITEMS NOT INCLUDED IN CONSTRUCTION COSTS:-

- Range or stove to kitchen areas (because of the varying cost differences).

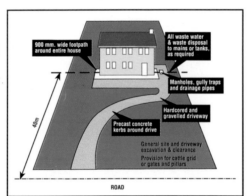

900 mm. wide footpath around entire house

All waste water & waste disposal to mains or tanks, as required

Manholes, gully traps and drainage pipes

Hardcored and gravelled driveway

Precast concrete kerbs around drive

40m

General site and driveway excavation & clearance
Provision for cattle grid or gates and pillars

ROAD

- Wardrobes
- Internal decoration to walls or ceilings

BRICK OR STONEWORK FINISH:

Construction cost does not include for complete stone or brick external finish to houses, as these types of finishes will be dependent on context of the house on the site.

Small feature panels in the form of quoins, or recesses, would be included.

WORK TO SITE:

Siteworks, drainage, water supply etc., included, as outlined on attached diagram, and amounts to approx. 6%-8% of the overall Construction cost.

Section E

Section E similar in spec to Section D with the following adjustments:-

- Driveway tarmac finish. Specialised finishes - an additional 5% included for specialised finishes, i.e. hardwood floors, plaster moulds, etc.

Specific to Section D

External wall finish	smooth rendered with 3-cts. masonry paint
Roof finish	fibre cement slates
Facia, soffit and barge	in upvc or aluminium finish
Windows	upvc, double-glazed
External doors	upvc, double-glazed
Internal doors	hardwood panel doors
Architrave and skirtings	hardwood, sanded and varnished
Stairs & railings	Hardwood thru' out with softwwod treads & risers
Fire surround	Tiled fire surround and hearth
Wall tiling	Bathroom complete, 1200mm. high to all w.c's, & en-suites, plus showers to ceiling, plus 3 row over all worktop areas.

DESIGN NUMBER	REGION A	REGION B	REGION C	REGION D	REGION E	REGION F	REGION G
1120	£99,911	£111,900	£126,886	£133,880	£155,861	£169,848	£187,832
1121	£93,500	£104,720	£118,745	£125,290	£145,860	£158,950	£175,780
1122	£97,000	£108,640	£123,190	£129,980	£151,320	£164,900	£182,360
1123	£87,434	£97,926	£111,042	£117,162	£136,398	£148,638	£164,376
1124	£77,457	£86,752	£98,371	£103,793	£120,834	£131,678	£145,620
1125	£95,711	£107,196	£121,553	£128,253	£149,309	£162,709	£179,937
1126	£93,785	£105,040	£119,107	£125,672	£146,305	£159,435	£176,316
1127	£101,553	£113,740	£128,973	£136,081	£158,423	£172,640	£190,920
1128	£107,484	£120,382	£136,505	£144,028	£167,675	£182,723	£202,070
1129	£94,826	£106,205	£120,429	£127,067	£147,929	£161,204	£178,273
1130	£106,116	£118,850	£134,767	£142,195	£165,541	£180,397	£199,498
1131	£82,746	£92,675	£105,087	£110,879	£129,083	£140,668	£155,562
1132	£89,231	£99,939	£113,324	£119,570	£139,201	£151,693	£167,755
1133	£87,016	£97,458	£110,510	£116,601	£135,745	£147,927	£163,590
1134	£95,144	£106,561	£120,833	£127,493	£148,425	£161,745	£178,871
1135	£84,947	£95,140	£107,882	£113,829	£132,517	£144,409	£159,700
1136	£93,563	£104,790	£118,825	£125,374	£145,958	£159,057	£175,898
1137	£96,393	£107,961	£122,420	£129,167	£150,374	£163,869	£181,219
1138	£88,245	£98,834	£112,071	£118,248	£137,662	£150,016	£165,901
1139	£92,857	£104,000	£117,929	£124,429	£144,857	£157,857	£174,571
1140	£105,400	£118,048	£133,858	£141,236	£164,424	£179,180	£198,152
1141	£80,412	£90,061	£102,123	£107,752	£125,442	£136,700	£151,174
1142	£142,068	£159,116	£180,427	£190,371	£221,626	£241,516	£267,088
1143	£112,742	£126,271	£143,183	£151,075	£175,878	£191,662	£211,956
1144	£91,344	£102,305	£116,006	£122,401	£142,496	£155,284	£171,726
1145	£113,877	£127,542	£144,623	£152,595	£177,648	£193,590	£214,088

Section E

DESIGN NUMBER	REGION A	REGION B	REGION C	REGION D	REGION E	REGION F	REGION G
1146	£176,606	£197,799	£224,290	£236,652	£275,505	£300,230	£332,019
1147	£162,870	£182,414	£206,845	£218,245	£254,077	£276,879	£306,195
1148	£114,747	£128,517	£145,729	£153,761	£179,005	£195,070	£215,724
1149	£98,030	£109,793	£124,498	£131,360	£152,927	£166,651	£184,296
1150	£113,298	£126,894	£143,889	£151,820	£176,746	£192,607	£213,001

Amounts shown are in the currency of the house location.
Prices are to be used for guideline purposes only.
Allow for variations of +/-6% depending on location, etc.
Note: in the interest of ensuring that your budget would be sufficient, we decided to use a detailed comprehensive specification and have deliberately tried not to under-estimate the construction cost shown.

Irish Oak™

THE FLOOR FOR A LIFETIME

– 'tis fit for a king!

Ireland's great tradition for using oak has been revived. And now the trend is toward hardwood flooring, in top business premises and in private homes.

Aesthetically beautiful, naturally non-allergic, Irish Oak is much more hygienic and easier to maintain than carpets – and once laid, lasts a lifetime. In fact, it improves with age!

You'll see Irish Oak in Tallaght Shopping Centre, Clerys, Easons and many other Stores – including Harrods of London. In hotels like the Conrad, the IFSC, Government Buildings, embassies and prestige offices too, Irish Oak sets the mood with warmth, colour, character and style.

Irish Oak is environment friendly. Many other types of flooring are based on non-renewable oil products, but Irish Oak comes from managed renewable forests.

Irish Oak enhances decor with the natural colours of timber or a range of wood stain finishes. The wood is impregnated with an oil wax solution making it water repellent and dirt resistant. So the need for periodic resanding and resealing is greatly reduced.

So the beauty of it lasts – and lasts!

- The only Irish hardwood flooring.
- Choice of natural timber or woodstain finishes.
- Hardwearing Uv, cured Acrylic or traditional Woodwax finish.
- Solid wide plank or narrow strip effect available.
- Installation systems for secret nailing over existing wooden floors or joists, or metal clip fixing over concrete surfaces.
- Cleaner, easier to maintain, longer lasting.
- Available exclusive from Buckleys branches nationwide.

HEAD OFFICE
Irish Oak, Church Road,
Glenties, Co. Donegal.
Tel 075 51145 Fax 075 51402

Buckleys
The Builders Providers Nationwide

DUBLIN
Robinhood Road,
Clondalkin,
Tel 01-507770,
Fax 01-508087,
Telex 30700.

DUBLIN
Swords Road,
Santry,
Tel 01-8425299,
Fax 01-8425917.

CORK
Ardarostig,
Bishopstown,
Tel 021-544099,
Fax 021-546176.

GALWAY
Wellpark,
Tel 091-53220,
Fax 091-51474.

LIMERICK
Ballysimon,
Tipperary Rd,
Tel 061-416844,
Fax 061-416418.

SLIGO
Finisklin,
Tel 071-61701,
Fax 071-60683.

To save time and expedite orders, clients may utilise this pre-enquiry form to ascertain whether or not the changes you require are viable and practical.

After examination of your alterations, we reserve the right to make any other "knock-on" alterations which we would consider necessary to rectify the layout.

Should you require a sketch showing the outcome of the alterations (scale 1:100) then enclose £45 with this form. This is not an additional expense as it is refundable on Mail Order when confirming your order. *(Note: in exceptional circumstances where alterations are extensive, we may have to request additional money for supply of sketches).*

We will reply immediately to your enquiry with any further relevant alterations, and advise on any additional costs for plans.

Sketch or plan indicating alterations plus any additional information may accompany this form if necessary.

DESIGN NO

QUICK REFERENCE GUIDELINE:

The following are three general conditions applicable to most sites, but in some cases there may be other overriding factors governing these:-

1. Main entrance to house located so as to be clearly visible on driveway approach to house, and sheltered from any prevailing winds where applicable.
2. The main living quarters designed and positioned to avail of maximum sunlight.
3. The living quarters designed and positioned to maximise on view. In most cases, compromise on points 2 and 3 are required.

ROOM DETAILS Description	*LENGTH Increase by		*WIDTH/BREADTH Decrease by		OTHER DETAILS
Lounge					
Family/living room					
Kitchen/dinette					
Dining rm.					
Utility rm.					
Sunlounge					
Study					
Bathroom					
W.C.					
Shower					
En-suite					
Bedroom 1					
Bedroom 2					
Bedroom 3					
Bedroom 4					
Bedroom 5					

Length of overall house *Increase by* .... *Decrease by* ....

Width of house *Increase by* .... *Decrease by* ....

* Length - Measured horizontally on page * Width/Breadth - measured vertically on page

Client's Name:

Address:

Additional information:

Changes to garage layout:

Signature:

Telephone Number *(Daytime):*

(Evening time):

(Only insert phone numbers that you wish to be contacted at).

I enclose payment of £45 for a provisional sketch showing alterations Yes ☐ No ☐
(this amount will be refundable in confirming order).

☐ Cheque/Bank Draft/P.O. made payable to Plan-A-Home
☐ Credit Card ☐ Master/Access ☐ Visa Card

Account no: ☐☐☐☐☐☐☐☐☐☐☐☐☐☐☐ Card expiry date: ....

Although it is impossible to indicate the effect the alterations will have on plan costs, we assure you that they will be competetively priced and worthwhile.

Please forward to:
Plan-A-Home,
Glencrow, Moville, Co. Donegal,
Ireland.
Tel. 077-82258 Fax 077-82341 Int. code 01035377.

THE SITE

Your choice of site, will undoubtedly influence the design of your home, so therefore, should you have a particular style of home in mind, you are advised to ensure that this would be suitable before purchasing site.

The following considerations are important before purchasing a site, and you may need some special advice to assist you in making the correct decisions:-

1. Size
Ensure that your site is large enough to:-
a) Comply with your local planning office's conditions for site size
b) To accommodate comfortably your preferred size of home
c) Ensure that it can adequately disperse with all storm and foul drainage on site if mains are not available
d) Suitable entrance can be provided to comply with all safety aspects of road openings
e) Accommodate where possible future extension/garage, etc.
f) That all necessary services, especially water supply and electricity, are available, as the remoteness or unavailability of these services can costs thousands later. Your local electricity office will be able to assist you in obtaining an estimate for the provision of electricity on site where necessary.

2. Serviced sites
Serviced sites should mean that all drainage, water, electricity and any other relevant services are provided on site. Sites may initially appear expensive, but in the long run can prove quite cheap. It is advisable to ensure that the developer in charge, is bound legally to complete all these services if they are temporary or unavailable at the time of purchase.

3. Site conditions:
The nature of the soil and site gradients are of upmost importance when deciding on a site, in that, a site that requires excessive filling or excessive excavation, can result in thousands of pounds expenditure, which you may not have been envisaged, therefore, a flat site with good soil conditions can often prove to be the best purchase bargain.

4. View/aspect:
The view is probably the first thing people consider when choosing their site, so therefore, it is natural that prime consideration should be given to maximising the use of the view when selecting a design. This should also be considered in conjunction with the availability of sunlight to the living quarters.

SITE LAYOUT & LOCATION MAP

Site layout and location maps are necessary for planning permission, building regulations, and contract purposes, etc. The accuracy and details on these are every bit as important as your house plan, so therefore, you should ensure that you get the proper professional advice on same to avoid any delays with your planning application.

We at Plan-A-Home provide a survey service in the Donegal and immediate area. Should you live outside of this area we would be unable to provide this service, but can, on receipt of the proper information from a suitably qualified person, prepare the actual map for planning permission. Details required are as outlined below.

ORDERING OF SITE MAPS
Information request:-

1. A freehand sketch with all dimensions as indicated on diagram below, so as to accurately locate any existing adjoining dwellings, and indicate entrance to adjoining dwellings. Same applies to dwellings within 100m. radius of your site, including dwellings on opposite side of road.

2. Location of (if any) septic tanks, serving adjoining dwellings.

3. The proposed source of water supply
a) Well - please indicate position
b) Public mains - please indicate location (which side of road)
c) If group scheme please indicate name of scheme.

4. Method of waste disposal
a) Mains - please indicate mains pipeline route
b) Septic tank

5. Exact location of dwelling on site

6. Any E.S.B., P.& T., or underground services which run over, under or adjacent to the site.

7. Site contours or spot levels, indicating relationship of site with:-
i) road entrance
ii) adjoining dwellings
iii) show proposed floor level.

8. An extract from an Ordnance Survey sheet showing your site location in relation to any nearby crossroads, Churches, or any easily identified landmark.

9. The precise address of your site.

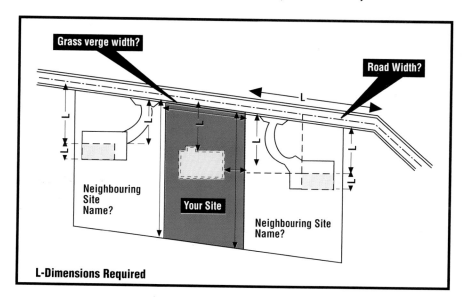

Grass verge width?

Road Width?

Neighbouring Site Name?

Your Site

Neighbouring Site Name?

L-Dimensions Required

① Detailed construction drawings with layouts, elevations, sections, and brief spec.
Ireland 8 sets, U.K. 12 sets

② Specification and detail sheets for tender and Building Regulation purposes.
Ireland 4 sets, U.K. 8 sets

NOTE: Plan orders include items 1 and 2 above.

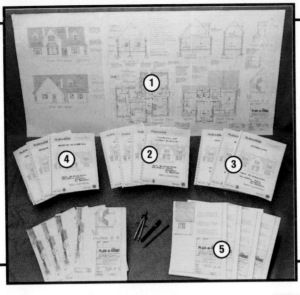

③ Detailed "shopping list" of materials and suggested labour costings.
Ideally suited for the self-build enthusiast.

④ Bill of Quantities - useful in it's priced form as a budget guideline, or as an additional tender document in it's unpriced form.

⑤ Site layout and location map, indicating relationship of dwelling to entrance, other structures and site, drainage layout, etc.

COST OF PLANS	1. Plans/Spec.	2. Site Maps	3a Material List	3b Bill of quantities	3a & 3b (both)	4. Perspective
Section A						
Below 1000 sq.ft.	£235	£45	£50	£50	£75	£60
Over 1000 sq.ft.	£270	£45	£55	£55	£85	£60
Section B						
Below 1600 sq.ft.	£295	£45	£65	£65	£100	£80
Over 1600 sq.ft.	£320	£45	£70	£70	£105	£80
Section C						
Below 2200 sq.ft.	£360	£55	£75	£75	£115	£100
Over 2200 sq.ft.	£390	£55	£80	£80	£120	£100
Section D						
Below 3000 sq.ft.	£445	£55	£85	£85	£125	£120
Over 3000 sq.ft.	£495	£55	£90	£90	£130	£120
Section E						
By agreement						

8. CUSTOMISED DESIGNS

Customised designs, i.e. preparing a house design "from scratch", is a major part of our service at Plan-A-Home, and is indeed a very sensible way of going about designing your new home. The ingredients required to provide a house that meets your own personal requirements are as follows:-

a) Details of site location including all surrounding developments and environmental landscape

b) Your input:
A complete list detailing all your thoughts and requirements. Part of this may be done in sketch form, if you so wish. Making direct reference to designs or parts of designs in this book showing any preferences in elevations or parts of layout, would also be helpful.

On receipt of this we can contact you for any further information required, and proceed to prepare sketched designs to a scale of 1:100. On your approval of these we can then discuss finer details, specifications, etc., and to prepare the complete construction drawings for planning and tendering purposes.

The approximate cost of this service is as outlined below, and the exact cost can be agreed on approval of the sketch designs. One third of this cost would be required for the preparation of sketched designs, with the balance due should you decide to proceed.

4. PERSPECTIVES

An artist's impression of your finished house, showing suggested landscape and garden concept. Similar to those illustrated throughout this book, perspectives would be prepared on cartridge/water colour paper, using mixed colour media, size A2. Site map, or photograph of site would be helpful, but not necessary.

5. GARAGE PLANS £40
List of materials £20

Garage plans as illustrated on page 16/17 can be supplied to whatever dimensions you may require. A photocopy of your preference with sizes would be helpful when ordering.

6. Reverse hand layouts (mirror image)£35

All the plans illustrated in this book are available in a mirror image to suit your site orientation. You should seek advice from your engineer/architect in regard to the most suitable handed layout to suit your site.

7. ALTERATIONS

Any feasible type of alteration is available to illustrated designs in this book. This can be prearranged by phone or fax for minor alterations, but the use of the Pre-Order Enquiry Form would be advised for more major alterations.

CUSTOMISED DESIGNS - PRICE LIST

Section A	up to 1345 sq. ft.	£250 - £390
Section B	1346 to 1900 sq. ft.	£390 - £590
Section C	1901 to 2500 sq. ft.	£550 - £790
Section D	2501 to 4000 sq. ft.	£700 - £1000
Section D	split level /specials	by agreement

1. **HOUSE DESIGN NO** ☐☐☐☐ *per set of 8 (Rep.Irl.) 12 (U.K)*		£
(See column 1, p.182) **ADDITIONAL COPIES** - *plans and specification @ £10 each (max. 4 additional copies)*		£
2. **SITE MAPS** *(p. 181)* **Set of 8 (Rep. Irl.) 12 (U.K.)** *(See column 2, p.182)*		£
3a. **LIST OF MATERIALS** *Please tick* ☐		£
3b. **BILL OF QUANTITIES** *Please tick* ☐ *(See column 3, p.182)* **Both** ☐		
4. **PERSPECTIVE** - *optional requirement* *(See column 4, p.182)*		£
5. **GARAGE PLANS** *(p. 16/17)* **State type No.** **8 sets (Rep. Irl.) 12 sets (U.K.)** *(See p.182)* **Note:** *roof style will be chosen to match dwelling.*		£
LIST OF MATERIALS FOR GARAGE *(See p.182)*		£
6. **REVERSE HAND LAYOUT (MIRROR IMAGE)** Yes ☐ No ☐		£
7. **COST OF ALTERATIONS** - *(if any) as agreed per Pre-Order Enquiry Form* *(See p.179)*		£
Postage & Packing		£10.00
Sub-total:		£
Deduct (if applicable) payment for sketches from Pre-Order Enquiry Form		£
TOTAL:		£

ALL PLANS TO BUILDING REGULATIONS STANDARD.

NAME (Capitals):

ADDRESS:

SIGNATURE:

Telephone Number (Home)

(Work)

SITE ADDRESS:

METHOD OF PAYMENT:

☐ **Cheque/Bank Draft/P.O. made payable to Plan-A-Home**

☐ **I prefer to pay by Credit Card.**
Please charge my: ☐ **Master/Access Card**
    ☐ **Visa Card**

Account no. ☐☐☐☐☐☐☐☐☐☐☐☐☐☐☐☐

Card expiry date:

Payment to be in currency of country in which site is located.
Allow approx. 21 days for delivery.

Please tick off your specification overleaf and detach or send photocopy of same, along with Mail Order Form, and payment to:
Plan-A-Home,
Glencrow, Moville, Co. Donegal, Ireland.
Tel. 077-82258 Fax: 077 82341 (International code 01035377)

Please tick the following to enable us to complete a detailed specification to suit your requirements (otherwise we will allow for a standard, good quality finish throughout).

ROOF COVERING:
Tiles:
- Concrete ☐
- Clay ☐

Slates:
- Synthetic (Fibre cement) ☐
- Natural (Stone) ☐

Other ☐

WINDOWS:
- Softwood ☐
- Hardwood ☐
- uPVC ☐
- Aluminium ☐
- Other ☐ ....

GROUND FLOORS:
- Sandwiched conc. floors ☐
- Suspended timber floors ☐

FIRST FLOOR:
- Timber joists & ply flooring ☐
- Timber joists & deal flooring ☐
- Hollowcore floor slabs ☐

EXTERNAL DOORS/FRAMES:
- Softwood ☐
- Hardwood ☐
- uPVC ☐
- Aluminium ☐
- Other ☐

GLAZING:
- Double glazing ☐
- Feature glazing ☐
- Please detail

GARAGE DOORS (if applicable):
- Hardwood sheeted door ☐
- Up & Over pressed panel ☐
- Roller shutter door ☐
- Overhead, remote control ☐

EXTERNAL FINISH:
- White roughcast ☐
- Smooth masonry ☐
- Brick ☐
  - " colour
  - " areas
- Panel features as per artists impression
  - Yes ☐   No ☐
- Other ☐

WALL INSULATION:
- Standard cavity insulation ☐
- Dry lining ☐
- Other ☐

DO YOU REQUIRE ANY OF THE FOLLOWING (please indicate room)

"Irish Oak" flooring to

"Knotty Pine" timber ceilings to

"Parana Pine" timber ceilings to

FACIA/SOFFIT:
- Softwood ☐
- Hardwood ☐
- Aluminium ☐
- uPVC ☐

STAIRS:
- Hardwood throughout ☐
- Hardwood sides & carpeted ☐
- Standard red deal ☐
- Other ☐

Floor tiling to

Gypsum ceiling coving to

Ornate plaster coving to

GUTTERING:
- Aluminium ☐
- uPVC ☐

EXTERNAL FINISH TO DORMERS:
- Rendered ☐
- uPVC ☐
- Aluminium ☐

Additional glazed int. doors to

SECOND-FIX JOINERY:
- "Sapelle" hollowcore flush doors ☐
- "Regency" raised panel hollow doors ☐
- Hardwood panel solid doors ☐
- uPVC doors ☐

SECOND-FIX JOINERY TIMBERS:
- Softwood ☐
- M.D.F. ☐
- Hardwood ☐
- Other ☐

Gas fires to following rooms

Central vacuum system
Yes ☐   No ☐

METHOD OF CENTRAL HEATING:
- Gas ☐
- Oil ☐
- Solid fuel ☐

PERMANENT VENTILATION:
- Wall vents ☐
- Window vents ☐

ANY OTHER REQUIREMENTS:

BARGE DETAILS:
- As per illustration ☐
- SKETCH 1 - 200 overhang ☐
- SKETCH 2 - flush pointed ☐
- SKETCH 3 - raised parapets ☐

BARGE DETAILS

SKETCH 1   SKETCH 2   SKETCH 3
(e.g. design 1008.)